As We Wait

in

Joyful Hope

For the Second Coming of
Our Lord and Savior Jesus Christ

SPIRITUAL PREPARATION FOR THE
PURIFICATION, TRIBULATION, CHASTISEMENT
AND
REIGN OF ANTICHRIST

CAROL AMECHE

With an Introduction by Bishop Roman Danylak
Toronto, Ontario, Canada

The publisher recognizes and accepts that the final authority
regarding these messages rests with the Holy See of Rome, to
whose judgement we willingly submit.

--The Publisher

FOREWORD

So much has been written over the past few years about locutions, apparitions, and the end times. Many writers have applied themselves to the task of interpreting the apocalyptic Scriptures or the messages of the approved and unapproved apparitions of these past two centuries and especially the contents of the third secret of Fatima. This modest book *AS WE WAIT IN JOYFUL HOPE* contains the fruits of prayer of Carol Ameche and her interaction with the prayer experiences of the parish of Saint Maria Goretti in Scottsdale, of its pastor Fr. Jack Spaulding and a group of teen-agers, now young adults, who first responded to the call of Our Lord to a life of prayer, in the spirit of the invitation extended by Our Lady of Medjugorje. It is not my task to discern the authenticity of the messages either of Carol or the prayer group in Scottsdale and their supernatural origins. But as I read and reflected upon the messages of Carol I was struck by an affinity of her messages to those of Fr. Gobbi, whom she also quotes in her book. The messages or *locutions* (as has become the custom of labelling them) seem to come from our Lord or the Blessed Mother. Although they speak of future chastisements, they speak of hope, and the fidelity of Our Lord and His blessed Mother to their promises. In this they ring true with the message of the Gospel. They mirror the hope that Scriptures convey to us even amidst the direst warnings of Christ. "Were not our hearts burning within us while he was talking to us on the road while he was opening the Scriptures to us." (Lk 24:32)

The Words of our Lord in the Gospels and the message of the Apocalypse are frightening. They confirm the prophecies of Ezechiel and Daniel about the end times. Christ clearly addresses the issue of a future general apostasy from the faith. "And yet when the Son of Man comes, will He find faith on earth?" (Lk 18:8) Jesus continues with the horrendous picture of the final judgment and the eternal punishment (Mt 25:31). No less frightening are His words that describe the signs preceding His second coming, and the trial that shall be sent upon this earth (Mt 24).

This is that same Lord of infinite love, mercy and forgiveness who often "has desired to gather together" the children of Israel "as a hen gathers her brood under her wings, and you were not willing." (Mt 23:37) These messages cause no little concern for us living in these times, which many hold to be the times of the apocalypse, the times foretold by our Lady in La Salette and Fatima. Add to the messages the graphic images of bleeding statues and icons, many weeping tears of blood, that are appearing in our times. They present Mary appealing to the world for mercy for Her divine Son, who bears the lash of divine justice, and takes upon himself the Sin of the world. They present Mary coming as the Mother, pleading for Her children that will be lost for all eternity. A general feeling of bewilderment, confusion, dismay and hopelessness grips those that still believe. What are we to think of the younger generation, the Theo's? What is their blame for the state of today's world? What can stop this mounting specter of a world gone mad, that is selling itself out to the evil one. What hope is there for our children and the future?

We know the reasons why Heaven has been appealing not only for sinners to return to their God of mercy and forgiveness. It has appealed to the 'righteous' to make reparation for their brothers. Yet, how many of those, who consider themselves the faithful ones, have failed to respond to this plea for prayer, for peace, the call to carry our cross for those of our brothers, intent on their own self ruin.

There is no power that can stop this hurtling to doom.

At the same time both Scriptures and the Church cry out in hope. The apostle exhorts us to look to Jesus. "Come, Lord Jesus!" (Cor 16:22) he cries out in hope and confidence. And the beloved John, as he portrays the picture of our day in the Apocalypse, reminds us that the victory is Christ's. Fear not for the Lord has overcome. All these things must come to pass as it has been written. But the victory is ours. And again the Lord encourages us: "Do not be afraid little flock, for it has pleased my Father to give you the Kingdom." (Lk 12:32)

The messages of Carol Ameche communicate this two-fold truth, of the inevitable chastisement that must befall the world that turns its back upon its Creator and Savior, and the need to purify God's people for the kingdom of the new heaven and the new earth. At the same time it presents the hope that the Blessed Mother extends to her children, whom she bears on angels' wings into the spiritual wildernesses of this world, to save them from the jaw of the beast (Rev 12:6).

Bishop Roman Danylak
Apostolic Administrator
Diocese of Totonto
Titular Bishop of Nyssa

PREFACE

While praying and interacting with the young adults at St. Maria Goretti parish, especially at their Friday night prayer group, the idea came to me to use a young person for this story of mostly fact who would be just like the *'kids'* here whom I have grown to know and love. A character who is a composite of everyone who comes here asking the same questions. The experiences related here are a collection of actual stories shared with me by young people who struggle to pray and change.

The need to understand the background of so many events occurring around the world in the last 12 years and the request of Jesus and Mary to share their warnings has resulted in a scenario which reflects all that happens each day here at St. Maria Goretti Church in Scottsdale, Arizona.

In prayer, on the morning of May 5, 1992, an interior locution welled up within me, as though our Lady and our Lord (and on subsequent occasions, the Father) were speaking to me. It is these I have recorded in this book. Where I say, 'Jesus says' or 'Mary said', I do not claim direct contact with Them, as in an apparition or vision, nor an auditory sound or voice. It is rather that way of communicating which God seems to sometimes use, in order to request, teach, strengthen or console his people.

This has not been, in my experience, answers to questions I posed, but a free flowing communication, seemingly initiated interiorly by the person speaking, resulting in the contents of the *messages* presented here. The belief in these locutions is a matter of personal choice, in which we must always be submissive to the teaching authority of the Roman Catholic Church.

I have, within this text, occasionally quoted from people of my own acquaintance who claim to be receiving interior locutions, and who are also sharing them.

These messages are in a certain sense apocalyptic warnings of an almost immediately grave future, with a call to prepare even more intensely for battles against the evil one. They are balanced, as they are received, with hope and joy. They seem to me to be words of joy, not anxiety and fear; a call to look beyond the trials and tribulations to a future filled with renewed beauty on a renewed earth. A future where sin and evil have all but disappeared, a time just prior to and in preparation for the Second Coming of Jesus.

The material in this book is about salvation . . . *yours* and all people in the world, and the difference we can make by *praying for them. There is no easy way to present all of this. These messages have been read, prayed over and discerned by more than one priest, who have judged them to be in conformity with Catholic truths and within the realm of possibility.*

This book is offered to you that it might open your mind and heart with the help of the Holy Spirit (no matter what religion you are or are not), and impress upon you the urgency to take seriously all you will read; to be moved to change, to become a new creation, to take action according to the requests of the Blessed Virgin Mary and her Son, Jesus Christ.

Carol Ameche
Scottsdale, Arizona
June 1, 1994

Chapter One

Preparedness

"Help us, O God our savior, because of the Glory of your Name; deliver us and pardon our sins for your name's sake." (Ps 79:9)

I caught the phone on the fourth ring and found Barbara from the Church just ready to hang up.

"Oh Hi, Carol, do you have a minute?"

"Sure, what's up?" I asked.

"There's a young man here at the office who has a million questions about the Young Adult Prayer Group, and I know you're the person to answer them. Could you possibly give him time today and explain some things?"

"Goodness. You must have me on your special antenna, Barb. I've just finished the last chapter of a big project that has taken months. Lets see, it's 1:30 now. If you'll ask him to wait an hour, I'll be happy to answer any question I can. And thanks for calling me. He must be very interested if you're trying to set him up so quickly. Please tell him the afternoon belongs to him."

I looked around the sunlit room to assure myself of some order. The warm reddish tiles of our Mexican floor reflected a cheery glow beneath the large sectional sofa. Moving around, I quickly removed cups and dessert plates, left after a late night snack, from the coffee table and turned on the lamps on each end table. Closing the doors to the tall armoire in the far corner gave the room a neater appearance and would allow us to sit at the smaller table and chairs to its left.

I checked the refrigerator in the kitchen and discovered enough soft drinks to carry us through the afternoon, whatever this visit would accomplish. Young people certainly don't usually mind a clutter, so I didn't bother to clear the long white kitchen counters. This was my favorite room, with its blue and white striped wallpaper and continuing red tile. Life in Arizona had introduced me to many new architectural styles, but the kitchen was still a holdover from life in the Midwest.

The young man on the doorstep had rung the bell tentatively and looked rather shy and uncertain. He was tall, with dark hair and a new sunburn, decidedly yuppie in his tailored shorts and pressed plaid shirt. A friendly nature peered through bright blue eyes already filled with questions.

"Hi, come on in. You're very punctual. I'm Carol Ameche. Welcome to Scottsdale."

He shook my hand, smiled and said, "Gosh, thanks so much for seeing me on such short notice. I'm very grateful. My name is Theophilus."

I was just ahead of him as we walked toward the living room. Stopping short, I whirled around and said, "You're kidding! Oh, I'm sorry. I didn't mean . . . how did you ever . . .?"

"Yeah, pretty heavy, huh? Actually, my friends call me Theo, and I hope you will, too," he said cheerfully.

"Well, of course I will. Here, sit down. What would you like to drink?"

"Anything is okay," he answered. "Water's just fine, really. Please, don't put yourself out for me. I'm just happy to be here. I do have lots of questions."

"Great, I'll be right back with diet soda and we'll begin. But I want to hear more about that name."

I quickly loaded a tray with glasses, ice and cans of soda and returned, eager to begin the conversation. We settled in two comfortable chairs across the small table from each other, and I invited him to begin with an explanation of his marvelous, but certainly unusual name.

"Well, it's really nothing. My dad has been a Scripture scholar and teacher at a large university in the East all of his adult life. I have a sister, Lydia and a brother, Luke. My Mom's name is Judith and dad calls her Jude."

I chuckled delightedly and said, "This is going to be fun. Your entire family is already invited to dinner. Are they all here in Scottsdale now?"

Theo explained that his father had just retired to the Valley of the Sun. Since Theo was the youngest child, he must make a quick decision about where to finish a final year of college. There was a school of international business in Phoenix that had the attention of this obviously bright and very pleasant young man. That was the reason for the rush.

It was already August, hot as it gets here, and not too inviting to someone used to the cooler Eastern seaboard. He also confided he'd just begun going back to church after a rather rebellious teen career, during which time attending anything Catholic was the first parental demand he fled. Now, it seemed, he had heard something about apparitions in the world and lo and behold, maybe even some right here in Scottsdale. He was all eyes and ears.

The fact that other young people his age were involved in events at St. Maria Goretti Church, our parish, intrigued him even more, so I said, "Well, what would you like to hear first? Do you already know about Medjugorje and the six young people there and their 'purported' apparitions?"

Just then the front door opened and my husband walked in from a game of golf. On Tuesdays he was usually able to sneak away to play at one of the many courses in and about Scottsdale.

"Oh hi, honey," I called. "Come and meet a newcomer to the parish and probably to Our Lady's Plan. He's here to gain a little info on the prayer groups. This is Theo, freshly arrived from points East and hoping to become an involved parishioner."

My husband is easy-going and has a great way of making everyone feel welcome.

"Hello, Theo," he said with a warm handshake. "May I join you for a few minutes and listen to your story?"

"Sure, Mr. Ameche, and I'm delighted to meet you. Your wife has consented to fill me in on as many details as I can handle, or perhaps as she can handle in one afternoon. I sure like that red sweater. How was your game?"

My husband gave him a menza-menza, got something to drink and sat in a third arm chair around the table.

"Please go on with your chat and I'll just listen and maybe learn something too."

"Okay . . . well, I must admit to knowing very little about anything, but I hear a lot of the same kind of talk at the edges of conversations everywhere I go. Has the Blessed Mother really appeared to people in many parts of the world? What does the Catholic Church say about that? What's this about punishment and chastisement? Why would God want to punish the world? It's already got enough terrible trouble. Would a loving God really try to destroy us? That's what I'm hearing people say. This is beginning to sound like Noah and all that Ark stuff."

"Whoa," I shouted, "do you have a few extra days to visit and hear the whole story? This is going to take more time than you realize, even though I'll give you a few books to read. Are you game to give it more than a few hours, or are you just mildly curious? You see, Our Lady often sends people like yourself here without them realizing she's working behind the scene. I suspect she's doing the same thing in your life. Are you interested in finding out? Would that make a difference to you?"

His eyes grew again and became thoughtful. A grin appeared.

"Oh gosh, yes, really, truly I'd be more than happy to, if you have the time. I had a funny feeling when I first went into the church and it was even stronger in that Tabernacle Chapel. Do other people mention getting a special feeling just walking in there? It's like a holiness or something. You know that God is really there, but it's more than that. What is that, anyway?"

Now it was my turn to grin. "Now you're cooking. I'm delighted you are so interested. Let's say a little prayer first, okay?

'Heavenly Father, we offer this time and conversation to You. Fill us with your Spirit and guide our words that all may give you glory. Amen.'

All right. We need to take a minute to go back to 1981. Actually, though, we in the Southwest didn't hear the news until 1987, if you can believe that. Someone gave me a book about apparitions of the Blessed Mother which began on June 24, 1981, in a small village named Medjugorje, in what was then Yugoslavia. A video tape tells the story of six young people she allegedly visits, giving messages for the whole world.

The belief that she was really appearing exploded inside me like a rocket, and I was there with two other friends in a month. Can you imagine? We rented a car and found our way from the Dubrovnik airport with a map that didn't even have Medjugorje printed on it. Gosh, that's eight years ago. Wait till you hear all that happened after that."

"Is the Blessed Mother saying the same thing here that she said to the people in Medjugorje?" he asked.

"Good question, and the answer is yes. Actually, she's asking for prayer, especially the recitation of the Rosary at least once a day; but also for fasting on bread and water . . ."

"Oh no, really?" Theo chimed in. "Why is that?"

"Hold on, now. Let me tell you how the whole thing unfolded. It's necessary for you to hear this rather slowly and deliberately. You see, she asked for five basic responses from the people of the world, and by 1987, the year of my first trip there, already several million people throughout the world had visited or heard about these special messages."

I got up from the chair and walked to the window to collect my thoughts. This was important information and the heart of all the the messages being given in the world. I wanted to remember every bit of it. Sitting back down, I addressed him again.

"The basic request given at alleged apparition sites in so many places is for *prayer, fasting, penance, reconciliation* and *peace*. Gradually, she has added the need to attend daily Mass and receive her Divine Son in the Eucharist, for those who are able. She requests that we pray to the Holy Spirit for guidance and read Scripture *very* often. You will notice, when you begin to read Her messages, that there is nothing new about any of her requests or the content of the messages. They contain the requests that have always been present in the message of the Old Testament, as well as the New. The difference is the seriousness of our times and the need for us to respond immediately. There is a great urgency for the world to listen *now*.

And then you have young adults here in Scottsdale responding in faith to an interior voice and believing that Mary, the Mother of God, wants them to help communicate her love and concern for her children. But let's come back to that after a few more basics.

Mary announced in Medjugorje that she had come as the Queen of Peace, and it was very necessary for people everywhere to pray for peace and conversion in the hearts of all of her children. By *children* she means every person in the world. She's not talking about the peace that exists between countries, but a reconciliation with God and each other and within ourselves that will give us peace in our hearts. It is in this way that peace will come into the world. Her words have made it quite clear that this call was to *all people*, not just Catholics; that we were all children of God, and only man had made the divisions.

Our Lady told the six young people (they were ages 10 to 17 in 1981), to tell everyone who would listen there was going to be a chastisement of the entire world because too many have turned away from God and are living in the worst state of sin since time began. She was here to warn us to pray and change and learn to put God back into the center of our lives. We had grown too independent and thought we didn't need God; thought all of our development and technology were the result of our own handiwork and not the gifts from God they really are.

And so Theo, God has sent Mary to get our attention with His words and requests and to point us towards her Son, Jesus. She isn't Mother Earth! She will *again* bring Jesus to us through our prayer, our listening to and living the messages.

She points out the danger of our times, teaching that the Supernatural does exist. Satan and his demons are real and have been given great power over the world at this time, these 'end times' before the appearance of the Antichrist and the Second Coming of her Son. She is also showing us how to resist the attacks of present evil by choosing good. She does not want attention and honor for herself, but for God the Father, through Jesus her Son, in the power of the Holy Spirit.

You are aware that the Virgin Mary appeared in 1917 at Fatima with warnings about world wars, if we didn't convert our lives and pray the Rosary, her chief weapon against evil. Not enough people listened and history tells us the rest.

The modern apparitions are actually understood to have begun with the Blessed Mother appearing to Catherine Laboure in Paris on the Rue de Bac in 1830. After that there were apparitions of our Lady to Bernadette Soubirous, a fourteen year old peasant girl in France in 1858. A miraculous spring of water appeared and since then many, many people have been cured physically and spiritually. Our Lady requested the recitation of the Rosary then, too. At Fatima in Portugal in 1917 she announced, 'I am the Lady of the Rosary.'

The Rosary is her weapon against Satan whose head, Scripture tells us, she will crush with her heal."

Theo looked thoughtful. "I remember mention of Fatima from the Nuns in Grade School. We used to make the First Saturdays and have May Altars. We crowned Mary with flowers and all that stuff. What else?"

I paused to reflect on the Fatima messages and requests, and walked over to the bookcase to retrieve more accurate information. My husband perked up and showed even more interest.

"I'd enjoy hearing those stories again too," he said. "I hadn't thought about the connection between all of these apparitions, since they are widely separated in time."

Leafing through pages, I came across an outline of facts. "Let's see, the Blessed Mother appeared for six months on the 13th of each month, to three peasant children, Lucia, Francisco and Jacinta, in a meadow where they were tending sheep. First though, they had been prepared for a whole year by an Angel, teaching them special prayers and praying with them. She asked for the recitation of the Rosary every day to obtain peace for the world and the end of the war (WWI).

Mary showed these young children the souls of poor sinners (together with many demons) in the fires of hell, groaning and shrieking in pain and despair. Our Lady told them God wished to establish in the world devotion to her Immaculate Heart. If we would pray, the war would end, which it did. If we did not continue to pray and fulfill her requests on the First Saturday of each month by saying the Rosary and contemplating the mysteries of her Son's life, a worse war would break out, and it did."

"So that was the second world war," reflected Theo. "I didn't realize that we had been warned ahead of time about that, or that we could have prevented it with enough prayer and a return to God. Sounds like the same thing she's saying today, don't you think?"

"That's not all," I answered. "Here, Meech, would you please read what else she prophesied. Notice how many of the events are happening now."

I handed the book, "*Her Own Words to the Nuclear Age*", memoirs of Sister Lucia, to my husband. "Sr. Lucia is the grown up visionary, Theo, and the only one still living," I said in an aside. He smiled as my husband began to read.

"When you see a night illumined by an unknown light, know that this is the great sign given you by God that He is about to punish the world for its crimes, by means of war, famine, and persecutions of the Church and of the Holy Father . . . She asks that Russia be consecrated to her Immaculate Heart, and for Communion of Reparation on the First Saturdays of each month."

"She still asks that, doesn't she?" he looked up inquiringly.

I nodded an affirmative.

"Anyway, she goes on to say that if we did all these things, Russia would be converted and peace restored. If not, Russia would spread errors throughout the world, causing wars and persecution of the Church; the good would be martyred; the Holy Father would suffer much, and various nations would be annihilated. Well, our generation has certainly lived to see all of that, haven't we?" he said rather grimly and looked at each of us.

Theo stood up and walked over to him, looking down at the book on Fatima. "May I see that?" he asked. Taking it from my husband, he began to read aloud.

" 'Finally, my Immaculate Heart will triumph. The Holy Father will consecrate Russia to me and she will be converted, and an era of peace will be granted to the world . . .' Gosh, we are seeing some of that happen right now, too. I didn't realize prayer to Our Lady had anything to do with the change in Russia and the downfall of Communism," he said with great excitement. Turning some pages, he continued. "Pray very much, Our Lady says here. Too many souls go to hell because there is no one to pray and make sacrifices for them."

Theo looked at us sadly and we could see a new compassion for the souls sent to Purgatory or Hell because of their sins, but also, affected by our lack of prayer and understanding for each other. He returned to his reading, and we both left the room to get a few snacks.

The afternoon sun was much lower now. We could see, through the large casement windows, long shadows behind a huge Saguaro cactus in the yard. Soon it would be time to start dinner and leave for meetings.

Placing pretzels and sparkling mineral water with lime on the table, we sat again to hear our delightful guest being opened to so many new workings of God through His Blessed Mother.

"Listen to this," he said. "There was a huge miracle on October 13th of 1917. Our Lady wanted to convince the rest of the world that she had really come to these peasant children, asking all they had reported. The sun spun wildly in the sky and suddenly lunged toward earth as if it were out of control. People were terrified and thought they were going to die. I guess so," he exclaimed.

"Mary also announced at Fatima that she was the *Lady of the Rosary.* I didn't know that. Was there anything else you can think of that she revealed back then that we are experiencing today?" he asked, and looked at my husband and myself.

"I remember one more important request," I mused aloud, "but it was later, in 1925 or so. Our Lady appeared to Lucia, who was in a convent by then, and promised to assist at the hour of death, with all the graces necessary for salvation, all those who would, on the first Saturday of five consecutive months, go to Confession and receive Holy Communion (the Eucharist), recite five decades of the Rosary while meditating on the mysteries, and keep her company for fifteen minutes with the intention of making reparation to her. Making reparation means offering the prayer and meditation time as a consolation to her for the sins committed against her Immaculate Heart and the Sacred Heart of Jesus."

Suddenly, as if by some tiny signal, both men jumped up and began to walk towards the TV. I figured some special male magic allowed them to intercept the sounds of a football game starting in some corner of the land.

"Are you trying to tell me something?" I asked rather cynically. "Does this mean you've had enough Church history for one day?"

They both laughed and continued to turn the channel until, of course, a football game appeared. "How did you know?" I asked in wonderment. "Okay, Theo. I don't want you to burn out with all of this new interest and information. How about tomorrow afternoon for another look at background material?"

He walked towards the front door through the darkening hallway and paused before leaving. "Thank you both for this special time today. I'd love to come back, if you mean it. And if I hurry, I can get home by the opening kickoff. See you at one o'clock, okay?"

I grinned and waved him out. Walking by the large arcadia doors and looking into the yard again, I thought about all of the incidents which had occurred since 1981 in Medjugorje, when Our Lady began these contemporary public visitations to her children here on earth. It was going to be my joy to reflect again and share them all with this most interesting young man. Blessed Mother's plan was unfolding again, I decided, and walked toward the phone to call a friend who might join us tomorrow.

A tiny movement outside the window caught my eye. Stopping, I watched a female Gambol quail lead her small family of five babies across an open space in the yard. I looked around for dad and, sure enough, there he was, walking along the top of the wall next to this precious procession. These birds are a favorite in Arizona, and protected by law. Intensely shy, they usually appear at feeding time, their lovely heads crowned with an even tinier comb. Papa usually walks apart, ahead or above, in order to protect his family.

The sight of this happy troupe sent a message to my brain. Follow the mother and trust her to lead you to safety. The father is somewhere nearby, ready to run interference.

Chapter Two

Renewed

"May he strengthen your hearts, making them blameless and holy before our God and Father at the coming of our Lord Jesus with all his holy ones." (1Thes 3:13)

"Hi. I'm really happy you decided to come back. Come on in and we'll do the soda routine first, before getting settled. What did your parents have to say?"

Theo followed me into the kitchen and then into the living room, the afternoon sun adding cheer to our meeting.

"Hey, I couldn't wait to get back and hear more. Today I promise not to ask so many questions, and you can just fill me in. Oh, and my Parents said I was probably taking up too much of your time, but that if it's okay with you, they'd like to come along sometime and fill up some of it too," he said with a grin.

"Ho-ho, that's wonderful, and I'm anxious to meet your folks. Bring them over anytime we plan to meet and chat," I nodded and smiled. "I've been thinking of where we might start today, and it seems a little more background on what we may have discovered in the last six years might be in order. If you'll have a little patience, we'll lay some ground work for a day or two, and talk about basics. I may even get 'preachy' now and then. Just stop me when that happens. Will you please? Lets begin, Okay?"

PERSONAL CHANGE

"The Blessed Virgin Mary has an oft-repeated theme, given in messages to several young adults here, chosen to be special messengers for her. *'Focus on my Son,'* she says. "We have come to know that this is an answer to all our problems, pain, anger, complexities of life, anxieties, fears, confusion, lack of understanding and trust.

If we are focusing strictly on Jesus, we will look beyond the slights, the hurts, the rejections, the different personalities, the snide remarks, things that make us crazy and cry for an equally snide response.

If we concentrate on and spend time with Jesus, remembering all He said and did, we have our behavior map. We'll 'keep it simple', cherish others, treat each other kindly and with gentleness. We are actually very fragile people.

Repeatedly her call is to pray more, become more like our holy Mother and *live with unconditional love, mercy and forgiveness.* On August 27th of 1992, during the Thursday Prayer Group at Church, Gianna Talone (a young woman pivotal to events here in Scottsdale), is believed to have received a very special grace. An interior inspiration attributable to Mary was discerned. The message is that all people in the world would one day soon have an opportunity to *see the condition of their souls* and the sinfulness there. This will actually be a huge act of mercy by God, Our Father, a chance to know that God exists. After a gift like that, how could we continue to fool ourselves about who we are and how we are to behave. Right?

However, Jesus has told us over and over again, *'I don't care what you have done, My people, just come back to Me. Don't worry about changing. Just give your heart to Me, and I will change it.'*

The basic understanding, Theo, is that God loves us right now, where we are, as we are. He wants to forgive and heal us; shower us with His love and gifts. That's not so bad. It's certainly nothing to be afraid of, something worth trying, worth fighting for, wouldn't you say?"

"I guess," he said.

"It is very true, as you will be hearing later, that God did not step into Arizona's present-day history to call *perfect* people to pray with His Mother, to ask them to serve Him and become instruments of His Will. None of those who said *'yes'* to many special invitations was without the need of God's mercy and healing, big time. Everyone agrees on that part.

There is no such thing as worthiness, by the way. We'll never deserve God's great love and mercy and approval. We can't earn it but we already have it. Of course we're inadequate, but we *are* capable of change. That doesn't happen instantly either. The healing and purification continues (to the end) for everyone in the world, Theo."

"Well, that's good news. Sounds like the pressure is off to be perfect," he said.

"I couldn't agree more. Because this parish, it turns out, has been called to be a place of mercy and the people instruments of His mercy, the Lord has given great evidence of His mercy by choosing us who, perhaps, had the most need of it. A rather worldly environment, filled with much less than perfect people, might have prompted the gratitude and willingness to say *'yes'*, and serve in whatever way He and His Mother requested. I found this in Scripture this morning, Theo, to read to you. It seems to apply to the situation."

'But you are "a chosen race, a royal priesthood, a holy nation, a people of his own, so that you may announce the praises" of him who called you out of darkness into his wonderful light. Once you were no people but now you are God's people; you had not received mercy but now you have received mercy.' (1Pt 2: 9-10)

"It's so comforting to find passages that relate directly to our experiences. Bet your Dad has mentioned that dynamic before," I said with a smile.

"Uh-huh, just a few times!"

"There were no ivory tower 'pray-ers' chosen here," I continued, "no people who had not made mistakes or had not bought into the world's promises of instant and plentiful gratification. No one was immediately converted. No living *without delay* in the perfect Will of Jesus with all (or even many) of Mary's virtues. To say that we have struggled would be to understate the case."

"Carol, what would you say have been major problems for people at St. Maria Goretti Parish in the last five years?" he asked.

The question ran around my brain for a few minutes. Then the phone rang so I ran out to answer it. On the way back to my chair, the final thoughts came together. Meanwhile, Theo had helped himself to a homegrown orange, surprisingly juicy and delicious for the desert.

"Wow." He finished the orange, jumped up to rinse his sticky fingers in the kitchen and brought back a banana. "You have to realize," he said smiling, "that listening to all this good stuff can make a person hungry."

I laughed and nodded, watching the banana disappear behind three cookies and a can of lemonade. I noted the goodness in his face and realized he would always be hungry, mostly for more understanding and knowledge of Jesus and His Mother.

"Okay, here we go again," I said to his now listening ears. "Change takes a long time: revaluating; reorganizing lives; rummaging through buried resentments, old hurts and angers; seeking reconciliation with family and friends (and ourselves) and God over and over again; falling, getting up; going forward, sliding back.

Then there's always the unhappy discovery of our less than lovely traits like jealousy, pride, vanity, selfishness and competition; new hurts, new angers, hidden sinfulness. Fr. Jack likes to say, 'I guess the Blessed Mother knew that if *we* could convert, anyone could.'

Now, I must tell you that every day I struggle against a nature that is selfish, self-centered and vain; one which seeks gratification with *more*. I constantly pray against temptations that will probably always plague me. Twenty years ago, the Lord had great mercy on me and instantly welcomed me into His forgiving arms.

There was never a time I did not experience Him as a loving, patient, compassionate, understanding, forgiving God. He has become a great friend, a deep source of trust, hope and joy. He is the One Who is always there; Who calls me constantly to more; Who shows me what is real, what is important, what is necessary. My struggle to maintain an ordinary spirituality, no different than that offered to everybody, will never end; neither will His love and acceptance.

There is nothing we encounter that Jesus didn't encounter first. He's totally familiar with human nature because He shares our nature. Hmm . . . and there's another great quote from Scripture right back here," I said turning pages quickly.

"Okay, here it is . . . 'For we do not have a high priest who is unable to sympathize with our weaknesses, but one who has similarly been tested in every way, yet without sin. So let us confidently approach the throne of grace to receive mercy and to find grace for timely help.' "*(Heb 4:15-16).*

"Right, I do like that one," he said.

"In reflecting upon our own journey through life, Theo, it's also good to use visuals, similes, allegories, to make the situation more alive for us, something to which we can truly relate. For example, when we move to a new city, we don't at first know our way around, correct? It might be necessary to make a 'dry run' before visiting a certain place (let's say for example, an important meeting), should we wish to arrive promptly.

Learning a route sometimes necessitates stopping and asking directions to save time, making sure we're on the right track. You may have already experienced that here in Scottsdale," I chided my new friend.

"Well, yes, I knew enough to stop immediately at church and ask Barbara all those questions. That shows the Holy Spirit might be working in my life right now, doesn't it?" he asked with delight. "I even found myself on a one-way street going the wrong way (You never did that? Oh, right). I needed to take the same route several times before knowing the way *by heart*. Lately, I've discovered which side roads to take in order to save time; the short cuts to travel for the least hassle. Is that the kind of thing you mean?"

Picking up the analogy, I hurried on to say, "Exactly. Some routes are busier than others at certain times of the day. Some bridges wash out during heavy rains. Some roads flood and become impassable. All these are signs with which we become familiar in order to make life easier for ourselves. Scottsdale has a lot of trouble with flash floods because of the clay soil. Tell your folks, Theo, that the run-off here is fierce.

There is no way to know all of these things about a different city until we spend time there. We know after a while what to do when the storms come.

Our spiritual journey is just like that. (Okay, "I said laughingly, "so you knew I was going to say that!) When the Lord moves us to a new *place*, we can't possibly know our way around. We get lost easily, and it sure helps to stop often and ask directions.

There aren't many short cuts on our way to the Kingdom. If we wish to move forward, make progress, stop getting lost or going up a street the wrong way, it helps to know who to ask. Mary begs us to hold her hand, call upon her often for help and then to listen to the direction she so anxiously gives. We must know when the traffic lights are red, green or yellow; learn the right roads to take, the ones to avoid. Jesus is a great crossing guard, Theo. The rules will be life saving if followed *religiously*."

I winked at my poor joke and he shook his head.

"Well, I think I do follow you. Maybe I haven't lived long enough and don't know the right questions to ask. But I know where you're going with all of that.

Do you think if I read the books you're giving me, I'll have a better handle on what's important? It seems to me people never grow up much, or change, until they're forced to by some event in their lives."

I sighed and nodded. "Theo, when you can come up with reasoning like that, you're doing fine. When we all learn to listen more, talk less, live the messages and prepare *now* for a time of purification, we'll be able to develop the kind of loving, healing relationships Jesus is talking about.

Tribulation and chastisement are the results of the way we live in the world: rampant sin; a growing schism in the Catholic Church which turns away from its inspired teachings and traditions and the Pope; civil unrest and world-wide violence unprecedented in our history.

This all sounds pretty glum, doesn't it? Yet, there *is* hope. People like to get stuck in fearful thoughts of possible devastation, but Mary and Jesus have promised there is a way to be protected.

PERSONAL COMMITMENT

" *'The salvation of the entire world'*, says our Mother, *'depends on those who pray.'*

Now that's something to spend time thinking about. *Now* is the time (before it is gone altogether) to give ourselves a holy shot in the arm (the one that holds the rosary," I nodded).

"We gather all of our energy and first fruits of endeavor and, with the help of the Holy Spirit, are *renewed, revitalized, reconvinced, recharged* with the strength being offered to everyone (not just Catholics, you know), who will *listen and reflect* on all that has been said and *look* at nurturing words from Mary and her beloved Son."

PERSONAL WITNESS

"Do you remember the first reading from today's liturgy? Well, it deals with this very subject: the dilemma of believing that you have been given warning material by God to share with *the world* who needs to listen, repent and return to God; or a punishment (the loving, merciful justice) of God is on the way, due to the existence of too much sin. Listen again to what this one says:

> 'You, son of man, I have appointed watchman for the house of Israel; when you hear me say anything, you shall warn them for me. If I tell the wicked man that he shall surely die, and you do not speak out to dissuade the wicked man from his way, he (the wicked man) shall die for his guilt, but I will hold you responsible for his death. But if you warn the wicked man, trying to turn him from his way, and he refuses to turn from his way, he shall die for his guilt, but you shall save yourself.' (Ez 33:7-9)

Oh, and one more word of caution, Theo. When a messenger of God makes a mistake in behavior; or causes scandal; or gives a prophecy that doesn't occur; we tend to deny that messenger's entire prophecy. It's interesting to note that some of the prophecies of St. Catherine Laboure, to whom the Blessed Mother announced herself as the 'Immaculate Conception' and gave us the Miraculous Medal, did not occur. Many did, but some didn't.

We mustn't try to box up God with *our own expectations* or qualifications. One of the first things Jesus said to us in special teaching lessons in Scottsdale was, *'Don't look at My messengers, listen to My messages.'*

If instead of focusing on Jesus, we waste valuable prayer time gossiping, we're missing the point. Blessed Mother told the young adult prayer group, *'You think you are not gossiping, but you are.'* She also pleads with us not to talk about her priests, but to pray for them constantly. We don't realize the brutally sinful state of the world. We're not believing the urgency, not acting with enough conviction on the need to totally give ourselves to the business of *holiness*." He shot me a look of dismay.

"Yes, I know," nodding my head. "The idea of holiness is a frightening one to most people.

We have the opportunity of a lifetime (present and eternal) to learn real truth, to acquire the tools and discover the "how to's" of an intimate relationship with Jesus by allowing Him to love us. Do you realize that our God is *begging* us to allow Him to love us?" I looked at Theo with amazement, and he looked absolutely flabbergasted.

THE END TIMES

"Please Theo, don't reflect upon doom and destruction, by the way. Our Lady is constantly telling us *not to fear!* And she uses the phrase 'end times' in enough of her messages around the world to get our attention."

"What on earth does that mean?" he puzzled. His face was full of wonder and concern. A true reflection of the reaction of so many people in the world to that phrase.

"It's important, Theo, to understand that what we are talking about is not _the end of the world_ but _the end of this time period_ as we know it; the beginning of a new, golden era for the church and the earth, an age of enlightenment and peace; a return to life on earth as it was meant to be before Adam and Eve sinned and were expelled from the Garden of Edan. This will be preceded by a purification and cleansing of the earth, including the appearance of the Antichrist and the time of the abomination of desolation, the ultimate battle, and the second coming of Jesus. Satan will be chained in the bowels of hell for whatever a thousand years means."

"Wow. Do you really believe that, Carol?"

"I do, Theo. Speaking to my heart in prayer I believe the Blessed Mother and Jesus have referred to this scenario a number of times in their gracious sharing with me. I'll read to you a sample of what I have written down.

'I am your Jesus of Mercy Who speaks to you. Praised be My Father Who gifts you with every sort of good thing. Praised be Him Who allows Me to speak to you in this way. Praised be His Divine Plan for the salvation of His children.

Thank and praise Him at every moment for His gracious goodness on your behalf. Give Him all the love in your heart and think of the Most Blessed Trinity every time you think.' (7/9/93)

Hope and joy are the armor we must put on, Theo. Anticipation for the 'Day of the Lord' will fill our hearts with gratitude, love, peace and trust, if we allow this to happen. Our time is short, running out, before love and mercy become lived out as the Father's justice."

"I don't know. It seems to me that's going to be a tough one, Carol," he said seriously.

"We're certainly being called to grow up," I answered.

Our Lady has said, 'do not dwell on chastisement, but on peace, the peace that grows and becomes the fabric of men's hearts,' the very air we breathe." I took a reflective moment and another deep breath.

"Perhaps we need to understand *time* in order to be at peace with the idea of '*time is short, running out*', phrases often repeated to special messengers throughout the world. Recently, a line from the Liturgy of the Hours caught my eye. It said, '*Time is the unfolding of truth as we know it.*' That was a new thought for me and, after running that around my brain for a while, I decided to look at the different eras, stages during which everyone lived in a particular way; the Ice Age, the Age of Dinosaurs, Paleolithic and Neanderthal times, the Stone Age, and so on.

The Flood of Noah's day was a time of cleansing and renewal of the earth. There are numerous eras recounted in scripture and the history of peoples which show us that each of these ages came to an end and another began, during which people lived and thought and had goals that reflected new discoveries, new understanding.

Before Jesus was born, people lived in expectation of the Messiah. After His birth, those who accepted Him did not live in *waiting* for the Messiah anymore, but in *fulfillment* of that promise. They collected and reflected upon His words and deeds. It was a time for living out all He had told them.

In the past 2000 years we have seen such eras as the Dark Ages, the Renaissance, the Reformation, the Industrial Age. Each one ended. People didn't continue living in those fashions (the roaring 20's for example) anymore, but dressed, acted, related, learned and thought in ways appropriate for the new era, modern times.

Right now such respected people as Father Stefano Gobbi, in mystical prayer through Mary, have come to believe that these are the end times referred to in Scripture: the Day of the

Lord of Daniel, Matthew, the Prophets and Revelations, to name a few. All of the events of history must occur to fulfill everything written in Scripture. It seems from prophecies and world events that we are now living in another time of expectation, waiting this time for Jesus' return to defeat the Antichrist and usher in a thousand years of peace. Life on earth will then be experienced as it was meant to be in God's original plan for His creation and creatures."

At that moment we heard the front door close and Theo stirred out of his reverie.

"Hi Mr. Ameche. How are you today?" He stood up and reached out to shake my husband's hand.

"Hi Theo. Say, it's my turn to like *your* sweater, young man. It's really a nice one." He cast an admiring glance at the navy blue cable knit topping khaki pants. "Hi honey. Sorry I'm late. I've got another meeting in an hour, but I can join you for a few minutes." Then, turning to Theo, with a twinkle in his eye, he asked, "How are you doing with all this holy propaganda?"

Theo loved that one, nodded and grinned broadly.

"I get no respect," I sighed, and shook my head, also grinning.

Then, taking on a more serious posture, Theo responded. "You know, Mr. Ameche, I have to admit that I'm still afraid of the idea of dying. I know in my head that heaven is a wonderful place, and if we live according to the commandments and now the requests of Our Lady, we will probably go straight to heaven. But I'm still afraid of death. What do you think about that?" Theo shared with my husband these serious feelings and questions with an equally serious tone of voice.

"I know what you mean, Theo. The more we come to know Jesus and Mary, the less we worry about life after death in heaven. However, that fear of death itself is one every human seems to struggle with. And that, I believe, is Satan's greatest tool against us, against our trust in God's promises.

To begin with, Theo, I seem to remember that C.S. Lewis said about Satan that one of his cleverest deceptions was to convince mankind that he doesn't exist. When that doesn't work, he goes on to try to frighten us any way he can, in order to weaken our resolve, line, our spiritual muscles. It's certainly not impossible for us, but we are all still a long way off from 'praying without ceasing.' (2Thess 5:17)

Prayer in order to surrender to the Divine Will is the best defense against Satan I can think of, son. I'm old enough to know by now that spiritual muscle gets built up just like physical ones. We lift heavier and heavier weights in order to develop muscles of any kind. Sounds to me like God the Father will allow us to struggle till the very last second, when everything looks absolutely lost, before He comes through with His heavenly cavalry to save us. Meantime, we better have lots of faith and trust going in His ability to save us without being afraid of anything.

Only thing I can suggest, Theo, is that you pray in Jesus' Name, to deliver yourself from all fear, because fear isn't from God. It's the evil one's trump card. We just can't let him get the lead anymore! How does that sound?"

"Gosh, Mr. Ameche. You've really helped me out. You sound like you might have given that one a lot of thought, and maybe worked at it a bit yourself," Theo said delightedly.

I looked at my husband who only smiled and nodded his head. It was my turn to smile and be warmed by feelings of gratitude for this manly philosophy. Suddenly looking at his watch, Don jumped up quickly and headed for the door. "Got to run Carol."

"Will you be home by six?" I asked the retreating figure of my beloved.

"Yep" he said. "Can't miss Monday night football."

I just rolled my eyes. He left us and we sat for a moment to allow a return to the quieter mood.

"Hear Our Lady today Theo," I began.

" *'My Son is coming again. The earth must be cleansed in order for Him to fulfill Scripture before He returns. All that is promised in Scripture will occur. All of you will be participants in these great events.*

Satan wishes to destroy the world and return it to the state of chaos in which He originally was cast. That is why sinful men who follow Lucifer wish only to destroy goodness and beauty and return to darkness. The forces of evil will not stop until they are completely destroyed by God at the appointed time. Until then, there will be many acts of violence against the earth and mankind who has chosen darkness and evil, and prefers to be ruled by the evil one.' " (8/27/92)

THE IMMACULATE HEART OF MARY

"We realize now that Mary has offered repeatedly, all over the world for many years, the opportunity to *take refuge in her Immaculate Heart,* to be wrapped in her Mantle and remain there in peace and safety. These are not just images she is using to create some sort of false sense of security. They are real possibilities for protection that we can believe in, trust and accept.

These words Jesus speaks about His cherished Mother may be what touches us anew, captures our hearts and keeps us prisoner in a love that wishes to save, to heal, to guide and to hold us in its grasp.

Would you do me a favor this time, Theo? Will you please read this to me? It's probably my favorite story from Jesus."

"Yes, sure, Carol. I'd be happy to do that."

The air was very still and Theo's voice filled with tenderness:

'In the warmth of the smile of My Mother, all is well.

In the shadow of her mantle, we are favored.

The love of My Mother will bring mankind to their knees to honor and adore the One, True, Living God.

It is My Mother who will bring the lost sheep back to the fold.

It is she who loves Me so much and soothes the grief I feel for My lost ones who reject Me.

Follow her manner, children. Learn from her gentleness.

Be still and listen to the soothing tones of Her voice, the melody of love which sings from her heart.

Be aware of the gentleness with which she accepts all who come to her; how she calms fears and tenderly wipes away tears.

Go with her into the depths of sorrow within each heart that comes to you.

Give courage and strength to Our dear ones in the Name of My Mother and Me.

Assure them of the ease with which they will be received by the grace reserved for them since the beginning of time.

Comfort them with the trust in My promises which is theirs for the asking.

Please, Continue to seek a closeness with My Mother.

Watch her. Listen to her. Be like her in all you do.'

(9/10/92)

There was a long period of quiet then during which we were held by the beauty of these words of love and encouragement.

"Thanks, Theo. It's beautiful, isn't it? Hard to believe that there are people today who refuse to recognize all the goodness contained in this most perfect of creatures.

St. Louis de Montforte had tremendous devotion to Blessed Mother. He has written several books outlining her life of virtue and ways we can hope to be like her in whom, he says, 'resides the ten principal virtues for us to imitate: her profound humility, her lively faith, her blind obedience, her continual mental prayer, her mortification in all things, her ardent charity, her heroic patience, her angelic sweetness and her divine wisdom.'[1]

Mary, the Mother of Jesus is here to lead us back to her Son, Theo. And in a like vein, just listen to what St. Paul wrote to the Colossians to encourage their fidelity." I picked up scripture and read:

> " 'So, as you received Christ Jesus the Lord, walk in him, rooted in him and built upon him and established in the faith as you were taught, abounding in thanksgiving. See to it that no one captivate you with an empty, seductive philosophy according to human tradition, according to the elemental powers of the world and not according to Christ.' (Col 2:6)

In the book I'm working on, I'm going to be inviting people to journey together and be led to a greater spiritual preparedness and *identity* as the remnant people of God.

God needs people who will stand forth to be counted, lift their heads high with love and faith in our Savior, *and accept His Mother* in order to fulfill the Father's plan of salvation for us, His children. Jesus has even warned us that if we do not come to know His Mother, we will not truly come to know Him.

---

[1] *True Devotion to Mary*, St. Louis de Montfort, TAN Books and Publishers, Inc., Rockford, IL

WHAT CAN WE DO?

"There's a great ten-point-plan for discipleship that I copied for you from Volume III of *I Am Your Jesus of Mercy* (pg. 7-8).

'1. *Put your trust in Me, your Lord God. Allow Me to care for you.*

2. *Never be self-righteous, but allow Me to be righteous in you.*

3. *The Will of my Father must always prevail for anyone to be My disciple.*

4. *Be joyful. Rejoice in Me and Him who has sent Me. Do not be somber or melancholy.*

5. *Never worry. I have said there is no justice in fear, worry or anxiety. I shall care for you, as I have devoutly told you.*

6. *Love unconditionally, and do whatever is necessary to avoid the poison of hatred or resentment from infusing into your soul.*

7. *Never give up hope. Remember, you are not perfect. It is I who perfects you in Me.*

8. *Carry your cross. If you suffer, then receive and offer your suffering for the salvation of mankind.*

9. *Seek the Kingdom of God. Allow your actions to speak for you.*

10. *Honesty. Always be honest and speak the truth with respect for one another.*

I have come to restore dignity and respect through My mercy. Those who practice these steps are My disciples in whom My mercy flows, restoring dignity to mankind.'

In a message to my heart Jesus gave a clear picture of our need for the presence of Mary living in our hearts:

'The essence of loving Me and being united to my Heart and Will is perceived and experienced by trusting all I tell your heart and request of you.

Take note of the changes within yourselves and give thanks to the Father for His many gifts to you.

Without the gifts of our Father, sustained by My love and the intercession of My Mother, you would be no better than the pagans who live in the world, worshipping false gods.' (7/2/93)

Theo, please understand that for those who don't respond to these invitations, life without the *extra* graces Jesus is trying to give us will not mean we are not loved by God. He will always love us. It is His Nature to do so, and He has promised to love and be with us always (Matt 28:20). It does mean that we are not living as fully as possible, or in full accord with the Father's Divine Will for us. And speaking of *full as possible*, let's take a break and get some food, shall we? In fact, why don't you take a chapter of this book home now? We'll plan another session when you're ready."

Snacking on cheese and crackers we agreed that he would return in three days. Could we get through all this information without gaining 20 pounds? I wondered.

Chapter Three

Responding

"The six young people have been phenomenal in their ability to see pilgrims who began going there immediately, answering the same questions form new groups every hour, every day since 1981. Imagine, having the patience to do that graciously, and being pulled at and pushed by huge crowds trying to get close to you and touch you."

She paused and I thought about how much we were impressed by this fact while visiting Medjugorje, watching group after group of pilgrims spend a half hour asking the very same questions over and over again, reaching out sometimes wildly to touch them, if possible. The Beatles had nothing on these kids!

It was nearly four in the afternoon, and we were sitting together again in the living room, with its marvelous cathedral ceiling, surrounded by colors and artifacts of the Southwest. Decorating in the warm mauves and soft shades of turquoise had been great fun and a total departure from the more severe Midwest climate, reflected in dark wood furniture and accent colors.

Theo had been prompt and my friend, Elsa, had joined us to add whatever she could to the details. She and I had been together in 1987 on my first of three trips to the tiny village in Yugoslavia. We would complement each other, I hoped, and enjoy the process. I nodded to her to continue the recollection.

"Anyway, the messages began to be given once a month in Medjugorje, for the whole world, through a young girl named Maria who still gives them to a translator on the 25th of each month to be distributed to millions of people waiting to hear what the Mother of God has to say. They have been collected in books over the years, along with commentaries by leading theologians.

Basically, the same requests have been repeated all these years, but in different ways. This is happening, Our Lady says, because she can't give us new messages until we learn to live the old ones. Mary has also been appearing in every country of the world with the same requests, although each place seems to have a different added focus. It can be understood better when you hear the portion of the story that includes Scottsdale." includes Scottsdale."

Theo looked at me with great excitement and said, "I'll bet everybody in Scottsdale must come to your prayer groups. There must be huge prayer groups everywhere in the country, in the world, and I didn't even know about all this. I can't stand it. What else?"

I gave him a calming glance before responding. "Well, no, not really, about everybody coming to pray, I mean, or not even huge groups praying everywhere either. That's one of the reasons Our Lady was sent by God to be His Prophet for our times. Too many people are indifferent and cold to the idea of private devotions to Mary or to public displays of prayer and affection to Jesus and His Mother.

The first thing she explained to the children in Medjugorje was that the chastisement planned by the Father to purify the world could be mitigated, that's lessened, or even prayed away completely if enough people would begin to pray and come back to Her Son. She was calling all her children to come back to her so she could lead us to Jesus. He would then help us to put God back into the center of our lives and assure our salvation. This was serious, and not many people were even paying attention.

After the chastisement, she told Mirjana (another of the young people), those who are still alive will live like the people in the days of the early church, right after Jesus ascended to the Father; when the Apostles were travelling and baptizing and teaching the known world.[1] If you read the book of Acts you can see that people in those days were living communally, sharing all they had with each other, very simply, without any of the advanced technology we enjoy today. They spoke to each other reverently and worshiped God with an appreciation and love for our Father and Creator. They were obedient to the commandments of God.

All this may sound frightening, however it's not meant to scare us, but to warn us to change and prepare us for the future. These events are necessary, Mary says, to fulfill Scripture. Isn't that how you understand it?" I said, looking at Elsa.

She nodded in agreement and I asked her to continue. While she related more to our guest, I left the room and made a few calls about an upcoming trip the following week, stopping in the kitchen to stir a bubbling batch of Chile, and then returned to listen to the story and watch the intense absorption of this young man lounging comfortably in one of our overstuffed chairs.

"And this is so important to understand: if we do all of the things Mary is calling us to, and stay wrapped in her Mantle (that's what they wore as an outer garment in her day and a term she equates with protection), *we have nothing to worry about*. We will be safe from the chastisement, although *all* people *will* experience the tribulations to come.

A lot of people don't want to hear this, Theo," Elsa said seriously, "but the state of sin in the world makes it necessary to be announced through the Mother of God. We have to take it seriously.

---

[1] From a homily given by Fr. Tomislav Vlasic, 8/15/83.

Now the people who really *heard* that and *believed* it, *got busy right away.* They returned to their homes and formed prayer groups in many, many parishes.

Expectations were high that the secrets pertaining to the chastisements, special signs from heaven and a great change in the earth, would be revealed quickly. That hasn't happened, as you've noticed. Blessed Mother repeated many times that *we shouldn't dwell on chastisement and destruction,* but on peace. When we become peace, we bring peace into the world. We're trying to do that.

There have been major natural disasters, however, throughout the world, which were also part of the scenario described by Mary. She pleads with people to begin to change and live her messages."

Elsa took a deep breath and paused for a minute. Holding up her hand to us, as if trying to organize in her mind other events that would support the fact that the Blessed Mother's prophecies were being played out already. She nodded to herself and continued.

"There have been major wars in different parts of the world all during the ensuing years. Who would have believed that she was warning the people in her beloved village of Medjugorje that war would visit their very homeland and such brutality occur between neighbors who had so recently prayed together as friends? We needn't be so shocked. The wars throughout the world are only a reflection of the hatred and violence in families and individual hearts. Would you agree with that?" she asked. Would you agree with that?" she asked.

"Sounds like this is a lot more complicated and serious than it looked at first," remarked our avid listener.

"You bet it is," continued Elsa, "and urgent, too; very, very urgent and serious, mainly because not enough people have begun to accept her presence among us, or the warnings she comes to give as a loving mother. Our Lady invites the whole world to accept her as Mother, to live her requests and receive the love and guidance she desires to give us.

"The single most important concept to realize," she said, "is that all of this is about the love of God . . . Hey, I've got to run," she said suddenly, jumping up and looking at her watch. "It was very nice meeting you, Theo. Sorry to skip out. You'll stay busy here," she promised with a smile. She winked at me and closed the front door behind her. Looking after her, I thought, 'yes, the bottom line here, the central theme, is the love of God . . . how He is loved and has loved us first.'

We regrouped, poured some iced tea and sat for a few minutes looking through the windows at several charming barrel cacti and a giant ocotillo. That was a new one on me and one of my favorite. A bunch of long, spiney, green branches ascend from the ground in a circle and end in bright red tips that wave gently when there's a breeze. At Christmas time, people love to outline them in green lights with red ones at the top.

I took some time to fill Theo in on local customs. He was fascinated about the fact that even the giant Saguaro, only found in the Sonoran desert, has an extremely small root system and can grow nearly two stories and weigh several tons.

"Are you game to continue? There's probably an hour left to the afternoon. Okay then. Mary has been sent by Jesus to get the attention of the entire globe in order to soften our hearts, open up our defenses, and listen to what she has to say." I looked up to make sure he was really listening.

"If we will do that, we can't resist beginning to love her in response to her incredibly tender love for us. If the world will allow her to teach us about her Son Jesus and His Father, it will turn to them and repent.

Jesus' Mother has announced that she comes to lead us back to God. She desires to acquaint us with a first hand knowledge of His great, unconditional love for each of us and prepare us to spend Eternity with Him in perfect happiness. Not bad, huh?"

I looked at him again and found his riveted attention.

"To attain all this we must begin by developing an intimate relationship with Him now. That's our inheritance as children of God, but most people don't even know that or refuse to listen or believe it."

Theo chimed in. "So what happened next to set in motion all the events that have led to you sitting here and answering all my questions?" he asked.

A big smile spread across my face and I sat back and took another deep breath. He smiled, too, appreciating the fact that he had asked the right question.

"Well, let me think. In October of 1987, nearly one hundred pilgrims from all over the valley, accompanied by Father Jack Spaulding, our Pastor, journeyed to Medjugorje. This was my second trip and even more filled with graces and Mary's presence than the first one. While there, we decided to form a prayer group on Thursday nights back home in order to pray for the salvation of the world.

Our first efforts were pretty good. About forty people gathered each week. Fr. Jack said Mass and led all 15 decades of the Rosary."

"Isn't that an awful lot of prayer?" he asked.

"It sure is when you aren't used to that much," I nodded. "Gradually we became accustomed to the increased time and, pretty soon, we were loving it. Turns out prayer is natural to us and since the Lord knew that, He wasn't worried about our making the discovery. Trouble is, humanity is an unfaithful lot as a rule. We get bored quickly and look for something new.

However, there were many great gifts of prayer in those early days. A commitment to prayer and a feeling of appreciation quickly developed within our new community.

By Spring of 1988, we had another group interested in visiting Medjugorje, so off we went, about 40 in number. This was actually the beginning of a new phase of Our Lady's Plan for the entire Valley of the Sun, but we didn't realize it then."

"Do you believe Our Lady brings people to certain places because she wants to use them for her own good purposes? There seems to be a large group of young adults here. Could she be bringing me here for a particular reason?" mused Theo. "I mean, when you look back, does it seem there was a scenario she knew all about, but only revealed to you one event at a time?"

Again, appreciation for this sponge-like mind sitting here washed over me. Jumping up, I circled the room several times, stopping now and then to keep my facts in order.

"Well, for heaven's sake, you picked up that one in a hurry. Mary certainly is a dear, holy Mother, and has more loving plans than we will ever keep up with. They all seem designed to save us from ourselves and the grip of Satan," I said seriously. "She spoke a lot about him in the early days in Medjugorje, and said how important it was for everyone to realize that he is real and wants to destroy our souls and bring us to hell.

Mary even allowed some of the six *seers* to make extraordinary visits with her: some to heaven, some to purgatory, some to hell. As a result, they could share with people what they saw, convince them these are actual places.

People in the world (which is the domain of the devil), who follow its teachings, want us to believe that hell and Satan don't exist, that it's nearly impossible to commit the type of sin that would keep us out of heaven for eternity. Men have gone from perceiving themselves as God's to thinking of themselves as gods.

She continues to warn us about the dangers of the evil one: his very real presence and temptations constantly offered each of us. By the way, would you like to break with something more to drink?"

"Gosh, yes, this is really getting good. Do you mind doing all this talking?" he asked innocently.

"Ho! That's a good one," I responded. "My husband would chortle and say, 'surely you jest.'

Invitations have sent me around the country lately, by the way, to speak to people who want to know more about the mercy and love of God displayed here at St. Maria Goretti. I love the warm experience of meeting huge groups of people who love Our Lady so much; who have all given their lives to her plan of enlisting our aid to pray for the salvation of the world. I especially love the talking part," I grinned.

"Many people in the world have professed experiencing Mary, our Mother, in prayer. They all seem to encounter the sweetness of her personality, the strength of her character, filled with purpose and the promise to protect and guide us. At the beginning of the talks around the country, I was questioned by a person who was obviously quite skeptical. At one point during the presentation, he jumped out of his chair and practically ran to the next room.

At the end of the sharing, I put my head down and prayed silently, 'Dear Mother, I hope I did not say anything wrong to offend that man.'

Immediately my heart filled with the words, *'Child, you have nothing to fear. You are my beloved daughter and you are wrapped in my Mantle.'*

I was surprised by this experience and filled with gratitude by her firm resolve. It left me feeling happy to be wrapped in that heavenly protection and delighted she had calmed my fears. It seems when Jesus and Mary say they are with us, it doesn't just mean spiritually or mystically. They are for us, on our side, in our corner, as long as we're in theirs.

The story is getting good alright. It's also getting late in her plans. Time, she keeps telling us, is short, is running out. So is my concentration, Theo. I need to work hard these days to hold on to my train of thought. Hold on now, lets continue. After that third trip in June of 1988, we came home more determined than ever to answer the call of Mary at Med- jugorje. During the return flight to Arizona, Gianna Talone was on board and claimed she had received a locution from the Blessed Mother.

Well, I didn't take her seriously at all and thought no more about it, until a visit one day to Fr. Jack who had some news that astounded me. He said the Blessed Virgin Mary had requested through several young adults in the parish that we hold a prayer group on Friday nights for young people, 18-35 years of age.

Many were already attending the Thursday night prayer group you see, but the fact that some of our young parishioners also claimed to be receiving locutions (an inner voice which speaks to the heart or mind, usually from Jesus, Mary, the Holy Spirit, the Father, an Angel or Saint, and heard inside or outside the head), increased the numbers to around five hundred. Yes," I nodded, "that many.

By the way, this special means of communicating has been experienced throughout church history by people whom God wished to touch, often to make requests of them. It was incredible news and spread quickly.

Fr. Jack was invited by Our Lady, through an interior locution to Gianna, to be the leader of the group and would discern any messages received. The other adult invited by Our Lady was myself. My reaction was great joy and delight, followed by nagging doubts and feelings of unworthiness. We have needed to learn a lot about worthiness. Please, remind me to mention that later."

Since there were so many facts to relate, I was beginning to realize the need to make lists of things to remember. Walking over to a low table between the overstuffed chairs I found paper and pen and began making notes as we talked.

"The young people were requested by Our Lady to pray especially for the conversion of young adults in the Americas," I continued. "These and other requests came principally through Gianna, Stephanie and Susan. So, for the past five years it has been my privilege to pray with them on Friday nights, lead the prayer when Fr. Jack is not present and become sort of a confidant to some of the group of nine young people specially chosen by Jesus and Mary. All of the particulars and people are mentioned in books I'll be telling you about."[2]

"Is that what all those stacks of paper in the next room are all about... the book you are writing? Are *you* writing a book?"

My eyes closed for a long minute. Theo seemed comfortable with my occasional retreats into thought, so I took my time. Looking up again, the conviction to share all of my own experiences was strong. This would be a good opportunity to share messages of my own with someone new to the whole story. Conviction flooded me and I leaned forward.

"Yes, I am writing my story, with mostly personal messages included. But we need to let that wait a little while longer. First let's finish talking about the young adults. Most of the early members stayed on, but a few left. We have learned to believe and trust that God has His special ways we don't always understand, and always works in each person to the very last minute of their lives to accomplish His Will. It's important to realize that God *never gives up on us* till the very

---

[2] *Our Lady Comes to Scottsdale*, Rene Laurentin, Riehle Foundation, PO Box 7, Milford, OH 45150

Our Lord and Our Lady in Scottsdale, Fr. Robert Faricy, S.J., and Sr. Lucy Rooney, Queenship Publications, PO Box 42028, Santa Barbera, CA 93140-2028

Return to God, the Message of Scottsdale, ibid.

last second, and continues to give us repeated chances to be saved.

We all have different prayer styles and Our Lord, more than anyone, certainly respects that. He also knows just exactly what each of us needs to be reached by His Presence, to discover our sinfulness, to be personally touched by Him. This is what begins people's conversion. We'll never be convinced by an intellectual presentation or argument. We must get to know Jesus Himself through an individual, tailor made experience.

St. Maria Goretti Parish has been given many gifts by God. Jesus has proclaimed it the 'Center of Divine Mercy' for the world, but especially this country. We are invited here to pray to the Blessed Mother as 'Our Lady of Joy.'

Lessons and subsequent messages from Jesus and Mary are collected in three volumes entitled, "*I Am Your Jesus of Mercy*".[3] A fourth volume, containing the last of the lessons and collected messages has just been published.[4] Many people in the world have read them and had their lives changed completely, Theo. It's truly marvelous how Jesus is working through these teachings.

Then in December of 1988, the Blessed Virgin Mary 'allegedly' appeared to Estela Ruiz, a mother of five adult children, who has worked many years for the Phoenix Department of Education. After years of resisting the idea of saying the rosary, though she was a good Catholic wife and mother, she willingly adopted this form of prayer, after a visit to Medjugorje by her husband Reyes.

Stella, who claims interior locutions and apparitions, relates her family was kneeling before a very old picture of the

---

[3] Riehle Foundation, PO Box 7, Milford, OH 45150.
[4] Queenship Publications, PO Box 42028, Santa Barbara, CA 93140-2028.

Virgin Mary when she began to repeat excitedly, 'que bonita! She's beautiful, she's beautiful.'

Mary told her during subsequent, frequent visits, that she had come to pray with us. To enlist the aid of all who would comply with her requests to pray specifically for the conversion of the Americas. It would take longer to convert us, she said, because of the degree of sinfulness; the abortions, murders, lack of respect and dignity with which we treat each other. She then asked that we pray to her as 'Our Lady of the Americas,' and requested that a shrine be erected in their back yard. This was attended by great numbers of people, and local media attention. However, as with so many prayer endeavors, the numbers have dwindled, and only a small core group of 150 people remain.

Stela claims her apparitions continue. However, on December 18, 1993, Our Lady announced that her appearances will now occur only on the *first* Saturday of each month and she invites us to focus even more on her Son and what God is asking of us personally."

The chiming of the hall clock broke the spell of these beautiful stories, so I announced that I'd be starting dinner now. Handing him a sheet of paper I said, "Why don't you sample an early message to Stela before we quit for the day?" Nodding to me, and accepting the outstretched material, he began to read silently.

'I cannot bear to see my children, my youth, lost to the evil one. I have come to claim for my children their rightful inheritance, which is heaven. I have come to battle Satan here in the Americas, and to help bring all my children, who will to do so, back to my Son's love. I have come to help my children enkindle their love, so that they can help me fight this battle.

It is through prayer and sacrifice that we will change many hearts. You who have answered my call and who

*have learned to pray from the heart, have already helped
me with many souls. I call on all the people of the
Americas to turn to prayer so that, together we will defeat
Satan and all his false promises.*

Satan cannot move against the strength of our prayers.

*Your sacrifice of fasting and giving up other activities
to be with me in prayer will help me to squash the
serpent's head.*

*We are living in tremendously evil times. God the
Father cannot possibly continue to allow this evil. He sent
His Son, my Son, to save the world, and the world ig-
nores this.*

*Help me, my children, help me. Time grows short.
Work with me to change the world, and your own lives
will change, and peace and love will prevail in your heart.
Sacrifice will turn to joy, and we will win the Americas to
my Beloved Son.*

*I thank you for being here. I send you my continual
love and my abundant blessings for answering my call.'*

Theo yelled to me in the kitchen, "Boy, I'd like to have been
there then. I never even heard of Stela. Does the Blessed Virgin
always perform miracles and give signs to people, Carol?"

"Hold on. I'll be right there," I shouted from the kitchen. I
walked out and led him back to the small conversation table
and chairs.

"Five minutes more," I said, "then back to supper prepara-
tions. Yes, conversions, some phenomena and healings have
occurred at St. Maria Goretti and in many places of prayer
around the world, as well as at the Ruiz' home. Extremely
important to understand is the fact that it's Jesus with His
Father, through the power of the Holy Spirit, Who call us;
convert and heal people; Who allow phenomena to occur. It
is Jesus' Mother who dispenses graces and favors, by the Will

of God, too, however, and serves as Prophet for these end times.

Accounts of the experiences of many of the young adults, and interviews with these visionaries have been written by Fr. Robert Faricy, Sister Lucy Rooney and Fr. Rene Laurentin. Those are some of the books I will be giving you to read, Theo, as well as, the four volumes of "*I Am Your Jesus of Mercy*".

Life goes on here and that is what these events are all about, teaching us how to live life in an ordinary way, but with extraordinary, unconditional love and mercy. Key words are *simplicity* and *perseverance*.

The profound love Jesus and Mary have for one another is reflected in the beautiful words they speak about each other. Jesus calls Mary, '*My Mother, My Heart.*' Mary's Immaculate Heart is the door to His Sacred Heart," I added.

"However, you certainly don't need to visit Scottsdale or Stela's house or any Pilgrim Site to have special prayer, to experience Jesus and Mary's presence, or hear their messages of hope. They're everywhere. All we need do is allow them to come into our lives and hearts to change us, cleanse us. We will then become more like God and the holy Mother. And one more thing . . ."

Theo looked at me intently again, as I took another breath and continued. "In May of 1992, Jesus and then His Mother began speaking to *me* in the form of internal locutions. They are telling me things to help my own transformation and healing, and facts to share with their people; facts that are being related in the contents of this fledgling book you have discovered."

"Carol, that's great. Can you share any of that with me now?"

I chuckled and nodded my head. "To begin with, Jesus and Mary have mentioned that we are living in the '*end times*'; that we must prepare for a time of purification (already upon us, by the way), and tribulations marked by wars and natural disasters on a grand scale. These will build up to an ultimate chastisement sent by God the Father, to cleanse the world and purify it for the Second Coming of Jesus into the world.

I am preparing this book in obedience to the requests of Jesus and His Mother in my heart, to share the messages They have given to me to help people *prepare* for the imminent future when many serious events will occur. What do you think of that? Do you still want to hear what I have to say, or do you think I'm one of those *'crazy people'* who go around announcing the end of the world?"

"*Are* you announcing the end of the world, Carol?" he asked softly.

"No, Theo, I'm NOT! This is definitely *not* about the end of the world.

Mary has explained that these are the times referred to in Scripture, preparatory and prior to Jesus' return and the defeat of the Antichrist, before a thousand years of peace. This is all detailed in Revelations.

It is *not* the end of the world. It is *the end of time* as we know it that they refer to and for which we must prepare; and it;s coming soon! The Triumph of the Immaculate Heart of Mary and the Reign of the Sacred Heart of Jesus will begin on the earth after this cleansing. It will be the actual return of Jesus to the earth when He, with His cohort of Angels, will defeat the Antichrist in the Battle of Armageddon. As I said in the beginning, this is very, very serious and urgent."

I stood up and walked around the room again. "To give you a clear picture of how direct Jesus and Mary can get, let me read a recent message. Since we have been backtracking anyway, we'll continue that pattern:

Blessed Mother: *'The time is over for talking. The Day of the Lord is upon mankind. The warriors of God ride into battle as the trumpets sound the battle cry.*

Harken to these words. Pray as you have never prayed before and be filled with love and joy and a fierce determination to hold out till the last moment of time that is left in this Age.

You will see unbelievable events and wonders worked by the hand of my Son. At the last possible moment, I will be victorious over the forces of evil, and Satan will be crushed and hurled into the burning pit. It is time for these events to begin and to play out to completion.

Blessed be the Lord, Our God.

Blessed be His Name.

Blessed be the might of His Arm." (6/13/93)

"But notice the message, even though it may sound frightening at first, is filled and balanced with the love of Jesus and Mary. They long for us to return to Them; to warn those who do not repent; to present new understandings of the spiritual darkness descending upon the Church and the world today. There are many reminders not to fear, but to be hope-filled *people of joy.*

Please do me a favor, Theo. Before you leave today, may I read to you one of the other messages Our Lady spoke to my heart in March this year? It won't take long, and will give you a better grasp of what I'm trying to tell you. Besides, it's wonderful to hear her own words of love and explanation. And, by the way, all of the messages I tell you about have been discerned by a spiritual director. Would you like to take some of them home with you and catch up even faster?"

"I would love that, Carol. Mom and Dad could read them too, and get a better look at what you've told me today. And I may be able to come back tomorrow. Gosh, there's really a lot to all of this," he said in amazement.

"Okay, hear what Mary is saying to us in this beautiful story, and then decide. It's fine with me for tomorrow. Now,

close your eyes and listen to her words meant directly for you."
I began to read in a slow, firm voice.

*'Now is the time for the triumph of my Immaculate
Heart to begin, as the darkness becomes nearly complete.
Without the mother, a child is lost and uncertain which
way to turn. Without the touch of her hand, the heart
grows colder and the heart is hardened from all that as-
sails it in this world.*

*There is no comfort like that of a mother. There is no
joy like that of a mother beholding her children at play, at
rest, learning and growing in the virtues of goodness.*

*I will defeat the evil one with my cohort of Angels, My
heavenly Angels, and my earthly angels who love me and
have given their lives to my cause. Oh child, rejoice with
me that a child has been born, the child of my longing. A
new heaven and a new earth are about to be born out of
the birth pangs of the world.*

*The labor and suffering of a godless world are about to
result in a new creature born of love and longing.
Without this labor, a child could not be born. This child is
a result of my love and labor in your behalf, Oh Alien
World. You have drifted far from the path of salvation and
have become a foreigner in your own land. You are not
aware of your birthright, purchased for you by my Son.*

*He is about to return and reclaim His rightful in-
heritance as King and heir of the Father. You will see
things as they were meant to always be in the Father's
great plan for His people. All is about to be purified and
rendered clean in the sight of God. Then it will be deemed
worthy to present to the Son upon His return. The Son
will, in turn, take all to His Father, and They will rejoice
together over your and their good fortune. Happy are you
who will see this day.*

*Please, give praise to Our Father Who so loves the
world that He will send His only Son, again, to save His
people and bring all to the completion of this Age.*

*You will look on in awe and wonder at these events
which will begin soon. There will be destruction of all the
evil which holds this poor world and all its inhabitants in
its mighty grip. Great will be the battle on that Day
which will see the return of my Son, the Great Warrior.*

*Be of stout heart and good cheer. Pray, child, pray that
many more will hear the call of their Lord and His
Mother before it is too late.'* (3/19/93)

We sat quietly for a while just to savor these beautiful and
powerful words. Certainly our own words would be a need-
less affront at that point. After several minutes I spoke again,
almost in a whisper.

"Here are the messages you'll want to take home. You
might want to read them more than once and get the true
flavor of Jesus and Mary's call to us at this very moment.
Before reading anyone's private messages, by the way, it's a
very good idea to pray to the Holy Spirit for help with your
own discernment and for protection. I've marked them all
with the dates they were received, but shuffled them around
to support the different themes that will be presented."

Theo nodded and started to get out of his chair. He looked
engrossed and a little sad and seemed to be listening deeply to
his thoughts.

"One more for today," I said, "even though it's time for you
to leave and for me to get busy again, but please, just listen to
this most poignant lament Jesus has shared about His world."
He nodded and sat back again listen to the beauty of Jesus'
words:

*'I, your Lord, am filled with joy and sadness for My
people: joy because of the increasing numbers who are*

turning to My Mother and listening to her plea; sadness for the many, many who do not listen, who do not believe and do not act on behalf of their brothers and sisters.

It is a world filled with greed and self-destruction.

It is a world intent to allow madness to rule and do nothing to change things for the better.

It is a world filled with its own need, mindless of the need of My beloved poor and starving children . . . starving for food and for the Light of Christ.

It is a world where chaos rules the hearts of godless men who fear nothing and no one, but their own fear of loneliness and emptiness." (8/19/92)

After a few more minutes of silence, I piped up again. "Besides trying to be obedient to Jesus and Mary's request to share all of my personal messages with their *children*, Theo, I believe it's important to take a good look at ourselves to see where we are in light of all that is being related to us in these urgent statements.

This is what will prepare us for the future: allowing Scripture, the Mass and the Eucharist, the strength of a prayer community and the solid convictions of our faith to nurture and strengthen us, help us to persevere in fidelity.

Gosh, I'm preaching. Go home, Theo. Here are the words from Jesus and Mary with some personal reflections that I'd like you to read before we meet again. Thanks for being such a good listener."

He gave me a quick smile and a hug. I shooed him out the door.

Homework for Theo

*'I, your Mother of Sorrows and Joy, am here.
Daughter, this was a week-end filled with many gifts
from God, Our loving Father. How He loves us all, as we
gather to plead with Him for the benefit of all His
children. Peace in the world has become a luxury of the
past, one which will not be enjoyed again until the end of
this era in which you now live.*

*The conditions in which you live cannot continue to
support life, true life in God. In order for the life of the
Spirit to be maintained, a proper atmosphere must exist,
one which will properly nourish the spirit and cause it to
grow.*

*Just as a flower requires sunlight, air and water in
order to blossom to its fullest, so the spirits of Our people
must receive the proper ingredients each day in order to
flourish.*

*There are certain laws of growth which are the same for
all living things, and when these laws are not fulfilled,
obeyed, proper growth cannot be assured. When constant
care and tending is not given a tender bud, it withers and
drops off the vine.*

*In a polluted atmosphere, the vine itself is choked and
unable to feed all the tender little flowers clinging to it for
life. This is the hostile environment in which all my*

*children find themselves today. Without a life of grace,
watered and nurtured by the Sacraments and supported
on the Word of God, each tender life, each growing bud
reaching out as a tender sapling reaches for the sky,
reaches out and finds . . . nothing.*

*The love of God, which once flowed vitally through
families, has dried up. The living waters of grace cannot
flow through branches that are broken apart and fallen
away from the main stem. The roots of family, which once
reached deep into the soil of faith, have dried up, as faith
has disappeared from the ground itself.*

*Daughter, this is a lesson for My people to ponder.
There is still time for My beloved children of the world to
beg God to cleanse the soil; renew the air; return the
waters of grace to their proper channels and build up the
Body of Christ, the Lifeline to the Father.'* (1/19/93)

Nearly seven months later on August 15, 1993, the Feast
of the Assumption, Jesus shared this point to renew our efforts
to watch, listen and pray. The time we were given in January
has passed. Have enough prayers been offered since then?

*'The delay afforded by My Father's mercy has not
brought about the results My Mother had hoped and
prayed for. It is necessary now for no more delay, for My
Father to execute His justice quickly and without ceasing
in order to hasten the day of My Second Coming and all
that needs to happen first. Time is a relative commodity,
My child, and there is no more. Compared to anything,
there is not one moment left in which to change the plans
of My Heavenly Father nor to effect a delay of His action."*

*It is time to go forth and call out again to the world
that Jesus Christ, the Lord of Divine Mercy, is coming
again and needs His children to prepare for this great
celebration on the day of the Lord.*

My Heart breaks at the coldness of hearts who turn from Me. What will reach the deaf ears of those who turn away? There are only a few left now who see the clear picture of Our needs, and whose hearts are fully prepared to respond with all they are and all they have to give.

My Mother has spent all of herself in an effort to speak throughout the world. Soon these manifestations will cease, and messengers are needed for the people who will falter. In the descending darkness, the only light that will shine will be the ones who will rally My remnant people around My Mother and protect her from the attacks of those who choose not to know her, hear her, listen to her words and invitations.'

'Doing Our Will is the greatest act of mercy you could perform for the world. Everybody wins. Most especially you are being merciful to My Father in Heaven when you allow Him to work through you His Will for His people.

Without an instrument of free will to use for His purposes, the Father chooses to remain helpless. Without your willingness to obey all He asks of you, the Father could not continue His plan of salvation for all of creation.

He has chosen to work through His people, as instruments of Divine grace and mercy and love. Unless someone says 'yes' to His invitation, nothing can be accomplished.

It is so true that you were created through no choice of your own, but you will not be saved without specific choices on your part.

This is the mystery of God's love. Everything you could ever need is completely at your disposal, but you must choose to love, to forgive, to have mercy.'

SUFFERING AND PAIN

'*Suffering is the vehicle by which My people become human. Their hard hearts are broken by certain events in their lives which cause great pain. This in turn causes them to stop and reflect in ways they never would otherwise.*

Pain breaks down defenses and postures, affects strength and rationalizations. One cannot present a false face to the world when that face is crumpled with grief or pain.

Pain is felt in the deepest recesses of your heart and soul. Nothing else will touch you at that depth. Joy is also felt deeply in your heart. This is only after pain and suffering have broken open the ground of experience in order to receive joy.

Pain and grief drop seeds of joy which ripen and burst into bloom only when they are watered by the tears of remorse and repentance. This process is the result of My Father's love for each of His children.

Without pain, man would continue to pursue lust and greed, power and ego, idleness and sloth. The pride which exists in the hearts of mankind is the sin of Satan's continued presence. As long as one continues to live a life of competition, anger and bitterness, selfishness and impatience, Satan will have his way with that soul.

It is not until that way is broken and the pieces of a life reassembled by Myself, through Our Holy Spirit, that a life begins to be lived according to the Creator's plan for it. Until then, the soul cannot find Me or My Way, because it is drowning in illusion, blinded by the false promise of the world.

One is healed only by being patterned after My life. This must happen for everyone before they can attain the salvation for which I died.

The vessel is broken and remolded many times because the action of change is very difficult for human nature to accept. The Father, in His gracious goodness, allows the soul to war against Him, resist and even run away, all the while calling to it.

The Father gathers the broken pieces once more and puts them together in a better fashion each time this process is repeated. Slowly, gradually, the finished works more and more resemble the Son, the image and likeness it was created to reflect. Gradually, there is less resistance, less tension from each vessel and it is then marked with My wounds.

The more a soul resembles Me and contains the marks of My life, My suffering and death, the more like Me it will become in every way.

Wounds and disease are caused by a split, a distance between the spiritual self and the worldly self. As long as this distance remains, wholeness and holiness cannot exist within the soul. The success of the world's promises will belong to its endeavors.

When you come near to Me on My Cross, you can see how much I loved you, and still do. When you accept your own cross: your weakness, defects, ineptitude, incompleteness, pain and wounds, you can bring it to me. I will press My wounds against yours to heal them.

You need do nothing but spend time with Me, the time it takes to fill you with peace after you have been emptied of the noise and chaos that lives deep within you. Only in the silence of contemplating My Cross and your own, and offering them to Me in unity, will healing begin.

Only by accepting each event the Father sends to you with obedience, and above all docility, will He be able to replace the lack of strength and discipline needed to be a child of God.

My suffering and death was the result of My love for you. Your suffering and all the little deaths, your crosses, are the result of My love for you also. They are the grinding stone which smooths the rough places, the hard edges, the brittle areas, the bumps.

My love for you also sustains you throughout your pain and suffering, just as My Father's love sustained Me. As you accept your life with its crosses, you will begin to discover the joy that can be yours in surrender.

Surrender to the Will of the Father is the gateway to joy. It is the narrow path which leads to the heart of the Kingdom. With it comes peace and contentment and security like you never imagined. These are all gifts which are experienced deep within the soul and are the results of allowing My Heavenly Father to lead you, to determine your life events according to what He knows is best for your soul to come most quickly to a state of perfection and unity with the Trinity.' (10/10/93)

'When a soul is in love, nothing is too good for, or too great a task to perform for its Beloved. Any suffering or hardship is considered no trial at all when performed at the request of the One who is loved.

The time spent serving the Beloved is a mere second on the clock of Eternal Love. The joy at serving the Master overcomes all fatigue, all thoughts of other plans.

In order to please her Master, the soul will wait in silent patience just to be available for the least desire of her Beloved.

What is necessary for you and what is pleasing to Me is what will be. Do not attempt to seek anything other than My Will. If you do not mention specifics, you will not be burdened with anxiety or questioning.

Peace is the result of total trust that all which happens is according to My Plan for you. Please, spend each day doing your work and accepting what comes as My Will and desire for you that day.

Stay in the present moment in a deeper awareness of My presence and be comforted by a knowledge of My love. The heart grows impatient when it is questioning and re-questing.

Be content with what is and know that this content-ment is the only way you can be aware of My presence and love for you. Seek Me in peace and docility. Be con-tent with My desires for your future and each thing that this will mean for you.

All have the opportunity to be renewed by My hand if they will only ask My forgiveness and pledge to Me their sorrow and eagerness to repent. It is a humble act to beg. It is a saving act to beg forgiveness for one's sins and con-fess them to Me.

Praise the Father and thank Him for His gifts, and above all, His Divine Will in your life. Whatever We re-quest of you is the result of His Will for your life. If you would live that Will totally, you will not ask questions regarding the future, but wait in humble obedience for all to occur. Docility is a difficult virtue. Only with the help of the Virgin Mother will you be able to live in this way.

Praise and gratitude to the Father for His gifts opens the way to more of His gifts. The Father's Will is always being fulfilled in each person and the events of each life. He knows exactly what each one needs to allow a full return to Him in sorrow and repentance. So do not question, but wait and see, love and serve all who come to you and trust that the Father's Will is being accomplished.

Please be at peace. Continue to wait in quiet acceptance. Offer each breath, each prayer, each action and word, to My Sacred Heart for the honor and glory of God, My Father. The knowledge that you are living in obedience to His Will gives you a peace and security like nothing else could.

A backbone of steel is developed by allowing Our words to build up in you a core of strength.

Only a peaceful, trusting waiting in My presence will equip you for your future. Again, it is not for you to do, but just to be. An instrument is picked up by the Master when it is needed, and laid down again after the fact.

You will help yourself if you focus only on the moment and what needs doing then. We can only accomplish in the present moment and none of your strength will be wasted through anxiety if you live in this manner.

The human will is a capricious sort which flies from one idea to the next. This flightiness must be tamed and stilled in order for it to wait on its God.

The Will of the Father is concealed until the right moment for it to be released. Then it goes forth to be accomplished by all those who will receive it with gratitude.' (10/11/93)

BATTLE PLANS TO STUDY AND IMPLEMENT

'A good soldier will be directed by her Savior and no one else.

A good soldier will listen intently for the commands of her Lord.

A good soldier will be attentive to the needs of her loved ones.

A good soldier will be compassionate and willing to do the Will of her God.

A good soldier follows the commands of her Commander.

A good soldier only acts upon the word of her Leader.

A good soldier is eager to serve the people.

A good soldier is patient and obedient to the end of the campaign.

A good soldier is willing to lay down her life for her duties.

A good soldier executes her Commander's orders without question.

A good soldier does not question an order.

A good soldier is faithful and honest and true.

A good soldier follows her Leader into battle, never running ahead or acting without His permission.

A good soldier displays courage and valor during combat.

A good soldier resists attacks on her person in silence.

A good soldier does nothing to interfere with the battle plan.

A good soldier lives with discipline and never challenges her Superior.

A good soldier does what is best for others without considering personal gain or loss.

A good soldier loves and cares for those people assigned to her care, and never betrays their trust in her.

*A good soldier is loyal to her Superior in spite of the
words and attitudes of others, even if this means dying
for His cause.*

*A good soldier is bound forever to the destiny of her Com-
mander.*

*A good soldier gives herself entirely over to the needs of
the Leader.*

*A good soldier does whatever it takes to stay in top shape
for the requirements of the job at hand.*

*A good soldier will never give in to coercion, or even tor-
ture, in order to remain true to the cause of her
Leader.'* (Jesus, 11/15/93)

*'Please continue on your present mode of giving all to
Me, coming to Me in prayer, holding My Mother's hand
and being aware of Our constant presence.*

*The days unfold in this holiest season of the year in
preparation for the celebration of My birth. As mercy is
born into the world again, let the love and forgiveness of
your Lord and Savior soothe your heart and cleanse your
spirit.'* (12/15/93)

*'The relevant forces of evil are gathering even now,
making their final plans for world domination. In their
viewpoint, there is nothing that can stop them, and they
will go forth with great courage and unabashed expectations of victory. There will be many different phases to the
Father's plan, so again I remind you, do not attempt to
figure things out. Do not waste time on speculation
please, but be prepared to respond in obedience.*

*Allow the angels to strengthen you with their love and
prayers and songs of praise. Join them for this holy season
in songs of thanksgiving to the Father.*

Bathe My infant body with your tears of love and gratitude. Warm me with your tenderness and love. Comfort me in the chill of the night with your prayers of love and thanksgiving.' (Jesus, 12/23/93)

'The minutes collect and go by and We are together as We await the Will of My Father. The time grows shorter, and We wait in hope for the fulfillment of His plan.

The time left before events shake the world is an instant on the timetable of My Father. You will know and feel My love for you just as often as you take the time to stop and be with Me and find out. Such serious times require preparation, and that includes much waiting.

Do you know what it is like to wait for Eternity? Ask the Saints to tell you what it was like for them to wait in their severe illnesses for the coming of angels who would release their bondage. Ask them what was the most difficult aspect of dying and the greatest source of pain.'
(Jesus, 1/94)

'It is by the Father's will that each little event occurs. If you will live in that awareness, peace will reign in your heart and so much can be accomplished. Your fatigue level will continue to diminish the more you can relax and trust that We are caring for you and helping you to finish each task.

The days move so quickly, My daughter, and huge changes are occurring in the world and in the lives of My faithful ones. You are all being brought together in order to pray and strengthen each other for the times about to unfold.

The goodness of God, Our Father, graces every action of those committed to His Divine Will. Please continue to pray for the gift of surrender to that Will, and all will be accomplished in union with it.

Do not expect certain events to occur at certain times. It has always been the Father's plan to keep the hour and the day reserved for Himself. Meanwhile, continue to give Him praise and thanks for all He does for you.

Your progress along the Way of Salvation is assured, child, if you will continue to listen and do the things We ask of you.' (Blessed Mother, 1/12/94)

'It is so unbelievable for one who knows Us so well to understand how people could reject the gifts being offered to them. Only continued prayer on the part of My faithful ones will assist the world through its final agony of cleansing.

The amusement of the moment seems to be the only thing on the minds of Our people, even as their brothers and sisters in foreign lands continue to suffer unspeakable horror.

The sadness in your own heart is only a shadow of the sadness in Mine. I am grieved so by the coldness of men's hearts who hurry by Me filled with indifference.

The self-serving of Our people has reached new levels unseen before in the history of humanity. It is impossible to reach them any other way now, and My Father's plans for the purification of the earth will be the only means to accomplish reaching through the walls of self-defense and self-seeking.

It is selfishness which is the greatest sin of this age.'
(1/30/94)

Chapter Four

Awareness

*"What we are aiming at in this warning is the love
that springs from a pure heart, a good conscience, and
sincere faith."* (1Tim 1:5)

In September of 1992, the Blessed Virgin spoke these
words to further understanding of the need to appreciate and
visit Jesus in the Blessed Sacrament *now.*

*'Soon the time will come when there will no longer be
an opportunity to visit My Jesus in His churches, or seek
peace before Him in the Sacrament of the Altar. Soon the
church will be overrun with darkness and decay, and man
will no longer be able to hear my voice or the voice of my
Son. Then will the hearts of all who love me be saddened
and heavy.*

*Then you must be filled with faith and hope in your
God Who has not abandoned you, but remains hidden in
order to purify His people and fulfill the Scriptures. This
will be a time of great suffering, for the feeling of abandonment will be very present in the world. Hearts will not
sing, nor will the worship of the One, True God be allowed.*

*I, your Mother, wish to warn my dear children and
help them and protect them; and they do not even know
my name. They will not acknowledge my presence in the*

world today, nor will they allow devotion to my Immaculate Heart.

Little do they realize that those who seek to destroy devotion to me are flirting with the fires of hell.

Little do they realize the implications of their actions and the results of their behavior. Doomed are those who reject me.

Lost are those who attempt to prevent my children from seeking their Mother.

Woe to those who walk in darkness, for they will weep and wail and gnash their teeth when my Son returns with His Angels on the clouds of glory.

Then the light will shine even more brightly for all to see their terrible deeds and witness their fiery descent into the deepest realm of hell, there to suffer torments forever.'

A mother always warns the children she loves. A mother always points out dangers of which they are unaware. A loving mother does not speak to frighten with mention of the freezing cold, but attempts to dress her little ones warmly in order to protect them against the penetrating wind and chilling dampness.

'Pray that somehow God's grace will penetrate the shields of all my children and light up the dark recesses of their souls. A soul who goes to hell suffers terrible torment forever, begging for even one drop of water to touch their tongues and ease their torment. This is not a torture to wish upon anyone. So, you must continue to pray constantly.

Continue to seek my Son and come into my arms to renew yourself for each new day's work.' (9/16/92)

Always there is tenderness, comfort, the dearness of a Mother who works and calls ceaselessly to train us for spiritual warfare and then renew us in the warmth of her love.

God, our heavenly Father, increases our awareness of His providence with His gracious message of October 5th, 1992:

'How I love My people and long to give them all My gifts. They must return to Me in repentance, and I will welcome them with open arms. Your world is about to be purified by Me for the great coming of My Son back into the world to lead all of you into My land of promise and plenty.

This time it will be Jesus, My Beloved Son, Who leads you into the land flowing with milk and honey, where former enemies will lie down in peace together, and all will live their lives in harmony, praising their God and loving each other.

Great will be the rejoicing, and songs will reach to the highest heavens.

No more will the hearts of My children be heavy with remorse and sorrow.

No more will the weight of sin pull you down.

No more will you need to be healed.

The rejoicing of all My people will raise the joy in heaven to new heights; and laughter and love will fill all those gathered to praise and adore the Living God Who has saved His people, once again, from the power of the evil one.

No more will he torment My beloved children. No longer will they weep and mourn, for peace and prosperity will fill the land. My people will be Mine forever.'

If we are receiving and understanding the words of Mary and her Son Jesus, given all over the world through special messengers today, then we must heed them as very *serious* and *urgent,* and become a new creation.

All of this involves a letting go, a death and grieving of our old selves; a slow rebirth and growth into the child of God we were always created to be. If we are becoming a new creation as a result of their call to *change* and *conversion,* we are no longer the same person we were when we began this journey back to the Father.

With the grace of God, we can be reformed and renewed, revitalized and elevated; or in some fresh new way, convicted with faith and trust in all we are hearing and seeing and experiencing with our new eyes and ears and hearts.

We can allow the words of our God and His Mother to fill us with an understanding of truth, a sense of awe.

Jesus calls again:

> *'My people, soon there will be much weeping and wailing and gnashing of teeth. Soon there will be but one flock and one Shepherd, but before that happens, there will be many who will wish they had listened sooner to My words and heeded the call of My Mother.*

> *Only those who come to know My Mother will truly come to know Me. Remain near to Her, learning from Her and allowing Her to bring you to My Sacred Heart.*

> *So many in the world do not listen to My Mother. They believe there is plenty of time for them to listen, and they go on about their chores in a carefree, mindless way. Do they not realize how near to the end* (of time) *they are? Do they not realize that all of My Mother's pleading all over the world comes from a knowledge of the Father's Will for the inhabitants of the earth?*

Pray that more will listen and turn to Her. Let your love, My love, flow out to all you meet. Tell them about My Mother and Me, and how much We truly love them. Tell them what glory awaits them in Heaven, and that I am waiting for them to come to Me and share My goodness.' (5/16/92)

Would not the fear of dying be erased if we allowed ourselves to accept these words of love?

Would our impatience not be soothed if we believed in goodness as our inheritance?

Would we not work and pray harder for the success of the Plan of Salvation outlined in Ephesians 1, if we acknowledged that the earth is truly the Lord's and all things in it, and that we are His heirs?

Would not complacency and lukewarmness then disappear?

'Blessed be the Name of My Father.

Blessed be His Holy Will and His Divine Justice.

Blessed be My Mother who mourns and weeps for her children at the throne of My Father.

Blessed are all those who pray unceasingly for the salvation of the world.

I wish for you to understand how very short is the remaining period of time, as you know it. Would that I could delay My hand, but I am unable to because of the many and great sins of mankind. They no longer believe in Me, or care that I call them back to the harbor of truth and unity of faith. They no longer care that I, their Lord, call again and again for My people to come back to Me. It fills Me with great sadness that man feels he no longer needs his God.' (7/3/92)

We know the feeling when our children reject us: when the children to whom we have poured out our love no longer desire our company and only come to us in time of need, in time of want. Our God feels this, only more so. And that is multiplied by tens of millions of people. No wonder it has been decreed by the Father that this can no longer be allowed to continue; not only for His sake, but for all of heaven and those on earth who are faithful to Him.

We have a loyal God, a loving God, one Who is faithful to His promises. No more will He stand by and watch his children be brutalized and experience their rejection. He must act on our behalf, for His own sake, for the sake of justice, and for heaven's sake.

These sobering words are offered to us as a warning to prepare. Let us pray to receive them.

> 'Our children must spiritually prepare as though the end is near. This is not the end of the world immediately, but it is the end of things in the world as you know it. The world is about to undergo an upheaval such as has never been seen before. Pray more and more that many more will be rendered worthy of salvation by the gift of the Father and the value of your prayers.

> The prayers of many are needed to purify the souls going into eternity. These times are most serious and call for the unity of all my children on this earth in order to offer one prayer of petition to the Father.

> He is greatly saddened by the need for this punishment. Please know that He does not wish to destroy, but only acts as a last resort in the face of a stubborn, stiff-necked people.

> Never in history has man rejected good with such a great force of will.

Free will was meant to be a good in the lives of Our people. Instead, it has become a weapon of destruction with which man batters God with his rejection of God and all His gifts. Man believes that man is responsible for all that he accomplished, without the realization that all is a gift from their Creator.

Man has become totally insolent and insufferable. It is no longer possible to tolerate this behavior.

Come back to Me, people. Time is running out, is gone, and your Lord and God can no longer hold back His arm of vengeance.

I long to take this people of Mine into My arms and calm their fears, soothe their worries; but they do not believe, therefore, they cannot come to Me, call on Me, their Lord and Savior Who died for love of them.

The time for My Father's hand to fall upon this earth is now, I tell you. The day is not important. Just be totally prepared at all times to live a long time or a short time. When you are prepared, it is all the same. When you are united with Me and serving Me here on earth, it is no different than doing the same in heaven. The discomfort you will experience here will be dulled by the joy of loving Me and serving Me.' (8/6/92)

'Children of the world, unite and come back to your God. Seize the moment and run to Me. Be assured of forgiveness and mercy. This has always been My promise to you. It has never been so important to believe and act on this promise. Soon all mankind will see their souls and the dreadful state of sinfulness.

Soon the adversary will redouble his efforts to win you away from Me. In his hatred, he will leave no stone unturned. No effort will be too great on his part, as he attempts to lure you with the empty promises of the world. Great will be the temptations and great will be the power to attract My chosen ones away from Me.'

Persevere in My love, and you will see how strong you really are, and how My love will protect and sustain you.'
(9/8/92)

Our Blessed Mother's heart reaches out to her children:

'Bring Me the lost and confused. Tell them of My love for them and of the comfort which awaits them in the Sacred Heart. Tell My children of Our concern for their souls and of how We long to hold and caress and comfort them. People do not believe Our love is real. Show them that love is the answer, and that the peace of My Son awaits all who come to Him without fear.

Tell all my children that We are longing for them to come often to Us in prayer. Warn them of the shortness of time, the little time that is left to repent and convert. Return to the rightful path towards your inheritance. A new day will dawn for all to see who will turn and be faithful to my Son.

The worst kind of pride is the kind that refuses to serve, refuses to love. It was in this milieu that the fallen Angels were cast into Hell and given dominion over the world.

My Son is coming again. The earth must be cleansed in order for Him to fulfill Scripture before He returns. All that is promised in Scripture will occur. All of you will be participants in these great events.

Blessed are they who toil in the vineyard of my Son. Blessed are you when you eagerly await His coming.

This event will be great, and the salvation of those who trusted in Him shall be fulfilled. Eagerly await this day. Long to see your Lord and beg Him to return soon.

All the earth will groan with birth pangs, as it awaits the dawn of a new day. This day will be glorious, for it will see a renewed earth and renewed beauty upon it. Our people will know their God, at last, and serve Him joyfully. All of Scripture will be fulfilled up to the Day of His Return.

Then laughter and joy will fill all hearts which have remained true to Him and to My desires.

Think of this day, child, and pray and long for it to appear. There will be many hardships and sorrows first, but a concentration on the happy events to come will strengthen you and give you courage from a knowledge of the happy times to come.

There is nothing to fear for those who fear the Lord, their Mighty God.

Satan is warring against the Father's plan to save His children and return the earth to its former beauty.

Satan wishes to destroy the world and return it to the state of chaos in which He originally was cast. That is why sinful men who follow Lucifer wish only to destroy goodness and beauty and return to darkness.' (8/27/92)

'The forces of evil will not stop until they are completely destroyed by God at the appointed time. Until then, there will be many acts of violence against the earth and mankind who has chosen darkness and evil and prefers to be ruled by the evil one.

Do not dwell on chaos, but on the love my Son and I have for you. Have no fear, my children, but be filled with hope because you have me to wrap you in my protective mantle.

Great protection is being given to each of you in this time of purification of the world. Great is Our love and longing for your return.

It is a time of Exodus, once more, out of the land of slavery and into the Promised Land. There will be great prodigies at the hands of my chosen children. It will be a time of unparalleled gifts from a merciful God Who calls out one last time for His people to come back to Him.

Blessed be God Who allows His Will to be done, even in His people who continue to reject Him. They do not know what they are doing.

Man must learn to honor his God and to listen to His commandments. Until the earth is cleansed of sin, there will be much weeping and gnashing of teeth. The hearts of many will be broken, and men will return to God with remorse.' (9/2/92)

Our God has a great longing for the love of His people. Are we convicted in our own hearts? Have we allowed His love to grace us, draw us into the Sacred and Immaculate Hearts?

'I await the return of My lost ones of the house of Israel to the home of My Father, where they shall be greeted with open arms and welcomed like the long, lost sons and heirs they truly are.' (1/10/93)

Our Mother teaches us to pray:

'Praised be the Father Who gifts His children.

Praise to Him Who continues to call His people to return to Him for more gifts.

Praise to Him Who allows me to come to all of you, and speak to you, and pray with you.

Praise Him with every breath. Seek to please Him in all you do.

Remain hidden with me, and you will learn quickly that to love is all.

Yes, it is sad that loving is so difficult for everyone. The very act by which you were created by Love Itself calls you to love as you are loved.

The very Love, which sustains and nourishes you, calls you to sustain and love everyone you meet with the same fairness and equality and acceptance that you have experienced from God. That same gift of love is free, my children, free to be enjoyed and developed and passed along to fill the world with beauty and carefree laughter and peace and safety.

The destructive forces which exist in your world today, children, cannot be allowed to continue. The Father has decreed that there has been enough suffering by all; and the cleansing power of His Love, His Divine Son Jesus, will rid the world of everything that is not of love, not of life. Pray, my children, and praise the Father.' (9/10/92)

A Scripture passage reflects:

"This is evidence of the just judgement of God, so that you may be considered worthy of the kingdom of God for which you are suffering. For it is surely just on God's part to repay with afflictions those who are afflicting you, and to grant rest along with us to you who are undergoing afflictions, at the revelation of the Lord Jesus from heaven with his mighty angels, in blazing fire, inflicting punishment on those who do not acknowledge God and on those who do not obey the gospel of our Lord Jesus.

These will pay the penalty of eternal ruin, departed from the presence of the Lord and from the glory of his power, when he comes to be glorified among his holy ones and to be marveled at on that day among all who have believed, for our testimony to you was believed." (2Thess 1:5-10)

Some are put off by the fact that the events, prophesied by Our Lady all over the world, have been delayed many times by the mercy of the Father and in answer to prayer. But the timetable for the cleansing of the earth and all people is still very much in place, and the 'soon' that we have grown to handle with care is now. St. Peter reminds us:

"But do not ignore this one fact, beloved, that with the Lord one day is like a thousand years, and a thousand years like one day. The Lord does not delay his promise, as some regard 'delay', but he is patient with you, not wishing that any should perish, but that all should come to repentance. But the day of the Lord will come like a thief, and then the heavens will pass away with a mighty roar and the elements will be dissolved by fire, and the earth and everything done on it will be found out." (2Pt 3:8-10)

"Therefore, beloved, since you await these things, be eager to be found without spot or blemish before him, at peace. And consider the patience of our Lord as salvation." (2Pt 3:14-15)

"Therefore, beloved, since you are forewarned, be on your guard not to be led into the error of the unprincipled and to fall from your own stability. But grow in grace and in the knowledge of our Lord and savior Jesus Christ." (2Pt 3:17-18)

Chapter Five

Awe

"Amen, amen, I say to you, we speak of what we know and we testify to what we have seen, but you people do not accept our testimony." (Jn 3:11)

"Theo! Hey, guy, haven't heard from you in a week. I thought you'd given up and left town. Of course you can come over this afternoon. See you, let's say about one."

A few hours went by and the lemonade was prepared for our new friend who had just arrived. Serving him, I listened to an account of his activity during the preceding days and was again touched by his quick mind and openness.

"Okay . . . is it alright with you if we pick up where we left things last time? Any questions about all those messages you've been reading?"

"Well, yes," he said, "and I've written them down to leave with you. You can answer them another time. However, there's one question I gotta ask," he looked at me intently. "Why you? I mean, this really isn't the sort of experience many people have. I don't mean to say you *shouldn't* be praying with the young adults or giving talks or receiving messages, but why did you get picked to be involved in all that has developed in Scottsdale?"

"Why indeed?" I responded. "That question certainly has come to me time and time again. And who ever knows all the answers, or God's plans. For one thing, I see God choosing the small and weak to confound the strong and proud. Certainly I've wondered myself so many times. Perhaps because the ages of our children are the same as those in the group and there is no trouble relating to anyone. I also have benefitted greatly from my time in the RCIA (that's for people who want to become Catholic or find out more about the Church), since there is such an emphasis and study of conversion. I know that helped me recognize and believe in the authenticity of the events here.

It's certainly not because of any resident piety that the Lord found in me just waiting to be tapped. On the contrary," I grimaced. "There have been many mistakes made during my lifetime, as I attempted to keep up with all the changes in our society. I was a real party girl and developed a drinking problem along the way because 'everybody was doing it.' My values were not great, to say the least.

Almost twenty years ago I was knocked off my high horse and experienced a very painful landing," I said wryly. "Coincidentally, God sent a special Nun into my life who acted as spiritual director. I could tell she was way beyond me and said to her, 'I don't have the kind of faith you're talking about. What can I do?' "

She just smiled then and said, 'Ask for it.' That was all, just ask. Then she said, 'and remember to be patient. It's going to take a long time.' And I thought of all the years gone by that brought me to this point. She introduced me to Scripture which opened up for me a profound sense of repentance, remorse and gratitude that has remained till this day. I didn't know much about Divine Mercy then, but knew I had been given mercy I didn't deserve, and could never earn. Worthiness would never be part of my re-entry, but an immediate conversion began, and a journey through Scripture and constant new discoveries about God. He was there waiting with joy and immense love to take me back, as He will for each one who returns to His arms.

It was not until my Medjugorje trips that Mary became a real person for me, and not just someone in a song or story. I knew her as the Mother of Jesus, but not yet the warm, loving, friend she has become since then.

Jesus and Mary did, however, also grant me several powerful experiences of Themselves, and a deep, heavy resting in the Spirit, from which I could not move. Several times I believe the Blessed Mother spoke to me through Gianna and Stephanie, moving me to believe the invitations to serve Jesus' beloved ones, and do other things in the future in Their behalf. This convinced me to accept the fact that I actually had been invited to work here in a special way. The Lord humbles us with gifts, Theo, and I would have to say now that my overwhelming feeling towards God is *gratitude* for all His goodness and patience and kindness towards me."

I looked up at him suddenly. "But what about yourself? How were you finally captured by God's relentless pursuit? I need to know what new understanding the Holy Spirit has given you, what change He has brought into your life to cause you to stop and listen."

Theo smiled, nodded, jumped up, and began walking about the room as he spoke. He waved his arms excitedly and described his gratitude at the discovery of a world filled with answers found only in God Himself.

"You're right about pursuit" he said. "As I mentioned the first day, it's been just recently that going to Mass on Sundays became important to me. I had told myself I'd have plenty of time to get straight with God after having the same college career as most people I know; get married and, maybe around the age of 40 or so, I'd give religion some thought. That worked pretty well for a long time and I never needed the help of anything or anyone.

Then it seemed like everything suddenly fell apart, although my folks have never been aware of that. First, my best friend at school got so sick he had to go home. The doctor said six months rest would bring back his strength, and he'd be fine. I visited him a lot, and we made plans for his return to the campus. Then, just like that, without any warning, he died.

I couldn't believe it. I wasn't even there. He'd been getting better and bam, he got pneumonia and was gone in twenty four hours. I still can't get over how fast it happened. I felt so helpless. I find myself going to the phone to call him with some new story or piece of information. I still feel so strongly that he abandoned me personally. That's not true, I've come to realize, but, gosh, the feeling just won't go away.

About a month after that, another close friend was forced to leave school permanently because of the death of her mother. She's taking care of her brothers and sisters now and doesn't know when she'll return. That was a bigger blow, I think, after Danny had just died. It made me feel terrible."

He was pacing and speaking even faster now, and I could feel the anxiety building in him from across the room.

"But why did he have to die? He didn't do anything wrong to anyone. He was going to be a person who would do great things for other people in this world. He never hurt anybody. He was a good guy! I just still don't understand," he said, shaking his head sadly.

"Oh Theo," I said gently. "Of course you don't. It really doesn't happen that way. By that I mean we don't die because God wants to punish us, or the people who love us. Someone, somewhere, I don't remember who, said, 'Life is not a series of questions to be answered. It's a mystery to be lived.' If you've lost someone you love, that part becomes apparent. We want so much to understand, reduce everything to neat answers, but if we only look at life from one dimension, here on earth, we will never see the truth that life is not over when we die, but only changed.

Sometimes we see immediately the reason a person dies. Often it's years later that we look back and realize that occasion brought us closer to God, or gave us a new appreciation of how fragile life is. We develop a greater respect for ourselves and each other. And, most often, we will not come away from a conversation like this with a new understanding. We need to live out the questions in our hearts, let life show us new mysteries, new truths."

"What do you mean by that, Carol?" Theo looked at me with concern. "Couldn't the Lord teach us in some other way besides taking a person we love away from us?"

Shaking my head sadly, I continued. "He doesn't take a person to be with Him in order to get even with us or punish us, Theo. Again, that person continues to live and grow into a new life in God. Often the Lord says of this period of time right now, 'many of our numbers will be taken to heaven in order to pray for those who are left here on earth.' That would not be the only answer about your friend, I think, but surely one of them. It's good to reflect on how your own life has changed and what you have learned since Danny died."

He looked at me for a long time without speaking. Then he said, "Will I ever understand, do you think?"

Gosh, Theo, I wish there was a way to assure you. I only know that understanding comes when we take those questions to Jesus Himself. In Scripture, answers are found to all our questions. In reading and listening to Jesus' words and how He lived His life, we come to many new awarenesses about why we live and die. Many people anguish over why Jesus had to die.

There's an encyclical that our own Pope John Paul II wrote in 1980 that sheds some light on that. He says that God, the Father, needed to show us how our life worked, as a series of dying and risings, so Jesus accepted death on the Cross followed by His resurrection, in order to give us a clear picture. God also wished to show us that He is more powerful than death, that death no longer had power over us, that the way to Paradise was reopened, when Jesus died to atone for the sins of all mankind, that we are only changed by death, as Jesus was changed in His resurrected body. A lot to think about, but our minds and understanding also must be stretched in order for us to grow.

If nothing else happens in your heart, Theo, please ask the Holy Spirit to help you believe that God has only good in mind for all of us. In Paul's letter to the Romans, chapter 8, he reminds them that God brings only good out of all things to those who believe in Him. Often a lot of time goes by for us before we can see that good, but we can pray and keep believing in that promise. And only the greatest good and happiness is given to those who are taken to heaven. We can be happy for them once we get past the terrible sadness of their departure. Time is the only healer, Theo, the only medium through which understanding and healing are given." I smiled at him gently again.

His face had softened now. Some of the anger and concern had ebbed away, leaving him visibly relaxed and at peace. He nodded his head again and said, "I guess I don't know very much after all, huh?" Then, as if he had satisfied some inner need to heal those memories, he took a deep breath, smiled, and continued:

"I guess part of what happened to me was I began noticing that many of the things I was doing and the ways I was acting were pretty stupid. I began to spend more time with one of the guys at school who we all knew went to church regularly and was really fun to be around. I asked him a few questions now and then about Jesus because we never really heard much about religion in grade school or high school, even in religion class. He told me a lot of good stuff which made me think going to Mass was less weird for people our age than I had imagined." He looked up for a moment and smiled ruefully.

"I told him about my other friends, and he explained I could pray for Danny and feel close to him again and maybe in that way develop a personal relationship with Jesus, too. I certainly never heard of having a personal relationship with God, but wanted to hear more, so I started going to church on Sundays with my new friend, Greg. Our priest gives great homilies and for the first time in my life, I was listening and learning something every week.

Greg explained that it was the Holy Spirit Who helped us realize new things about God and opened us up, he said. There have been so many new concepts, Carol, and I *have* begun to feel closer to Jesus. I'm still not sure how that works. We visited the Blessed Sacrament together sometimes, too, and the 'quiet' was so peaceful, I couldn't get enough of it," he said in a hushed voice.

I smiled through a few tears and nodded my head. His story was so powerful because of his sincerity and awe.

"Anyway," he continued, "that's how I began to hear stories about the Blessed Mother appearing, and that's when we moved here, of all places. God has been very good to me, too. The Sacrament of Reconciliation was actually much less difficult than I had expected, and I did feel better. Now that I've begun praying more, I can't get enough of these lessons and stories. It truly has gotten easier to pray the rosary every day. I guess it *is* just like football. The more you practice the easier and better it gets," he nodded. "I sure hope we can continue these meetings till I'm completely caught up with everything. What were you about to tell me next?"

I smiled again and motioned for him to sit down. It was alright for him to wander around talking, but I would never maintain enough concentration to present the important points that came next. I took a deep breath, a long sip of tea and launched into a new direction.

TESTING OUR SPIRITS

"The basic requests of prayers for peace and conversion of the world, fasting, reconciliation, penance and faith, have been given to us by Mary and Jesus. If I am truly living them, nothing more is needed, except perhaps a boost in commitment. I do need a charge for my batteries now and then, a further understanding of the need to be on guard and test all spirits, a keener listening for changes, for softly pedaled heresy. That's one of the advantages of Marian conferences held yearly around the country. People want to come together to celebrate their love for the Blessed Mother, and her incredible love for us." I could feel a deep conviction on these points.

"Obviously, we are existing in a time of war. The enemy is everywhere, and we're learning how to recognize him. The necessity for *testing the spirit* of each message we read is absolute. We've been attending, one might say, a holy boot camp. We've been tested and shown the value of testing.

We've come together in prayer communities with people we didn't know before and received weapons that shouldn't have been new, but in most cases were: the rosary, private and group prayer, scripture studies, the chaplet of Divine Mercy, Eucharistic Adoration. We discover who's trustworthy and those on whom we can't rely. Leaders develop and from time to time someone goes A.W.O.L.," I said with a quick smile.

"Everyone learns obedience to the Supreme Commander. A common goal is very cohesive, especially when lived out under the folds of a blue Mantle belonging to the Commander's Mother.

One of the most important spirits to test on a regular basis (believe it or not), Theo, is *our own*. How sincere am I? Why *am*

I attending prayer groups?" He nodded his head as if to agree and encouraged me to continue.

"Last year the members of the Young Adult Prayer Group said they felt Our Lady was asking them, *'Are you coming here for the glory of God or for your own glory?'* Now you see, when *she* asked that question, we had to confront ourselves. Actually all of us need to question our motives and pray constantly to be purified, fortified. We have a great ability to rationalize, to fool ourselves most of all."

"I believe that easily enough," said Theo. "I've been good at that."

"Haven't we all?" I agreed. "So, wouldn't you know it, in the First Letter of John there is a significant passage and guideline for our times. Would you please read it aloud so we can reflect together?"

He took the Bible from my hands and settled back to begin the passage I had marked earlier. First he read silently, sat quietly and seemed to think about it. Several minutes ticked by without a sound. Then he read aloud.

> "Let what you heard from the beginning remain in you. If what you heard from the beginning remains in you, then you will remain in the Son and in the Father. And this is the promise that he made us: eternal life." (1Jn 2:24-25)

FAITH ROOTED IN TRUST

We shared a long look of mutual appreciation before I continued. Now it was my turn to walk around. "In case you wonder why I chose this passage in Scripture, by the way, know that recently I attended Mass in another parish at which the celebrant said: 'Father, send Your Spirit upon these gifts of bread and wine that they may become a *symbol of our lives.'* " I stopped and turned to speak directly to him.

"The words that we have heard for centuries are, 'Father, send Your Spirit . . . that they may become *the Body and Blood of Our Lord Jesus Christ.*' (Not a symbol of anything!) The difference between the two prayers is enormous. That's one kind of subtle change I'm referring to. The Eucharistic Prayer said the first way is not what we have heard from the beginning. Here's another reminder from John." I reached down and took the bible from the table, opened it, and began reading:

> 'You belong to God, children, and you have conquered them, for the one who is in you is greater than the one who is in the world. They belong to the world; accordingly, their teaching belongs to the world, and the world listens to them. We belong to God, and anyone who knows God listens to us, while anyone who does not belong to God refuses to hear us. This is how we know the spirit of truth and the spirit of deceit.' (1Jn 4:1-6)

"The above is a famous quote, and one which could prove very important to each of us some day. When changes that have begun in the Catholic Church escalate, become more public and challenge our faith in the name of obedience to a pastor or bishop, we will know what is right, what is truth, if we are prepared by a knowledge of Scripture. It will always be a matter of our unflinching faith in Jesus Christ, the example of His life and teachings, and our *Tradition* (which contains revelations of God to the Saints), that will help us to persevere.

Truth will be preserved in our lives by embracing it, remaining one with it, defending it. Hmm," I looked at him suddenly, "your expression is a giveaway, young man. Are you thinking what our children often say to me . . . 'So, Mom, how do you *really* feel about all that?' "

Just then the door opened to usher husband home from the financial wars. "What are you two talking about today?" he grinned. "Want another set of ears for a while? I think you probably need some fortification, right Theo?"

"Hi, Mr. Ameche, it's great to see you. I could use a drink other than all this tea, that's for sure. Shall we go back to that Happy Hour idea?" he teased. Don quickly poured a glass of tea from the pitcher and sat down to join us.

YOUTH OF SCOTTSDALE RESPOND

Laughing at first, Theo quickly became serious and asked, "What else can you tell me about the young adults? Have they changed very much, do they pray a lot now?"

A picture came to my mind of the interior of the Tabernacle Adoration Chapel about fifty yards from St. Maria Goretti Church. Big enough for only seventy five or so people, the glass walls allow a merging with surrounding flowers and shrubs which are then enclosed by a white stucco wall. A beautiful mosaic of Jesus graces one side; facing one of Mary, just as beautiful, on the opposite wall. The night sky becomes a starlit ceiling above those gathered, and lights that can be dimmed set the stage for a peaceful visit with Jesus. It is perhaps the most unusual Monstrance (receptacle for the Host) in the country.

A sturdy, filigreed, hollow bronze cross holds a crystal bowl filled with consecrated hosts at its center and stands on a small rock formation. Light from the base illuminates the cross and hosts, affording a soft reflection on the faces of four attending Angels. They hold large vigil lamps and kneel at four corners. It always makes me think about how we discover, sooner or later, that Jesus is at the center of every cross, waiting in peace to be discovered.

All of this sits within a fountain that continually issues a low bubbling sound of the blessed water running into a tiny pool surrounded by growing, trailing greenery. The Angelic faces stare intently at their Creator with great awe and affection. After a while, the faces of human adorers reflect the same look. It is a place of great peace and beauty. Jesus must relish being present here.

"Every evening," I began, "from seven till almost midnight, Theo, the same young faces appear for nearly an hour. They spend time with Jesus talking about their day, mentioning petitions and just praying for the world and other youth in the Americas. This is all silent, private prayer with no formal routine, but a consistent return of the same people speaks of a strong and deep relationship with their Lord. They arrive and leave at different times and are quite recollected and peaceful looking, although they might be struggling over some very serious problem, just as much as anyone else.

We are very fortunate to have perpetual adoration at St. Maria Goretti. People are adoring Jesus in the Eucharist around the clock. There is an extremely active teen group, also. Members of that crowd drop in all day and evening too, and I know that many people from the parish spend a regular hour there every week. The charismatic group meets in there on Tuesdays, and visitors never want to leave.

That's pretty special, don't you agree?" Theo sighed in response.

"One of the most notable occurrences is the large number of young people at the daily Masses, at least ten times as many as five years ago. It's encouraging, Theo, just like the beautiful display of 700,000 orderly, prayerful youth who spent a quiet, respectful week-end in Denver recently to visit with Pope John Paul II.

The ministry and spirituality of this parish has always been alive and special, however. Just attending church here can prepare one for whatever God wills.

Fr. Jack had *always* emphasized the importance of the Eucharist. He would say over and over, 'We can't live the radical demands of the Gospel without the nourishment of Jesus in the Eucharist,' or 'Don't let being good keep you from being great in your relationship with God.' I think his favorite quote must be from St. Agustine, 'Our hearts are restless, O God, until they rest in You.'

Anyway, there are young people all over the country who have answered Mary's call, and other adults need to recognize and appreciate that. Those in the Friday prayer group here are becoming more serious about their commitment, more in love with Jesus and Mary. Jesus told them He is a romantic God Who seeks an intimate love relationship with each of us.

"Gosh, do you think I could fit in? I haven't even been back to regular Sunday Mass for very long. I feel pretty *out of it*."

My young friend's face was clouded and wrinkled with concern. I thought of all the conversion stories that had been shared with me. He would never believe and I couldn't tell him the contents of those stories, but each person had a special problem or pain to bring to the Lord. All of us were here now as a result of conversion from a much different lifestyle. Some of those stories were tragic, some poignant. All were terribly exciting examples of God's mercy.

"Everyone who prays all over the world is still struggling, please believe that, Theo. God must be allowed to penetrate our defenses in order to make us fruitful, to create Jesus in us over and over again. When Mary invites us to the same *'Fiat'* *(let it be)* which she gave, it means we can say with her, 'Be it done unto me according to Your word.' (Lk 1:38)

In another of the messages to my heart, I believe I personally received Jesus' promise, *'In listening, you will be led. In answering, you will be protected.'* "

I sat down again and stared in silence at my shoes and a thought suddenly came to me of an incident I could share.

With great excitement I nodded my head, leaned toward my avid listener and spoke warmly.

A CONVERSION STORY

"Now, let me tell you a story. It's an actual account of one person's experience here." He sat up straighter sensing something important.

"There's a young man living in Scottsdale who moved here from another state. He had a deep call from Jesus after visiting one time. After a lot of discernment and change in his life as a result of what he saw and heard here, reading material in the volumes of "*I Am Your Jesus of Mercy*", his decision to move was finalized by a divorce.

The pain and struggle to get a job, settle in, and spend the amount of prayer time he felt called to, resulted in his spending a lot of time in the chapel. All this had covered many weeks, and loneliness had been a constant companion. Even though he recognized a new presence of Mary and her Son in his life and was nourished weekly by their words, the change had brought with it a sorrow, a mourning of the old days, the person he used to be and the people in that life. He especially missed his two children.

According to his account, late one night he came into the chapel after being sick for several days. He closed his eyes as usual, and sat there for a while trying to settle down, to absorb some of the peace always present there. Suddenly, with his eyes still closed, he began to see continuous bursts of brilliant colors with a predominance of beautiful purple hues billowing across his mind's eye.

Then from the left of this picture, an outline that he felt was Our Lady came towards him. She was holding her hands cupped together and outstretched. In her hands was a tiny fetus which she was presenting to him.

He recalls not wanting to open his eyes, keeping them closed tightly and thinking, 'I'm really seeing this.' He sat there in amazement at this scene or vision, still surrounded by the brilliant shades of deep purple.

As he looked at the fetus, it came to him that the Blessed Mother wanted him to pray for an end to abortion and for the mothers of those babies. He said an Our Father, Hail Mary and Gloria, all the while colors were still swirling.

By the end of the last prayer, the figure of Our Lady had receded and only the fetus was there floating in the radiant shades of purple. Instantly, he says, he knew it was a boy and that it was 'the child my wife had miscarried when we were first married. I knew without any words it was my son,' he said with great excitement.

He cried for joy. Tears ran down his face from still closed eyes, and he started to ask Our Lady if what he was seeing was something real. Then he thought, *no!* Jesus has been teaching me about my faith. I won't ask, I will believe.

Later, Fr. Jack told him to ask his son to always pray with him and for him, and for his mother and brothers.

He has an understanding that his conversion which was so life changing, was facilitated by the special prayers of his infant son. Sometimes he feels a special closeness to him, as if he is kneeling down next to him while praying.

That's real, Theo. Let's not even talk now, but reflect on the beautiful mystical gift Our Lady gave to this young man. Perhaps tonight you can think about his story and the great mercy and goodness of God.

I think tomorrow I would be free to continue, by the way. Would you like that? Great. See you then." He left quietly.

Chapter Six

Alertness

"Be constantly on the watch. Stay awake. You do not know when the appointed time will come." (Mk 13:33)

"Theo, hi, come in. Be right with you."

I had motioned to him from where I stood talking on the phone. After hanging up and walking over to where he sat, I held out several papers.

"Listen, would you mind reading through these, Theo, since I have to make a few more phone calls? You'll enjoy reading them to yourself anyway."

I ran back to the hall and sat down. Occasionally looking up, I could see him sunk down in a large chair and completely absorbed. I nodded to myself, thinking for a moment about the messages I had given him, messages which I believe Jesus and Mary had spoken to my heart.

Jesus: *'The people of this generation are totally without the grace of God; totally disinterested in anything which speaks of holiness; totally without interest in the things which are necessary to save their souls for their future in Eternity.*

It is nearly unbelievable that so many refuse to listen to My words and those of My Mother, spoken through Our chosen ones in so many parts of the world. There have been many who prayed; many who fast and do penance for the conversion of the world and, still, not many have responded to those good works being offered on their behalf.

All of heaven is waiting for the sword of justice to be lowered upon the earth. All are in preparedness, and wait in silence for the battle to begin. It will be just as it is written, My daughter. Pray with Me for all who will suffer great trials and hardships.

There will not be one person who does not experience this tribulation in some way. My remnant flock will be saved for the glorious time of My Second Coming. All will be in readiness for My return, and Scripture will be fulfilled completely.' (4/26/93)

Blessed Mother: 'The time is over for talking. The Day of the Lord is upon mankind. The warriors of God ride into battle as the trumpets sound the battle cry. Harken to these words. Pray as you have never prayed before, and be filled with love and joy and a fierce determination to hold out till the last moment of time that is left in this age. You will see unbelievable events and wonders worked by the hand of my Son. At the last possible moment, I will be victorious over the forces of evil, and Satan will be crushed and hurled into the burning pit! It is time for these events to begin and to play out to completion.

Blessed be the Lord, Our God.

Blessed be His Name.

Blessed be the might of His Arm.

Jesus: 'See that you continuously defer to Me in all that you do and say and think. These are dark days, indeed, and I need you to be strong and courageous.' (7/25/92)

Blessed Mother: 'Always remember that it is Our plan and Our work that is being done and the Father's Will *that is being accomplished. Seek to defer to Our help. This will be given to you and all will go smoothly. You will not go astray if you follow this advice and stay close to my Heart.'* (8/19/92)

Blessed Mother: *'You are seeking a greater union with me, and that is the first step towards acquiring it. Continue to practice inviting me to be with you and pray with you at each moment of your day. I long to hold all my children in my arms and welcome them into heaven where they belong.'* (9/4/92)

Jesus: *'Please, continue to seek a closeness with My Mother. Watch her. Listen to her. Be like her in all you do.'* (9/10/92)

Blessed Mother: *'Gratitude is a necessary ingredient on our way to holiness. Appreciation of God's gifts will help us to realize more and more what a privilege it is to be allowed to serve God and His people. It makes us aware of the different gifts the Father has given to us, and how He is now allowing us to use them.'* (9/10/92)

Jesus: *'Doubt and darkness will exist regarding My real Presence in the Eucharist. This will be the cause of a major battle within My Church, and many will fall away for fear of their own safety. Many will be the Bishops and Leaders who will lead astray My poor sheep. They will wander aimlessly, and it will be to these that you must take My words of faith and encouragement.'* (11/28/92)

Jesus: *'Please, believe Me when I say time is short and the urgency is great. Satan is trying to wear you down. Don't let him. Fight with all of your might to avoid his clutches and distractions.'* (1/5/93)

Jesus: *'My remnant flock will be saved for the glorious time of My Second Coming. All will be in readiness for My return, and Scripture will be fulfilled completely.*

Come with Me now and stay at My side as we experience these events together. I need your love and comfort and prayers. I need for you to be My defender for Myself and My dearest Mother. Come and arm yourself with My strength and might. Take up the call to victory, but first, stand strong and firm against the enemy that is cunning and sly and evil.' (4/26/93)

Jesus: *'As you see events and natural disasters occurring, know that the plan of My Father is coming to pass. Each event will touch more hearts and turn them to Me.*

Is it not a pity that conditions in the world must bring about such punishment in order to purify My Father's Creation? My Heart bleeds anew for the inhabitants of earth. My soul is again sorrowful unto death.' (7/9/93)

God the Father: *'Please, have more patience for all to occur in your life. Each waiting, each letting go, each dying to self creates a new person born in you to the glory of My Name, My Heart and in My Divine Will.*

Each time you say, 'Thy Will be done,' you are lifted higher and become more purified, more blessed by that Will. Please, continue to be in the most perfect union with Me through the Sacred Heart of My Son and the Immaculate Heart of My Mother.

Dwell only in Our peace, continually denying your self and deferring to Me. Only by living out your promises can you adhere to the action of My promises.'

Jesus and Mary wish to speak to all of us, they have said in locutions recorded around the world. We must however *test* each voice we encounter in our hearts to make sure it comes from God and not the evil one, or our own imagination or longing. We are so weak and inept, such fledglings in our experiences with God, that we must be always on guard, cautious and careful about the messages we read and follow, though not unbalanced and fearful. And remember, the only *messages* we can completely trust are those recorded in scripture, believed to be Divinely inspired and guided.

The use of holy water while praying is important. Bless yourself before beginning to pray: 'In the Name of the Father and of the Son and of the Holy Spirit.' We used to add, 'Praised be Jesus Christ now and forever, Amen.'

Challenging a perceived *'holy voice'* is a *must* for all who pray, in order to be led by the *Holy* Spirit. It is Jesus Who has power over Satan, not us, and the authority to use His Name to expel demons is given to us by Him.

> 'I command you in the Name of Jesus Christ to identify yourself.'

> 'If this is not of God, in the Name of Jesus Christ I command you to cease.' *(To be used whenever we see a vision or hear a voice.)*

> 'Do you submit to the Lord Jesus Christ as your Lord and Savior?'

> 'In the Name of Jesus I charge you to say, "Jesus Christ is my Lord and My God." '

Words to become familiar with and comfortable using when we feel ourselves under attack or temptation are:

> 'Be gone, Satan, in the Name of Jesus Christ, and do not return!'

Or,

> 'By the power of the Name of Jesus, I command you to depart from here and return to hell where you belong. You have no power over me.'

Our belief, our conviction in the *power* of Jesus' Name further enables Him to be victorious on our behalf.

When we are fearful or angry, driving these feelings away in Jesus' Name is most helpful. Treat them as the *demons* they are. The evil one is subtle, cunning, sneaky, lower than we can ever imagine. He is mean, despicable and always on the lookout for the slightest crack in our defenses, a tiny waver in our resolve. We are no match for him and his demons, and must always begin and end our day asking for the protection of Mary and her Angels. This is meant to generate peace, not anxiety, a conviction in the supreme power of the *Name of Jesus.*

Nancy Fowler, the *'alleged'* visionary from Conyers, Georgia, has confided that she always uses this challenge, *'Say that you bow down to God the Father.'* On occasion, it is Satan who appears (disguised as Jesus or Mary), who responds, *'I bow down to no one!'* Then he vanishes. We can have total trust that Jesus is more powerful than any demon, and the Blessed Virgin, as well, because she has been made the enemy of Satan whom she will strike with her heel (Gn 3:15).

Theo put down his reading material just as I hung up the phone. Walking back to where he sat, I said to him, "Theo, something has just dawned on me. Would you read these principles of discernment while I go out and start dinner? They are a collection of my own ideas from the experiences of these past few years. You are free to use them or not."

He took them from me and began to read.

SPIRITUAL WARFARE

1. Be alert spiritually at all times. Be on guard, aware of the possibility of deceit.

2. Always be aware that I am operating out of some degree of pride and never be too sure of myself. Remember how *needy* I am.

3. Before any decision, ask for guidance of the Holy Spirit; count on it and give thanks for it before and after the fact.

4. As a general rule, before leaving home in the morning, ask for protection of God and His Holy Angels; invite Mary, Our Mother, to be with me and pray constantly with me. Offer all to the Father for His honor and glory. Pray for guidance of Holy Spirit throughout the day. Seek the help of Mary as Mother of Good Counsel. Pray to her daily under that title.

5. Before each conversation or task, pray that the Father's Will be done. Ask to do only this. Thank Him upon completion. Praise and thank Him often for His gifts to me. This should help me stay in the environment of discernment and trust.

6. Have all material and myself under the guidance of a *competent spiritual director* and have recourse to him often.

7. Before receiving or reading any message, ask for deliverance in Jesus' Name from any spirit that is not of Him. Request the protection of St. Michael. Afterwards, return to Jesus in prayer, thank Him for the message and ask again (in His Name) whether or not it's really from Him.

8. Be extremely patient for prophesied events to occur. Even Jesus and Mary do not know the day or the hour. Do not be distressed if they do not occur.

9. Know and keep in mind all the rules of discernment of St. Ignatius.

10. If I belong to a prayer community, ask them to pray and discern with me.

11. In sharing messages or decisions with another person, avoid anyone who is not mature, or who thinks I'm wonderful.

12. Be serious, but never take myself too seriously.

13. Be joyful. Seek to live completely and constantly in the Divine Will of God.

14. Remember that we never know if a message is real until it either does or doesn't occur.

We all may suffer demonic attacks or great temptations from time to time. The sensible attitude toward these is not fear, but one of *preparedness*. Here's a prayer we have permission to share. It was given during a time of great danger to a source who must remain anonymous:

'By the grace of God I recognize you Satan. You have no power over me, I am a blood-bought child of the lamb. In the name of Jesus Christ I command you to depart from me. Go directly to the foot of the Cross, where Jesus will deal with you, and bother no one on the way. Come, holy angels of the Lord. Come and minister to me in my needs and weaknesses, all for the greater glory and honor of God, the Father, Son and Holy Spirit. Amen.'

Back in the room again I watched Theo's face become more and more serious, so I said, "We need to be serious, Theo, and practical about the way we are living and interacting with our brothers and sisters. A daily reflection on our behavior is one of the biggest spiritual favors we can do for ourselves. But remember to balance that with the prayer, 'Jesus, I trust in you,' and a sense of joy and hope."

While he reread more of Jesus and Mary's words, I sat and reflected on some issues that had become important to me. The fact that we cannot see demons, who are conniving in every possible way to deceive us, is all the more reason *we should take every precaution to save ourselves from their influence.*

Several precautions came to mind:

Feel positive about all the things we're doing to answer the call of Mary.

Discover that serving others, treating them kindly and thoughtfully builds up unity with them.

Remember that forgiveness heals us and removes anger and bitterness, and at the same time removes walls and barriers. I can then more fully become one with my brothers and sisters.

Joy and hope are the fruits of faith and charity.

SPIRITUAL MATURITY

I remembered that recently the job of ironing had filled my day. Noting that different settings were needed for different types of material, it dawned on me that we wouldn't think of disregarding the directions on an iron so as not to scorch the fabric; but we think nothing of ignoring heavenly directions *(and the commandments)*, and scorching our souls.

Theo looked up and seemed ready to listen to more.

"Okay. Here's a thought to hang on to, Theo. Many people are sitting back and accepting heresy while doing and saying nothing about it. *Be on your guard not to be led into error.*

It's Spiritual Maturity we are being called to. *KNOW* some Scripture; it's not that difficult. *LIST* helpful sources to read when you need comfort for sorrow or anger, fear or anxiety. You get the idea. When you attend Mass or church services on Sunday, *LISTEN* to the readings. *PRAY* to the Holy Spirit to alert you to what He wants you to *HEAR* at that particular time. *PONDER* them, *REFLECT* upon what they mean to you and your life. Have the *COURAGE* of your convictions and continue to believe in the face of the ridicule and rejection of friends and loved ones. That's really a tough one, because we don't like the way it feels. It's going to be more and more difficult to remain true to our Holy Father and the traditional teachings of Jesus and His Church. This is the preparedness of Spiritual Maturity that results from our response, our commitment.

Realize that all the stories of people in the bible are meant to be a parallel for our history. Knowing that allows us to identify with them and learn more about ourselves. The experiences of Abraham, Job and Peter are outstanding teaching examples. When we associate with their lives, and reflect on the words and deeds of Jesus, the people of His time and Old Testament times, we discover models for our own lives.

Let God and yourself know that you've been touched, changed, nurtured by His Word, convinced in a new and deeper way. Stop and *respond* with appropriate words or decisions of your own.

Have your home enthroned to the Sacred Heart. There is a prayer ritual that's used for this, and any priest should be happy to comply with your request.

These are ideas that may be totally new for you, Theo. Much has been written about sprinkling holy water on visions or apparitions as a *test* of authenticity. It is also prudent to sprinkle the room where you pray with holy water. Have your house blessed by a priest and often sprinkle holy water throughout.

Today we believe that it is a basic and good foundation to make the "*Consecration to Jesus through Mary*" according to the directions of St. Louis de Montfort outlined in his books, "*Total Consecration*", and "*True Devotion To The Blessed Virgin Mary*".

There are wonderful promises of special graces and gifts from Jesus and Mary to those who practice special devotions. Visit Jesus in the Blessed Sacrament every day. Jesus has requested this many, many, many times.

Something young people might need to realize, Theo, is that the *Rosary, fasting* and *private devotions* such as Novenas, were down-played after Vatican II as being pietistic, going overboard and 'cultish'. They aren't, and all of heaven is praying that we, as a nation, as a world, return to these blessed practices.

The Blessed Virgin has asked all of us to *put on a Scapular* (brown or green) and wear it always. She has been quoted as saying to St. Simon Stock that some day she would save the world with the rosary and the Scapular. Our Lady of the Americas told Stela Ruiz that it was not only a sign that we belonged to her, but would be a protection against the evil one."

Theo sat back and refilled his glass. It was obvious that there was going to be a lot of reading in his future from the solemn look on his face. I allowed a few minutes for reflection and then continued the theme.

"If you read at least one of the Gospels and the letters of Paul, Peter, James or John, reading small segments slowly two or three times, they can become *part of you*, help you become strong."

I suddenly became quiet myself and thought about how we digest food better when we chew it slowly and calmly. We do become what we ingest. And once is not enough. We didn't drink just one bottle of milk as babies to build up all these bones. And now we were beginning again as little ones, growing on the words and graces and prayer being fed to us by a Mother who would see to it that we are ready to be on our own, face the world, do battle, but this time with her constant help.

It isn't as though we have no resource or warnings regarding the end times, I was thinking, and picking up the Bible on the table, turned to a passage that spoke strongly to me.

> 'Now the Spirit explicitly says that in the last times some will turn away from the faith by paying attention to deceitful spirits and demonic instructions through the hypocrisy of liars with branded consciences.' (1Tim 4:1)

I jumped up as the phone rang again. "You're on your own a lot today, boy! Here are some added messages of Jesus and Mary you can look over while I'm fixing dinner. My husband is bringing company home tonight."

Jesus: *'The salvation of so many of Our people is at stake, and We will do everything We possibly can to gain their attention. All is being accomplished for the glory of God and to hasten the coming of the Kingdom. Please, continue to pray for all My people that their hearts may be healed and they will allow Me to be their Lord and their God. The world is soon to learn the truth of My words: Blessed are those who hunger and thirst for justice. It shall be theirs.'*

Blessed Mother: *'The future of all who pray is bright with the light of Christ, my Son. Be filled with joy, as we work together for the good of mankind. Be filled with gratitude to the Father for allowing this extended time of grace.'*

QUESTIONS TO ASK OURSELVES

Do we have such hearts of stone that we cannot be moved with pity to pray and respond with our lives?

Do we know and do all we can at this moment to answer the tender heart of our Mother who is begging us to help her?

Are there not many who weep with the Mother of Sorrows at the plight of the entire world, filled with disease, war, natural disasters, greed, self-gratification and rejection of God? Am I one of them?

Do we need to pray and sacrifice more of ourselves, surrender to our Creator Who is beckoning us to abandon ourselves to Him?

There are many people praying, yet Mary says there are still not enough prayers being said.

We are invited to pray more, and to pray constantly. Two thousand years ago St. Paul prepared the Ephesians for battle:

'Finally, draw your strength from the Lord and from his mighty power. Put on the armor of God so that you may be able to stand firm against the tactics of the devil. For our struggle is not with flesh and blood, but with principalities, with the powers, with the world rulers of this present darkness, with the evil spirits in the heavens. Therefore, put on the armor of God that you may be able to resist on the evil day and, having done everything, to hold your ground. So stand fast with your loins girded in truth, clothed with righteousness as a breastplate, and your feet shod in readiness for the gospel of peace. In all circumstances, hold faith as a shield to quench all the flaming arrows of the evil one. And take the helmet of salvation and the sword of the Spirit, which is the word of God'. (Eph 6:10-17)

I walked back into the room just as Theo seemed to finish his reading. "By the way, have you decided to go back East, or complete your last year here in Arizona?" I asked him.

Looking at me, he replied, "I attended the Thursday and Friday night prayer groups last week, Carol, and they were such a peace-filled and beautiful experience. I never have felt anything like the quiet in my heart those two nights. And Friday, after prayer, some of the young adults invited me to join them for a bite to eat, split a bean, I think they called it. I'm hooked on Scottsdale as well, Carol. What a sharp place to live. I've also never met nicer people anywhere. Even in the stores they're the friendliest of any place we ever visited. No, you're stuck with me, too."

He had risen and was again walking slowly towards the front entrance.

"Good, good, Theo. Call me whenever . . ."

Chapter Seven

Prayer

"Thus will I bless you while I live; lifting up my hands, I will call upon your name. As with riches of a banquet shall my soul be satisfied, and with exultant lips my mouth shall praise you." (Ps 63:5-6)

The next two days were spent refining messages, passages and thoughts to share with Theo. These continue to derive from my experiences in prayer.

Blessed Mother: *'My dear one, the events foretold by me all over the world are about to become a reality, and set the stage for the return of my Son, Jesus. I am filled with grief at the events about to unfold, but filled also, with joy that this purification will set the stage for Our Hearts to be glorified upon the earth.'* (11/16/92)

Blessed Mother: *'Nothing could possibly be as important as the salvation of the whole world; preparation for the Second Coming of my Son and the battle in preparation for that great day. It is with great excitement that I contemplate the coming of my Son into a purified Kingdom on earth. Remain in constant communication with me, your Mother who loves you, my children.'* (5/4/93)

'Our children will not seek Us without many prayers of preparation for them. They need support now so that they will be guided by the Holy Spirit in order to hear Our words meant especially for each particular heart.

Nothing is accomplished without prayer.

Each person, chosen by the Father before their birth to serve Him in a special way, requires someone's prayers for them to enable God's Will to be done in them. It was necessary for your parents and relatives to pray for you, and for me to say special prayers, and for my Son to pour Himself out to the Father on your behalf before the graces and gifts reserved for you before you were born could be released. So you see why it is now necessary for you to pray on behalf of others that graces and mercy and healing may be released on their behalf.' (8/12/93)

In early August of 1993, Jesus spoke these words:

'Notice, My people, how quickly the time is running its course. Time and these days, these opportunities, can never be recovered, and so efforts need to be redoubled, the focus of your prayer greater than any in your life so far. Continue to invite My Mother, the Angels and all the Saints to pray with you, for in this way your prayers are greatly multiplied.'

Jesus: 'Focus on Me and My Mother and all the horrible suffering of Our dear ones throughout the world. Notice the difference constantly between your life and theirs, and allow their pain and suffering to be the impetus for your industry on their behalf.' (8/15/93)

Jesus: 'Listen and lament the fate of all those who will not watch and pray and listen.' (8/19/93)

Blessed Mother: 'Blessed are all who work for the coming of the Kingdom. Father, Thy Will be done.' (1/8/93)

Blessed Mother: *'Praise God for His mercy and generosity. Thank Him for giving you the means to be saved and to return to Him, though there is no one on earth found worthy of His grace. It is a great gift of the Father, given with unconditional love and mercy'. (1/9/93)*

Jesus: *'Watch, listen, pray.' (1/10/93)*

Each of us is aware, hopefully, of the urgent need to pray for the salvation of the people who are distant from God at this time, the ones Jesus and Mary continually refer to as, *'Our poor lost ones.'* We have a better idea now of how much we can do at prayer.

It is good to pray alone at home, or out enjoying nature, driving the car, alone at church, or in front of the Blessed Sacrament; in prayer communities (even just two or three gathered in Jesus' Name), in homes or special groups, visiting the sick or shut-in, or worshipping at Mass or special week-end services, the Sabbath.

INFINITE VALUE OF THE MASS

Pope Paul VI said, 'The Mass is the most perfect form of prayer.' Padre Pio, the stigmatic priest, said the world could exist more easily without the sun than without the Mass. The Cure d'Ars, St. Jean Vianney said, 'If we knew the value of the Mass, we would die of joy!' Pope Benedict XV tells us, 'The Holy Mass would be of greater profit if people had it offered in their lifetime, rather than having it celebrated for the relief of their souls after death.'

Once, St. Teresa was overwhelmed with God's Goodness and asked Our Lord, 'How can I thank you?' Our Lord replied, 'Attend one Mass.'[1]

---

[1] Quotes from the blue Pieta Prayer Book, published by Miraculous Lady of the Roses, 1186 Burlington Dr., Hickory Corners, MI. 49060.

ONE STEP AT A TIME

Notice that Our Lady at Medjugorje and in our personal lives has led us through the dynamic of change and conversion one step at a time, all we can handle at a given time. First she requested one rosary daily, then added daily Mass and receiving the Eucharist.

The call for prayer went from one hour a day to three for those who could respond. This included prayer to the Holy Spirit, daily reading of Scripture, and frequent reconciliation. From private prayer, the call to develop prayer groups, or attend them regularly, rearranged our lives again.

First, she asked for a one day a week fast on bread and water, then two. Wearing the Scapular was requested, then other sacramentals: medals, carrying the rosary at all times; holy water in the house; a crucifix on the wall; a small altar where we could pray with a minimum of distractions and where she and Jesus would be specially honored in the home; pictures of Jesus and Mary, the Saints and Angels to remind us of our *'new'* Family.

Mary began to encourage us to visit her Son more often in the Blessed Sacrament. Now Jesus asks, begs us, to visit Him *every day* in the Blessed Sacrament where we will be emptied of the *world* and the results of living in it for so long: the pain, the betrayals, the disappointments and discouragement, the loneliness, the fears and anxieties, angers or even rage, the defenses and hardness of our hearts. We will be welcomed, our beloved Lord promises, heard because we will be listened to, appreciated, healed. We will find approval, love and acceptance. Didn't He always tell us that?

> "Fear not, for I have redeemed you; I have called you by name: you are Mine." (Is 43:1)

The word *broken* has become more familiar to those trying to change, deal with their own humanity and reality. Mary continually repeats the call to come to her Son in the Eucharist. In getting to know Jesus intimately, we begin to understand that He constantly has His Heart broken for love of us, by the rejection of His people.

Jesus and Mary must break through our defensive walls, our protective barriers built against those who are simply different than we are. Our own hearts are broken by those in life who betray us. In turn our resentment and bitterness is broken when we begin to forgive and love all people again. The chains and bondage of sin are broken when we return to the Sacrament of Reconciliation and attempt to live in a new way, free of all the old enslavement. Bad habits and companionships are broken when we turn in faith to the grace and goodness of Jesus and His Mother.

We break out of darkness into the Light of Christ when we allow the Holy Spirit to lead us. We celebrate our brokenness and are content when we unite it to the sufferings of Mary and Jesus on the Cross. *Heart to heart.* We repeat along with the words in Scripture,'...I am content with weaknesses, insults and hardships, persecutions and constraints, for the sake of Christ, for when I am weak, then I am strong.' (2Cor 10) We believe that, united to Christ, our suffering and brokenness is redemptive. That is, it can be *offered* to God *for* the redemption and salvation of others.

And now our Mother, who guides and counsels us, is sending us out to evangelize, with our lives and love, all those we meet. Certainly this is nothing new. It is the central theme of the New Testament. As He said to Peter, Jesus has said to us a hundred and three times, *'Do you love Me, My child? Feed My lambs, feed My sheep.'*

And so we are called to reflect the *unity* of the Hearts of Jesus and Mary in our own lives.

It has so often been requested in the apparitions today, that we *consecrate ourselves* to the Sacred Heart of Jesus through the Immaculate Heart of Mary. Mary has shown us that consecrating ourselves often, every day, all day, is the path towards living in their constant presence. This would be very difficult, she said, but she will help us if we ask her assistance, hold her hand. An awareness of the presence of Jesus and Mary is what tells us we are not alone, that we are *in* this world, but not *of* it, that we are living in the Kingdom as fully as is possible for us here and now.

Jesus reminds us not to look for Him in the past or contemplate Him in the future because we can only find Him in the present. He can only touch us in the present. We can only reach Him in each present moment.

Become a *'house of prayer'* and realize with St. Paul:

"If our earthly dwelling, a tent, should be destroyed, we have a building from God, a dwelling not made with hands, eternal in heaven." (2Cor 5:1)

Always we are invited to pray more: *'Pray, pray, pray.'*

Please God, we will learn that we were created to praise thank and love the Lord for everything, even and especially the struggles, the defeats, the deaths, small and large. *Fidelity, trust, perseverance, endurance* are words to live by.

Every help we can find, understand, appreciate, will be an impetus to better prayer and growth in virtue. The four components of the Mass are a great framework for our prayer: *Praise, Adoration, Love,* and *Thanksgiving.*

TEACH US HOW TO PRAY

There are prayers particular to all times of worship and devotion, but we often wonder where and how to start. The answer to questions about what to do for sick people, enemies, lack of faith, a concern of special importance is always, 'pray'; but how to begin, what to say?

For me, asking the Holy Spirit to pray in me and help me to pray with my *heart* is the way every prayer or Scripture time must be started. Also, it may seem mundane to many, but the words *'In the Name of the Father and of the Son and of the Holy Spirit, Amen,'* ought to start every meal, every endeavor, every conversation with God, His Mother, the angels or saints. A good way to begin, for those who are not used to lengthy prayer time, is with prayer of petition for five minutes, followed by another five minutes of listening. Gradually this time may be extended as the Holy Spirit leads you.

Here are more words of Jesus and Mary. First of all, they are grouped in what seem to be helpful suggestions about *how to begin* prayer. Then, *prayer intentions.* Finally, reminders about our prayer which enrich us and deepen our understanding of prayer and showing the *effects* of prayer in our lives and the lives of others.

HOW TO BEGIN PRAYER

Jesus: *'Give to Me the first fruits of your energy, of your time, of your talents. Be still and know that I am God. Listen, as I mold you into My instruments of mercy, of peace, of forgiveness, of love.'*

(I take this to mean, get up early and pray before one is too tired to do it very well, don't you?)

'Only those who come to know My Mother will truly come to know Me. Remain near to Her, learning from her and allowing her to bring you to My Sacred Heart.'

(This sounds like the very atmosphere, the total environment of prayer we are invited to by St. Paul who says, 'Pray without ceasing.')

'I wish for you to love Me, your Lord, with all your heart and soul. Give Me all that you are. Pray that more will listen and turn to My Mother.' (5/20/92)

Jesus: *'Ask for the grace of being emptied before you begin to pray. Ask for union with Me every moment of your day.'* (3/29/93)

Blessed Mother: *'Spend time praying to the Holy Spirit, begging for the gift of openness. Continue to invite Me to pray with you.'* (11/16/92)

Jesus: *'If you remain peaceful and low-key, it will be easier to be recollected and prayerful.'* (1/5/93)

Blessed Mother: *'The gift of quiet, nurtured during times of silent communication with my Son and Myself, will develop a poise within you that will soon be second nature.'* (5/14/93)

Blessed Mother: *'Come with Us at every minute in quiet recollection and study what you have been given. Pour out your gratitude in supplication, praise and adoration, love and thanksgiving to God, Our mighty Father.*

If you will only pray much and surrender all, while at the same time working hard, you will see a quick resolution and completion of all that I am asking of you. Offer each step to my Son to bless and purify.' (3/22/93)

Jesus: *'Time spent in quiet will develop your inner quiet and a silence of spirit.'* (9/1/92)

Blessed Mother: *'Practice praying to me and thinking of me at every moment.*

You will be calmed and quieted in this way. You will be modeled and formed into my image very quickly, if you allow me to be present to you at all times.

My presence will change you, strengthen you and keep you close to me and my Son. Please, try again and again to do this, as it will be very difficult to accomplish. With practice and the help of our Holy Spirit, you will make great progress.' (9/1/92)

Jesus: *'Remain as quiet and recollected as possible. Spend more time in silence before Me and allow Me to heal you. Avoid all that would disturb your spirit for your own sake and dwell in Me in My Sacred Heart. You are safe in the silence of My Presence. I promise to heal you quickly if you will allow Me the opportunity.'* (9/2/92)

Jesus: *'Please, spend more and more of your day in union with Me. This is the only thing that will ultimately give you inner peace. As you are emptied, more of My grace and love can flow through you to others. Continue to come to Me and just rest and BE with Me in comfort and quiet. Your willingness to serve is a grace in itself.'* (9/4/92)

Blessed Mother: *'Seek me every moment of your day, but especially in the quiet times. Come to me, and I will console and strengthen you. Seek my will and the Will of the Father. Pray more and offer sacrifices to my Jesus. We are always with you and will never abandon you.'* (7/22/92)

Jesus: *'As you work, offer each breath, each movement, each thought to My Father in thanksgiving for the many gifts He is giving to you. Work diligently and quickly to prepare.'* (1/27/93)

PRAYER INTENTIONS

Jesus: *'Bring Me the things you feel need healing. Listen intently for the sound of My voice and join your petitions to those of My Mother for Our poor lost children of the world.'* (3/27/93)

Blessed Mother: *'Ask me to pray constantly at your side, as you walk with my Jesus into this time of witness and confrontation. Thank the Father more and more for all the gifts He gives to you.'* (5/3/93)

Blessed Mother: *'Before you leave in the morning for Mass, please, say as many prayers as possible to prepare yourselves for the day to be open and listening for Our* voices. *Immerse yourself in the sound of my voice. Be attuned to my presence and the touch of my hand.'* (1/5/93)

Blessed Mother: *'When you have finished each task of your day, and before you go on to the next one, please, stop and give thanks to the Father for that task and all that He allows you to do for Him.'*

Gratitude is a necessary ingredient on our way to holiness. Appreciation of God's gifts will help us to realize more and more what a privilege it is to be allowed to serve God and His people. It makes us aware of the different gifts the Father has given to us, and how He is now allowing us to use them.

'Praised be the Father, child, Who gifts His children.

Praise to Him Who continues to call His people to return to Him for more gifts.

Praise to Him Who longs to gift us with Himself for eternity.

Praise to Him Who allows me to come to all of you, and speak to you and pray with you. Praise Him, child, with every breath.

Remain hidden with me and you will learn quickly that to love is all.' (9/10/92)

Blessed Mother: *'Blessed be the Lord, our God. Blessed be His Name. Blessed be the might of His Arm.'* (6/13/93)

Jesus: *'Praised be My Father Who gifts you with every sort of good.*

Praised be Him Who allows Me to speak to you in this way.

Praised be His Divine Plan for the salvation of His children. Thank and praise Him at every moment for His gracious goodness on your behalf.

Give Him all the love in your heart and think of the Most Blessed Trinity every time you think.' (7/9/93)

Blessed Mother: 'My dear one, nothing is more important than your prayers.

Please, continue to unite yourself to me and be assured of my love and protection. Be in good spirits as you work and pray each day, all the while holding my hand.' (7/9/93)

Jesus: 'Stay close to Me and My Mother so as not to be deceived. The evil one will try anything to distract and confuse. Do not give him a moment's attention, but quickly pray and drive him away in My Name. You will be blessed and protected in the Mantle of My Mother.' (3/22/93)

Jesus: 'Please, seek to become one with Me in the Trinity.' (6/9/93)

Jesus: 'Please, offer all your fears and doubts to Me here in front of My Blessed Sacrament.' (5/16/93)

Jesus: 'I invite My children to spend more time in silence before My Blessed Sacrament. Please, say nothing and begin to listen more. You must work hard at this and learn to be still. Your mind will be purified and your heart healed the more you spend time just being in My Presence.

Please, come and pour out these concerns and then be still and allow Me to take these hurts, these concerns, these old resentments and jealousies away from you, so that you may be filled with My peace and truly cleansed. I desire you to be at peace and emptied of harmful residue of the past.' (8/28/92)

Blessed Mother: 'Please my child, continue to spend very much time in prayer and in front of My Son in His Blessed Sacrament. Only there can you be completely prepared for your future. After you have spent time in prayer, thank the Holy Spirit and ask Him to tell you *what it is He wishes you to do at that time. Please, practice listening and following the requests of the Spirit. Please, be available to do Our Will at all times and listen for the guidance you need.'* (10/31/92)

WHAT WILL HAPPEN IF WE PRAY?

Blessed Mother: *'Daughter, please try to pray more and be less busy with people and things which keep you from visiting my Son in the Blessed Sacrament where He waits to speak to your heart and heal your wounds.'* (6/16/93)

Blessed Mother: *'Continue in a prayer mode and with great reflection and recollection, My daughter. This will strengthen your inner self and build up a reserve of energy and a core of strength on which to call in the future.*

It is not without compassion that I speak, for I know of the fatigue which plagues all of my children who are praying and working for the success of my plans and preparing for the Second Coming of my Son. Please know that my strength and love are at your disposal. We shall pray and praise together.' (7/11/93)

Jesus: *'Continue to come to Me and spend time listening and loving Me, and a great mutual love will grow between us. It will be nurtured by praying for the Will of My Father to be accomplished. You are beginning to perceive the necessity of being in constant communion with Me, constant prayer.*

I see every instance of your life. I am aware of all that worries you.

When you are weary, seek rest in My Sacred Heart.

When you are lonely, seek comfort in My arms.

When you feel empty, take courage and be filled by My Presence in the Blessed Sacrament.

When all looks bleak and overwhelming, come to My Mother and Me, and We will refresh you.' (9/16/92)

Jesus: *'You are doing My Will when you pray often and come to visit Me in My Blessed Sacrament. Many are the hours when I long for My people to come to Me. It brings Me such joy when you take time out of your day to spend some of it with me. This is a time for strengthening, a time for storing graces and My blessings for the days to come.'* (7/22/92)

Chapter Eight

Objectives

". . . *we even boast of our afflictions, knowing that affliction produces endurance, and endurance proven character, and proven character, hope, and hope does not disappoint, because the love of God has been poured out into our hearts by the Holy Spirit that has been given to us.*" *(Rom 5:3-5)*

Blessed Mother: '*Please, continue to pray that the request for as many available priests as possible for the Sacrament of Reconciliation be granted, and that Our people will have the opportunity they will need to confess their many sins and return to my Son.*' *(7/25/92)*

Blessed Mother: '*I weep so often tears of blood for my children who will be lost. Please, daughter, continue to pray for them and to do special penances on their behalf. Many will still be saved because of the prayers of my faithful. Spread my words to all of Our children and encourage all to pray without ceasing.*' *(8/6/92)*

Jesus: '*My child, never cease praying and offering My people to Me. Persevere to the end and never give up on them, for they need a champion, a warrior, a one who pleads their cause until the last possible moment with her last ounce of breath. Pour yourself out, as I have poured Myself out for you.*

The Father's Will is the foremost desire of your heart when you pray constantly and offer each little act and each step of this new journey to His honor and glory.' *(8/19/92)*

Jesus: 'Bring My poor lost ones to Me, their Divine Physician, and I will heal their wounds and dry their tears. My Mother will care for them with all the tenderness in her heart and, together, We will prepare them to meet My Father as We present them to Him.

Call upon the Angels and Saints at any time. They are at your disposal and praying for all My children constantly and will help in your time of need.' *(9/4/92)*

Jesus: 'Bring Our lost ones to My Mother and, together, bring them to Me. I await you in My Blessed Sacrament. I long for My children to return to their Lord.' *(9/8/92)*

Blessed Mother: 'Your interest and prayers for my intentions bring great peace and comfort to me, and I am grateful, daughter. Praise our Heavenly Father with me now and thank Him for His many gifts to His children Who love Him.' *(9/16/92)*

Jesus: 'Please, continue in peace to attempt to reach all My people and continue to pray that hearts will open more to My Mother and Me. This time is most serious, so please take each task most seriously, My children.' *(9/28/92)*

Blessed Mother: 'Let us continue to pray constantly together for this worthless generation, that they may at last listen to my words and return ever-so-quickly to the Father God. Great care and tenderness await all those who seek the love of God.' *(9/28/92)*

Blessed Mother: 'The intentions of the Father are to save all of His people. This can be accomplished only if *enough prayers are said, if enough lives are changed and turn back to God, their Creator.*

Please, impress upon Our people the need for constant prayer and vigilance against the attacks of the evil one. He is relentless in his pursuit of souls. Remind yourselves, my dear ones, of the desperate state of the evil one and how he will stop at nothing in order to entice people away from Us. Call on all the Angels and Saints to pray with you as we pray for the people of the world.' (11/6/92)

Blessed Mother: *'The plan of Our Father is so great. Continuously give Him thanks and praise that We are allowed to continue to reach out to Our people until the last available second.'* (1/5/93)

Jesus: *'My child, when you allow your heart to fill and expand, this in turn, increases your capacity to love more and hold more of Our people in your heart. Soon, your heart will encompass the world. There will be no task you will refuse for the good of Our people. It is in this way that you will become more and more like Me and the love I have for you.*

Begin each day asking Me for a greater capacity to love; to heal; to reach out and touch the hearts of all those who come to you. Woe, child, to those who have contributed to destruction through their greed and callousness. This behavior must be cleansed from the world, so that peace and a true love of the Creator reigns in the hearts of all His people.' (1/15/93)

I like to think of our stomachs here, and the fact that we know how a hollow sac like that can be stretched to hold more and more, so this should be easy to believe about our hearts.

Blessed Mother: *'The prayers and good works of My chosen ones will work miracles in the lives and hearts of*

My poor, weak, lost, lonely children. It will be a time of redemptive prayer and suffering for all of you for all of them.

Do not worry about any shortcomings or imperfections. It does not matter, but only saying 'yes' to Our Will for you will enable My Son to work within you.' (5/3/93)

Blessed Mother: '*When you think of how beautiful a day you celebrated,* (Mother's Day '93), *remember all those who choose not to accept me and my call to them all over your world. Pray for those who refuse a Mother's love, and reject my words and my presence in so many places.*

Please be aware of each crisis which develops in the world and pray for mercy on those who are suffering now, that they may be urged to to respond to the call of their God which comes in the midst of the storm.

Be aware of the countless who suffer and die in each corner of the globe, and offer them to the Father for His mercy and forgiveness. Be assured that this prayer will be most effective. Spend every minute in prayer and preparation.' (6/9/93)

Jesus: 'Pray together with Us, children, for the coming of the Kingdom. The salvation of the entire world is in the hands of those who pray. Will there be enough interested in saving their brothers and sisters? It is the central thought of all Our prayer requests, My child.' (6/16/93)

Jesus: 'It is always a great comfort to My heart to see My children praying together and lifting their hearts and voices to My Holy Spirit. The more you pray for each other, the more you will be healed yourselves.

It is important that you practice silence and humility, all the while praying for sincerity and joy.' (6/23/93)

WORDS AND LOVE TO SHARE

Blessed Mother: *'Please, tell My children of Our love, and that We are longing for them to come often to us in prayer. The Blessed Sacrament is a most healing place for them to come to speak to my Son and offer Him all their hurts and broken hearts. Warn them of the shortness of time, the little time that is left to repent and convert.'* (7/29/93)

Blessed Mother: *'You are seeking a greater union with me, and that is the first step towards acquiring it. Continue to practice inviting me to be with you and pray with you at each moment of your day. I long to hold all my children in my arms and welcome them into heaven where they belong.*

Remember that the most important duty is that of prayer and living in the presence of your God. With this awareness, a new peace will descend upon you, and you will go from one task to another with ease, making of each one a prayer to offer to the Father.' (9/4/93)

Jesus: *'Please, My dear one, call upon Our Holy Spirit to give you the right words for people. Tell them they must prepare to fight evil with weapons of prayer, penance, and fasting. Much can be accomplished by obeying Our directives. Much can be accomplished by listening with your heart.'* (11/16/92)

Jesus: *'When you come seeking peace and healing, it shall be yours. Many are the times you will wish for the opportunity to visit Me like this, and it will not be possible. The opportunities will be fewer; the places which honor My Sacred Heart will be fewer and at greater distances. Alert all who will listen one last time with warnings of a grave future.*

There will be no peace to be found, as My churches will be used for other purposes, and My Sacred Host and Dishes will be desecrated; no, not forever, but the darkness will be great for a long time, and you will be desolate without My Eucharist to comfort and nourish you.

Your prayers and constant presence with Me now will build you up for the time to come. Be completely immersed in My strength and the belief that I will never fail you. Many will need to be filled with courage and faith and pointed in the right direction.' (3/31/93)

Jesus: 'All of heaven is waiting for the sword of justice to be lowered upon the earth. All are in preparedness and wait in silence for the battle to begin. It will be just as it is written. Pray with Me for all who will suffer such great trials and hardships.' (4//19/93)

Blessed Mother: 'I am grateful when my children pray as seriously as they can, in earnest, to prepare them to better serve Our people. They truly are like lost sheep with no one to guide them. They bleat and run in all directions without sense or pattern. They react to the tiniest noise and are bothered by everything and everyone. The anxiety is high today in the world, child, because of fear and lack of proper direction.' (5/3/93)

Jesus: 'I, your Jesus of Mercy, love you with a love which will last forever. You are being healed by this very love of Mine which washes you clean and returns you to state of purity. Please, ask My Mother to lead you to a deeper appreciation of the gifts of My Father. Continue to thank Him more often with all of your strength and remain in simplicity and peace as much as possible.' (7/25/93)

Jesus: 'My daughter, please tell Our dear loved ones the Lord, their God, is waiting to receive them into His love, into His fold, so that He may shepherd them and bring them back to the one true Church of Jesus Christ. I wish for you to bring them to Me in the Blessed Sacrament and tell them that I am present there, waiting to hear all their hurts and tears and shame.

Tell them I love them, no matter what they have done.

I need for them to come back to Me and love Me.

I need their love.

I wish for them to be united to My Sacred Heart, where they will be healed, but they must spend much of their time in prayer and remorse with Me, their physician, much like they would spend time in a hospital being healed of physical wounds. Their wounds are deep, and time is short.

Please, ask them to spend all the time they have with their Beloved Doctor Who longs to bind those wounds with His Love.

Please, give them all the assurance you can that they are forgiven when they come to Me to be reconciled.

Please, children of the world, reconcile with your God before it is too late. Reconcile with each other and forgive each other . . . now.' (7/14/92)

Blessed Mother: 'Seek the Kingdom of God, and all else will be given to you. These are words I wish for you to ponder and present to all My little ones.' (7/14/92)

'My dear child, this is an urgent plea to you and to all the nations of the world. Now, more than ever, it is important to impress people with the urgent need for prayer. Because events have been delayed by prayer, many think the events forecast by me are no longer real.

Please, beg them to listen. Beg them to be serious about my requests to the world for prayer and fasting. It is no

*longer a matter of time left. It is a matter of living in the
moment with your God and being united to Him in
prayer, one in mind and body; one in heart and soul; one
in the holiness of God; one in the neediness of man.*

My heart begs you, my people. Pray. pray. pray.'
(1/27/93)

The commitment to prayer, be it group or private, is not
unlike a marriage. We go into the arrangement, the covenant,
the promise of this kind of relationship with God and during
times that the excitement and magic are gone, we don't shop
around. We stay and grow through the daily repetition, the
sameness, the *routine*, the dull times, the decision to hang in
there, knowing that the potential for magic and excitement is
still there, and will return according to the Lord's Will and our
personal investment.

Our Lady has said, *'Your prayers and charity are manifestations of My Immaculate Heart within you and within the world.'*

In case we need one more reminder of our heavenly
Mother's love, this is shared with you to read. Consume,
digest, assimilate, absorb and grow up with it.

There is nothing that can be added to all the food for
thought presented here. It's potential is limitless to cause
within us profound transformation into a new creation.

AT THE FOOT OF THE CROSS

Blessed Mother: *'My child, please write. It is I, your
mother, who comes to you now. You are seeking a greater
union with me and my Son. Please, child, continue in this
fashion, for of such is the Kingdom of God.*

*All of heaven contemplates the beginning of my Son's
Passion this night, and you will be more surely united to
me if you walk this way in my company.*

*Allow me to bring you to the foot of the Cross, my
daughter. Allow me to show you the depths of my love, as*

I followed my Jesus from a distance through the streets lined with shouting, jeering people, whose only thoughts were to kill my Jesus.

Allow the feelings to penetrate your heart, as you hear these sounds and terrible words. See what they are doing to Him Whom I love. See how they push and taunt Him.

I long to run to Him and shield His bruised body with my own. A mother would always try to do this for her child, but I must stay away and allow all of Scripture to be fulfilled.

My Son, the Lamb, must be slain for the very people who are screaming for His death. They are intent on destroying the One Who has loved and served them, taught them and healed them, eaten with them and visited in their homes; Who only wished to bring them knowledge of the Father and His great love for them.

Can you bear to watch this scene, child? Can you bear to see His Sacred Blood poured out on the filthy streets to mingle with the dust and dirt of the crazed people yelling for my beloved Son's death?

I was all alone when I met my Son in the street on His way. I approached Him slowly and with great trembling, for my own sorrow was so great; but I knew it would be the last time before His death, so I hurried to Him to touch and caress His face. He was nearly dead then.

When we looked into each other's eyes, the greatest love passed between us, and a new strength, a new sense of purpose seemed to pervade His being. I knew He would survive all the cruelties and impossible pain in order to fulfill the Father's Will for Him. As much as He loved and longed to comfort me, it was His Father's Will which gave Him the strength and courage to continue on His way.

The love of my Son for His Heavenly Father is more than anyone could ever comprehend, my child. Please know that it was this love which gave life and breath to every single thing He did while on earth. It allowed Him to be single-minded in the face of a truly impossible human situation.

I knew of the longing of my Son to fulfill every word that had been written about Him, and so I too bowed before the Will of Our Almighty Father God, Who in His plan of salvation of His people, emptied Himself of His precious Son in order to redeem mankind.

Dwell on this thought, my daughter, and allow it to fill your heart with love and gratitude. My Son did not suffer alone. The Father and their Most Holy Spirit suffered each pain; each humiliation with Him, although humanly He had been abandoned to the lust and greed of a crowd, a mob gone mad with the taste of blood.

Love for my Son allowed me to find the courage, the strength to follow Him to the foot of the Cross. It was a night that had begun earlier than I could remember. Perhaps for days we had not slept, in preparation and prayer for this solemn event. There were no tears left in me, only a living out now of the things foretold for my beloved Child, since the fall of Adam.

It was now time to behold His Crucifixion, and it was only through grace and the help of Angels that I was able to behold this horrifying scene. Imagine one of your own children nailed to the cross. The blood which was left in His body spurted afresh, as the nails pierced Him, and my heart broke completely with each sound of the hammer.

I do not know what allowed me to stand in that place, yet I could not bear to leave Him alone with that hatred. You can never imagine such a scene, my daughter, and I *will never forget it. Until the day I left this earth, it was before my eyes at all times. Even though I knew He had risen and was now in heaven with His Father and the Saints and Angels, standing at His right hand pleading for the world, it was with sorrow that I continued to contemplate that terrible scene of His agony.*

My heart was always filled with great longing to be reunited with my Son, and this was a longing which gave me an energy and love to serve His friends who also missed Him so; and spoke of nothing other than His words and recounted stories of His time on earth with them.

Each day new marvels would be recorded, as an awareness grew within them of all my Jesus had done for them. I was able to be comforted by the recounting of all these times in my Jesus' life with His beloved ones. It brought me comfort to hear the love and gratitude in their voices, and for a brief time He would live for each of us again.

We lived for the day that each of us would be called to heaven to be with Him, all the while learning together from His words that were remembered.

This was the way our days passed, child, in love and longing; never quite recovering from the horror of those dreadful days when my Son, the Lamb, was crucified.

Join me now, my child, as we walk the streets behind Him and watch Him suffer and die.

I love you, my child, and thank you for wishing to accompany me on this awful journey.

It begins . . .' (4/8/92)

Chapter Nine

Reconciliation

"Lord, wash away my iniquities, cleanse me from my sins." (Liturgy of the Mass)

Two weeks later Theo returned, this time with his parents. I should have known the material on prayer might have peaked their interest to the point of wanting to investigate more. With genuine delight I welcomed them. They were both tall and still trim, and dressed in matching colors of tan, black and white. He wore tan dress slacks with a white knit shirt and black pullover. She accompanied her black culottes with a tan cardigan over a white blouse. Their outfits reflected an Eastern attempt at casual, with a holdout for more conservative color combinations. I smiled inwardly and noted a reflection of unity as well. These two were very close I felt.

"How do you do, Mr. Dunne, Mrs. Dunne. Hi, Theo, it's good to see you. Please come and sit in here while I fix some lemonade, then we'll start with a prayer."

The next two hours were spent answering questions and filling in more details on the last five years.

"Listening to the direction of your remarks, I realize the three of you are believing what you are hearing, but there is something that needs clarifying. The messages I have received since May of 1992, and am recording in this book for publication, are strictly what I believe to be receiving from Jesus, Mary and the Father, in addition to and outside of the experiences that Theo has been relaying to you about St. Maria Goretti's.

The messages which were given to us through Gianna, through Fr. Jack and other young adults here do not contain much information about the end times or the coming of the Antichrist nor the Second Coming of Jesus. Guess I'm just saying, don't think, please, that all that is being said to me is also being said to others at the Parish. Jesus and Mary seem to be giving different people different ministries and messages that, while we might begin together, like me being here at St. Maria Goretti, don't necessarily continue in exactly the same vein."

"Carol, I'm glad you brought that up," said Mr. Dunne, "and please, call us Thomas and Judith. We are certainly fascinated by all that you have told Theo, and have been reading the books and messages you're sending home with him. It's very good of you to give us so much of your time. We hope you will continue for a while," he added in a eager voice.

"Well," I answered, "its important that you do understand, thank you, Thomas. And what do you think, Judith? Are you comfortable with all you have read and heard?" I turned toward her and smiled.

"Well, my goodness, it's like a dream come true even being here. I fussed so much over moving and leaving everyone I've known all my life, and, well you know what that's like. I was talking to one of my friends from back home just yesterday and I told her . . ."

"Now, Jude, why don't you let this kind lady continue with her story? We can talk about our problems later. Seems to me she might just have a whole lot more to say about what Jesus and Mary are telling people. We feel we pretty much have the background down pat. What's next, if you don't mind moving right along?"

"Yes, you're right, of course," I chuckled. "Since time running out is one of the issues here, we should fill each minute to our advantage. I'm grateful that you are believing what you have heard, given your background, Thomas. With your knowledge of Scripture, reading the signs of the times and conditions in our world, I guess it's easier for you to see the possible unfolding of what the Prophets and Revelation proclaims.

The next messages, according to my outline, have to do with reconciliation. This Sacrament of Reconciliation (going to Confession we used to call it)," I spoke in Theo's direction, "is also believed by Catholics to impart graces that will help us live better lives, turn away from sin. If we really mean it when we profess our sorrow and contrition, promise a firm purpose of amendment and to avoid the occasion of those sins in the future, we know we have just taken a giant step toward deep spiritual healing. This takes no small amount of decision making.

Gianna claims that Jesus has said, *'It takes time for My people to change and time is running out. Begin now.'*[1]

'Come to my Son now, as a God of Mercy, not a God of Justice,' Stela reports.

Where do you think might be the place to begin?" I looked at father and son.

"Oh, well," piped up Thomas, "seems to me honesty is the place. We have such an ability to rationalize, try to fool others, that we end up believing the false face we present to the world. We probably need to pray something like . . . *'Holy Spirit, fill us with your truth, lead us in truthfulness.'*

To repent and confess our faults is necessary to have them forgiven and healed. To pray for the Spirit of God to enlighten our minds will assist the process. Am I right?"

"Oh, but dear, I thought you were always right. At least that's what you always tell me," Judith said with an innocent smile. "Are you going to begin reading, son?" She looked at the

---

[1] *I Am Your Jesus of Mercy*, Vol. 1, Riehle Foundation, Milford, OH 45150.

boy and this time she was beaming. He had been scanning the pages and commenced in a clear voice filled with emotion.

Blessed Mother: *'Please warn Our people of the shortness of time and the little time that is left to repent and convert. The Sacrament of Reconciliation is the place to begin. There is so much healing offered to my dear children through this sacrament. Pray that my dear ones return to this sacrament soon and often.'* (7/29/92)

Jesus: *'Our lost children must be reconciled and return to Me, for I wish to present them to the Father.'* (8/23/92)

Jesus: *'When you are emptied of your sinful ways and harmful resentments, you can be filled with My peace and My power.'* (8/28/92)

Jesus: *'I long for My children to return to their Lord.'* (9/8/92)

Jesus: *'Our children are so dear to us, and We wish to give them every opportunity to return to their Lord and God.'* (9/16/92)

Blessed Mother: *'Confess your sins often, child, and seek to remain constantly in the state of grace.'* (9/16/92)

Blessed Mother: *'In these times, neighbor does not love neighbor, nor do people hold each other in esteem. On the contrary, there is no peace in men's hearts, and neighbors seek to destroy each other in hatred and violence. For thousands of years the Father has warned His people to return to Him in repentance. Now He will no longer wait for a hard hearted creation. He lowers His arm in great sorrow in order to cleanse the earth and fulfill all that Scripture has foretold.*

The Lord, God, is waiting with open arms to receive the millions of Our children and nourish them back to health. The sickness of your day is a result of a lack of God in lives given over to earthly pleasures without the love of God to sustain the health of mind and soul. Great care and tenderness await all those who seek the love of God.' (10/13/92)

Jesus: *'When you enter heaven, you must be white as snow and pure as a lily. Each of the trials you meet with resignation and trust will prepare you that much more for the glory which awaits you in Eternity.'* (10/31/92)

Blessed Mother: *'Times are critical. The goal is everlasting salvation or everlasting hell fire! The choice is freely offered to each one who is free to accept or reject. Leave all of your sorrow with me, my child, for I am the Mother of all Sorrows.'* (11/8/92)

Blessed Mother: *'I see the sin and corruption in the world and watch my children continue to reject me and my Son. Oh, if they only realized. 'Father, forgive them. They know not what they do.' I tell you, child, this is a depraved people who think of themselves as the source of all good. Come back to me, children, lest you perish forever.'* (1/5/93)

Jesus: *'Woe, child, to those who have contributed to destruction through their greed and callousness. This behavior must be cleansed from the world, so that peace and a true love of the Creator reigns in the hearts of all His children.*

We love you, people of the world. We long to save you and bring you to an earthly Paradise prepared for you from the beginning. We are begging, pleading with you to hear Us; to repent and come back to Us, the Triune God. We reach out, call out to you until the last possible moment of your lives, 'Come to your senses. See your folly.'

The love I have for My people is choked by the sorrow of their rejection.

People will not acknowledge what they do not wish to hear.

Hear, O coastlands. Hear and prepare. The Day of the Lord is upon you. Alas, My people. You do not hear, so you cannot prepare.' (1/15/93)

Jesus: *'Grow in My wisdom and love and grace, My child. Events will serve as a light to darkness that still exists in your soul. It is only through testing and learning that you are tried in the furnace of My love. The flames of purification will burn away the dross of imperfection if you will allow this to continue.'* (3/19/93)

Blessed Mother: *'Soon a new reign of terror will begin to sweep this beautiful country of yours, and a time of unparalleled suffering will begin.*

Before my Son returns, this world will be purified. People will be tried for their faith, and only a remnant will remain faithful to God. This will help to purify those who turn away from God in order to save their lives.

All people will live in danger and fear, and think only of how to survive this great time of holocaust. Those faithful to Me and to Jesus will be protected in my mantle until the time comes for His return.

Some of your number will be brought to heaven to pray for those remaining on the earth.' (4/16/93)

Jesus: *'My words and the words of My Mother will touch many hearts and return them to their rightful place as heirs of heaven. Even those who then turn against Me will hold the truth deep in their hearts and have another chance at salvation.'* (5/9/93)

Jesus: *'Read Scripture. Come before Me and listen to the words your heart needs to hear for its healing and renewal. Return to Me, that you may be better formed and molded into My chosen ones.*

The light is nearly snuffed out completely in this darkening world, and it will be more difficult for you to find each other in the coming days.

Hearts are hardening again, as the evil one fills each one with bitterness and suspicion.' (6/9/93)

Blessed Mother: *'Count on your Mother to be ever-present with you, children, and be aware of this. Strengthen yourself with the knowledge and faith you have in my Son and myself. More graces will be available to those who heed the call to return immediately to the House of God and raise their hands and hearts in supplication for their sins.'* (6/16/93)

Blessed Mother: *'My people grow cold and indifferent again. The condition of the world is so serious, only a direct act of the Father will alert Our people to the dreadful state of their souls and the destructive behavior which exists everywhere.'* (7/2/93)

Jesus: *'Talk to people about their struggles, My dear one, about the brokenness that so many share. Remind them of a Savior's understanding of humanity, since He has shared all it means to be human. Simplicity is the key to reaching My people.'* (7/27/93)

Jesus: *'The mind of God is so great, and His plans for each of His children are tailor made to each individual need. Who could know each one better than their Creator? Who could know, and want to give to each one, that which he or she most needs?*

Appreciate the Father and His gifts. Praise and thank Him with all of your strength.

Ask to be healed according to My Will, and it will be done. Seek and you shall find. Knock, and We will open unto you. I am your Jesus Who loves you. Amen. Amen.' (7/28/93)

Theo stopped and sat back with a sigh. "Are you ready for a break," I asked him. We all stood up and moved around. I showed them the house with its three bright and airy bedrooms, tiny dining room, long serviceable kitchen, and our many Medjugorje artifacts. A statue of Our Loving Mother from Conyers, a large replica of the Tilma from Guadalupe, and a magnificent crucifix from Ecuador recently sent by friends. Like many of our friends there were books on all the alleged apparition sites world wide, lives of saints and modern day spiritual writers. I offered to lend any they might choose to read. We sat back down finally, and continued.

"Reconciliation," I said, "is the first step to change, conversion. Here are compassionate words, which I believe are from Jesus, reflecting the difficulties of reforming our lives, attempting to alter our behavior, allowing Him to work within us.

Jesus: *'A new routine wars against our nature as an invading virus disturbs the calm of our body functions. Daily, the new process will be accepted more easily, and cause less and less disturbance within you. Please, trust these words and simply try it.*

Focus on Me and My Mother and all the horrible suffering of Our dear ones throughout the world. Notice the difference constantly between your life and theirs, and allow their pain and suffering to be the impetus for your industry (struggle to change, begin to form new habits, better ones.) *on their behalf.*

Pay no attention to the negative thoughts and feelings which assail you. That is simply an attempt by the evil one to divert you, to dissuade you from continuing on your path (back to Me, serving Me).' (8/15/93)

Blessed Mother: *'My daughter, I your Mother, wish to speak for your heart. Now, I wish for you to listen closely to what I am about to tell you.*

In the beginning of the world, when darkness and chaos ruled, it was a dreary and empty place. There was no beauty, no color, no loveliness of nature to brighten the dark places of the earth. There was only the sound of the wind and the rain. Oh, how it rained, with lightening and thunder to fill the air.

It was necessary for the earth to begin like this because the forces of evil had already been let loose, and were ruling the great chasm between heaven and earth. The difference was so great between heaven and earth so that Satan would realize all that he had lost by rejecting God for all eternity.

There was much sadness in heaven after the fallen Angels had been driven out of Paradise. There was no rejoicing except for the victory of Michael, the Archangel, who had defeated Lucifer. All the Angels were appalled at the sinful pride of the Angels who dared to follow Satan and refuse to worship God.

This was the beginning of the worst kind of pride, the kind that refuses to serve, refuses to love. It was in this milieu that fallen Angels were cast into Hell and given dominion over the world.

God, the Father, knew that He would create man, and it was at this time that He formulated all His plans for salvation. These included our first parents who would sin and be cast out of Paradise because of the sin of pride and disobedience. The Father knew this would happen and that the gates of heaven would be closed until His Beloved Son would come upon the earth to reopen them.

He loved His Son so dearly that He wished to reclaim mankind from all the harm and damage that would befall them in order to make a gift of them to the Son Who would then present them back to the Father, their

Creator. He wished to create a suitable place for His people, whom He loved, and provide a beautiful world to give to His Son. It would be necessary to send His Son to redeem His people and restore a reign of peace.

At this time, He saw all that would happen throughout history and, in that moment, His plans were formulated to save each age as it came near to total destruction, instead of learning to love and serve their God and Creator.

The Father saw each one of you who has responded to My call. He chose each one of you then for the roles you are fulfilling now. Some of His chosen did not respond or fell away after a short period of time. These were replaced whenever possible.

Daughter, I have told you this short version of the story of the world, so that you will understand that Satan is warring against the Father's plan to save His children and return the earth to its former beauty.

Satan wishes to destroy the world and return it to the state of chaos in which He originally was cast. That is why sinful men who follow Lucifer wish only to destroy goodness and beauty and return to darkness. The forces of evil will not stop until they are completely destroyed by God at the appointed time. Until then, there will be many acts of violence against the earth and mankind by those who have chosen darkness and evil, and prefer to be ruled by the evil one.' (8/27/93)

I stopped and looked around at each of them. There was a long silence filled with deep reflections on Mary's explanations.

"Well, what do you think? Doesn't it give you more understanding of the senseless killing and brutality and destruction around the world after hearing that story? It's Satan himself and his demons driving their followers to such inhuman behavior. Of course, it's not a story we can check up on, but why wouldn't Mary continue to help us, with a story like that, to hear the reasons Our Father will be working in such a powerful way to cleanse and purify the world? When we consider the conditions which exist today, we can better appreciate why God's wrath has spilled over."

"Oh, I just think it's a marvelous story Carol," Judith chimed in with a deep sigh. "Who would believe that we'd be sitting here listening to a . . ."

Thomas jumped out of his chair and began pacing. "Now, Jude, hold on. Let's not get carried away. We've got to get serious about the urgency of *praying* and *fasting* and *reconciling,* just like Our Blessed Mother is telling us. The Scriptures are full of wonderful quotes to remember which bolster our courage for the return to the arms of God. The mere fact that confessing our sins is made easier for some by talking face to face with a priest can be a great help for those returning after many years. Don't you agree," he asked in a pleading tone?

Nodding my head I picked up the ball again. "Recently, I believe, Jesus requested that people be reminded that since He is everywhere, they must not be afraid to confess those serious sins. He said, *'Tell them I was there. I already know all about them and I love them anyway. I'm waiting for them in love to come back to Me.'* " I told them.

"I remember being terribly nervous early in my conversion, considering the nature of my sinfulness and pride. The priest was so patient and helpful. There was no judgementalism in his voice. In fact, he kindly reminded me that it was truly Jesus present to whom I was confessing my sins. That helped a lot.

People returning to the church after many years can still talk to the priest (the presence of Jesus) kneeling behind the curtain if it makes them feel more comfortable, but the darkness is gone. The gloom and doom atmosphere has been replaced by light in the confessional. I happen to like that very much myself."

We all sat again in quiet reflection for some minutes. Then our scripture scholar spoke up. "Do you mind if I share some of the quotes that come to my mind?"

Judith's face lit up, "Oh Thomas, would you, dear?"

"Yeah, Dad, who would know better?" his son noted with pride.

Thomas looked grateful. "This one from John always gave me comfort. I repeat it to myself before confessing my sins.

'If we acknowledge our sins, he is faithful and just and will forgive our sins and cleanse us from every wrongdoing.' (1Jn 1:9)

And here's a banner statement for the sacrament:

'Let us hold unwaveringly to our confession that gives us hope, for he who made the promise is trustworthy.' (Heb 10:23)

It helps me to say these little phrases. It calms me down and builds me up," Thomas confided.

"I can think of another one I'd like to share, but it's too long for me to remember. Could I borrow that bible, please? Yes, here it is." In comforting tones he read:

'By your stubbornness and impenitent heart, you are storing up wrath for yourself for the day of wrath and revelation of the just judgment of God, who will repay everyone according to his works: eternal life to those who seek glory, honor, and immortality through perseverance in good works, but wrath and fury to those who selfishly disobey the truth and obey wickedness. Yes, affliction and distress will come upon every human being who does evil, Jew first and then Greek. But there will be glory, honor and peace for everyone who does good, Jew first and then Greek. There is no partiality with God." (Rom 2:5-11)

"Gosh, Dad, that really sums up all that Jesus and Mary are saying today about these end times," chimed in Theo, delightedly." Jesus tells us to come back to Him and doesn't care what we've done. 'Just come back to Me,' He says. *Don't worry about changing. Give Me your hearts and I will change them.'*

It's so reassuring to hear those words and believe that this special time of Divine Mercy is still active, and it's easier than ever to return. The graces are available for the asking, but we must ask *now*.

It's interesting that we begin by praying to the Holy Spirit to show us what we need to remember, to know about ourselves and to confess our sins. He will do that. Then He makes us aware of the gifts of the Spirit and the virtues we lack. We return and request from Him, again and again, graces and strength and those much-needed gifts. We certainly can't do anything by ourselves. The Holy Spirit is our Great and Holy Enabler."

"Gosh, you're right, Theo!" I said with delight. "We'd be nothing without the help of the Holy Spirit. You are very fortunate to realize that already. One thing we could all benefit from is to go to Mass early and ask the Holy Spirit to enlighten us as to what to confess and ask forgiveness for before receiving the Eucharist. That we ask Jesus' Blood to wash us that we may forgive ourselves and others, resolve not to repeat a sin, and to bring us to holiness, purity of spirit and a more mature spirituality."

Then turning to his dad I asked, "Have you found any more quotes that might benefit us, Thomas?"

There was great excitement in his voice as he answered. "As a matter of fact, here's one we can perhaps close this visit with today. What a God we have. What comfort He offers us if we will seek Him. Listen:"

'He will not always chide, nor does he keep his wrath forever. Not according to our sins does he deal with us, nor does he requite us according to our crimes. For as the heavens are high above the earth, so surpassing is his kindness toward those who fear him. As far as the east is from the west, so far has he put our transgressions from us.' (Ps 103:3-4, 8-12)

"Thomas, that's just beautiful," I said to him. "Would you please do me a favor? Would you make a list of scripture passages that deal with forgiveness and bring them next time we visit? I hope you'll all come back together again. But there's one more thing to share before you go. I need to tell you about a memory that came back to me the other day.

While playing in my neighborhood as a small child, my mother used to call out the window, 'Carol, it's time.' That's all she needed to say, 'it's time,' and I knew what she meant. Time to come home. It was getting late, getting dark and time to come back to her and the safety of the house, partake of the nourishment that had been prepared for me.

I never questioned that. I was an only child and knew the value of obedience in those days. That repeated experience has been ringing in my ears. Our Mother is calling out of her heavenly window to all of her children in the world, *Come home, children. It's time'.*"

Again there was silence as we digested that thought and its urgency. The afternoon sun cast new shadows throughout the room and seemed to emphasize the passing of time, the disappearance of light and end of this day.

"One more story, and then we get back to chores. Judith, you'll like this one, I think. You sound like a person who loves antiques and ancestral treasures."

"Oh I do, my dear, I do. How nice that you realized that about me," she said.

Everyone took a sip of lemonade and got comfortable again, and I began.

"One of my favorite allegories for reconciliation is shared when I ask people in an audience to picture themselves going into the attic and walking over to the corner where a huge, old antique trunk sits covered with dust.

They are invited to lift the lid and realize they can only see the top layer; then notice you can't see what's underneath until you remove it. Taking off the first layer exposes the next. You proceed through each item and get sort of wrapped up in them, reminiscing, reliving events. You spend more time over some than others, and time goes by. In fact, you probably need to leave and return again, when time permits and the urgency is upon us."

"Are you with me, Judith? Can you see it," I asked her pointedly?

"Oh, I do, I can. It's my grandmother's trunk, full of old things I've been saving forever. Land sakes, I haven't thought about a lot of this old stuff for years."

"Exactly, Judith! You get down into the deep layers and say, I didn't know I was hanging on to that old thing, or, I had no idea this was in here."

Everyone was listening intently now and nodding their heads in agreement.

"Going to confession can be just like opening an old trunk after years of neglect. You have to remove the top layer before you can see what's packed below it. You have to dig way down and, after a while, it begins to get musty and even pretty smelly. The light and air hasn't hit those layers in a long, long time. The *stuff* can even affect the inside of that poor old trunk."

"We're like that with life experiences. We've stuffed so many hurts and resentments, anger and bitterness (*old stuff*) way down deep inside us where we can't even see it. After a while, we forget it's there. It gets moldy, for sure. It all begins to settle in and gather dust and smell bad. It can affect the soundness of our insides. We must allow the air and light of

God's grace to penetrate those layers, one at a time. The Holy Spirit in His wisdom, might show us just one layer at a time. We need to return often and continue to work through all that's buried there. If those things are rank enough, they could make us ill."

"Have you ever seen what mold and mildew does to the inside of a once-lovely trunk? It's ugly."

"Our souls are like that. Different areas of our lives can contain material that harms the rest of us, eats away at our insides, may cause real damage."

"Unless and until we expose all those saved 'treasures' to the light, we can't decide what to take out of the trunk and what to keep. Until we expose all our old *junk* to the Light, we cannot allow Jesus to remove it for us. We do however, have a great advantage. All the grace we need is available to us. If it's too dark down there, if we are too weak or frightened to discover more or continue, Jesus is right there to hold our hand, to help us. What else is grace, but holy strength given for moments of need, when we falter? Jesus doesn't ask us to move along any faster than we are able. Believe that one, for sure.

Stella relates that in 1989 the Blessed Mother reflected that many of us, her children, have so much pain, so much hurt buried deep inside, we will never have time to work through the forgiveness for our own healing."

> 'You must just let it go,' she said, 'Just let go of your unforgiveness, your resentments and betrayal. This will be impossible for you to accomplish without help. I will help you. Just come to me, the holy Mother, and I will give you the ability to let go of these long held feelings.'

I thought to myself, What an offer. Once the wounds have been exposed and cleaned, Jesus cauterizes them in the fire of His Love. Then He pours the oil of gladness and grace on them to prevent reinfection.

At this point Theo and his father got into a heated debate about forgiveness. Thomas thought it would be more difficult for an older person to forgive others and most especially themselves. Theo said, "no, young people have hotter tempers, and more judgmental, cruel behavior. They would require more time to let go of personal hurts, attacks and poor self images."

Judith and I eyed each other, then sat and waited. After a while they quieted down and began to listen again, so I continued. "Just as to love is an act of our will, so to forgive is a decision we make, an act of the will," I said to the three of them.

"That is most convincing, young lady, but you must be weary now. I think we need to go home now, Jude, Theo. Could we stop by the church on the way? I need more time to digest all I've heard today and think Jesus might just facilitate that process, too."

I looked at these new friends and felt joy filling my heart.

"If you continue to call me young lady, Thomas, the three of you are welcome any time. But please, could we say a Rosary together before you leave here today? We've been talking so much about it. Now, let's do it. Okay? Good. Would you lead us, Thomas?"

We all took out our rosaries and bowed our heads. Then his resonant professor, teacher voice began . . . 'I believe in God, the Father Almighty, Creator of heaven and earth. And in Jesus Christ His only Son, Our Lord, Who was conceived by the Holy Spirit, born of the Virgin Mary, suffered under Pontius Pilot, was crucified, died and was buried . . .'

Chapter Ten

Trust

"Only in God is my soul at rest; from him comes my salvation. He only is my rock and my salvation, my stronghold; I shall not be disturbed at all." (Ps 62:2-3)

The phone rang. "Hello, Theo. How is everyone there?"

"Fine, Carol. How's it going with the book? Would you be able to spare an afternoon this week? We really hope to get together with you again. My Dad has some more Scripture quotes he's dying to share with you."

"You know, I can't see all of you any day this week. Could you make it next Monday? We'll catch up quickly. I really enjoyed your parents, by the way. Your Dad is right out of central casting for professors. I'm anxious for a visit, myself. That's okay? Great. Have a good week, Theo, and let's keep each other in prayer. Bye."

The search that was going on in my office for certain material continued and the work that was such a joy was renewed.

At this point it seemed important to reflect on passages from Scripture that deal with God's promises to us; that He is a God who keeps His promises. That means we can trust what He tells us, believe in what He is saying through certain messages in these terribly serious times of grace, mercy and preparation. By grace and God's design, we grow in certitude by allowing the Holy Spirit to teach us through the Word of God.

143

REFLECT ON GOD'S ACTIVITY IN OUR LIVES

When we trust in God we are more content to *wait and see.* Contrary to our usual way of doing things, we allow the Lord to take over, work His Will in our lives, most importantly, on His timetable. Looking back on our own lives to discover how God *did* come through for us is an immense help to bolster our security and confidence in His promise to be always with us (Mt 28:20). It's good to consider writing a quick account of some way God worked in our life that fulfilled a promise.

It is only in reflection that we come to a true appreciation of the way God is continually working in our lives, supporting us, leading and guiding in a gentle way. Without appreciation, there is no gratitude. Without gratitude, we are dried up shells, far from being enriched by the waters of life-giving grace.

There is a phrase something like this: 'A life not reflected upon is a life not completely lived.' Surely we will be more *alive* if we are living at a more deeply reflective and grateful level. We cannot be grateful if we do not love. Just as surely, we cannot love without a grateful heart.

Isaiah and his magnificent poetry (49:15-16), reminds us that the Lord will never forget us, even though our mother should; that our names are written on the palms of His hands.

The Lord said to Isaiah:

'Hear me', you who know justice, you people who have my teaching at heart: Fear not the reproach of men, be not dismayed at their revilings.

They shall be like a garment eaten by moths, like wool consumed by grubs: But my justice shall remain forever and my salvation for all generations.' (51:7-8)

'Blessed is the man who trusts in the Lord, whose hope is in the Lord.' (Jer 17:7).

This phrase, repeated daily, can afford us flight from anxiety; a return to serenity, peace. We are going to need the

Lord more than ever as a source of strength, His Word as our comfort and consolation.

There is reason to trust, have hope, be stilled in the peace of Jesus.

> 'Only in God is my soul at rest; from him comes my salvation. He only is my rock and my salvation, my stronghold; I shall not be disturbed at all.' (Ps 62:2-3)

When we fill ourselves with the sweetness of such words, we become that sweetness. A grasping, arguing, ungrateful attitude is sour, sets our teeth on edge, our hearts empty.

Scripture is full of stories about waiting on the Lord. It is an oft-repeated theme. Patience is the single most difficult virtue to develop, most people seem to agree. We know we don't even practice very well without lots of grace from the Holy Spirit. We can identify with the Psalmist:

> 'How long, O Lord? Will you utterly forget me? How long will you hide your face from me?' (Ps 13:2).

We can relate to a feeling of *never-endingness* and that makes trust all the more difficult.

One day at a time, step by step, is the best observation and suggestion ever made to people in this age.

The Divine Mercy Prayer, given to Blessed Faustina Kowalska, a Sister in Poland to whom He gave many teachings about His Divine Mercy in the early 1930's, is the Lord's solution: 'Jesus, I trust in You'. [1]

Doesn't it often seem to be a part of God's plan to make us wait until we're barely breathing? This is the scenario which strengthens and develops our trust, our ability to hang in there, go the limit, 'fight the good fight' (2Tim 4:7). It's good to look back on successes, times when we realized God was there, holding us up, adding His fortitude to ours.

---

[1] *Divine Mercy in My Soul, Diary of Sister Faustina Kowalska.* Marian Press, Stockbridge, Mass, 1987.

Perhaps the quickest way to become acquainted with Abraham and his great trust, or the Exodus story (when the Israelites wandered in the desert for forty years), is to read Psalms 105, 106 and 107. In order to bolster our own confidence, we literally need to know where to turn. These pages of Scripture and many other stories found there will come to our aid, will shore up our flagging efforts, will restore our sinking spirits. Probably the most famous passages are found in Romans 8, a favorite of so many people. To quote here some of those wonderful lines might lead us to look for more to feed our hungry souls:

> 'We know that all things work for good for those who love God, who are called according to his purpose. For those he foreknew he also predestined to be conformed to the image of his Son, so that he might be the firstborn among many brothers. And those he predestined he also called; and those he called he also justified; and those he justified he also glorified. What then shall we say to this. If God is for us, who can be against us?' (Rom 8:28-31)

> 'For I am convinced that neither death, nor life, nor angels, nor principalities, nor present things, nor future things, nor powers, nor height, nor depth, nor any other creature will be able to separate us from the love of God in Christ Jesus our Lord.' (Rom 8:38-39)

If we trust in Jesus, then we trust Mary, His Mother, and we listen to Their words. At the wedding feast of Cana, Mary said, 'Do whatever He tells you.' (Jn 2:5) This has become a basis for many theological thoughts and explanations about accepting God's Will in our lives, trusting in His choices for us, listening to Mary and allowing her to lead us to Jesus, always her primary action in this world.

If we trust in Mary, we believe that she is (as well as the Mother of God), His 'Prophet' for our times. Through proper prayer, discernment and the gifts of grace and mercy, our hearts will open to accept the fact that she is speaking in many places in the world (every country).

She is calling all people back to her Son; appearing to chosen messengers for the purpose of getting our attention; teaching us how to love; drawing us to the Sacred Heart through her Immaculate Heart in order to prepare us for the Second Coming of Jesus.

If we trust God, our Father, we believe that all of the events being foretold by the Blessed Virgin Mary are a part of His great plan for the salvation of all people. We can pray to Jesus with conviction that His final victory over Satan and the powers of evil becomes a reality.

> "Dying, you destroyed our death. Rising, you restored our life. Lord Jesus, come in glory."

When we more totally trust, we answer more totally God's call to holiness. Holiness, we are told, is also translated as *wholeness*.

> *'If you are holy, you have such a strong self confidence in your love for Me that the judgment of men will not disturb you.'* [3]

This certainly speaks of the sort of love for ourselves in Christ that will protect us from the harmful judgments of mankind, make us whole.

When Jesus said to His disciples (and us), 'Be perfect as your heavenly Father is perfect' (Mt 5:48), He was also inviting us to the wholeness and holiness of the Father, not perfection according to the world view.

When we can completely trust in the Divine Will of God for our lives, we will probably be standing face to face with

---

[2] Memorial acclaimation from the Roman Catholic Mass.

[3] *I Am Your Jesus of Mercy*, Vol.1, Riehle Foundation, Milford, Ohio.

Him. However, by degrees and with His grace, we believe that slowly our trust grows and His Will becomes less terrifying, less a matter of tension with our control, more a place of refuge and peace, lived out quietly and consistently.

Scripture tells us that God has loved us first (1Jn 4:19); that He has chosen us, we have not chosen Him (Jn 15:16). Belief in these thoughts alone should be enough to convince us of the final victory of God's Plan for us: living this life in adoption to Him through Jesus (Eph 1).

To be comforted, uplifted and led to greater trust by what we read is possible as described by Paul to the Ephesians:

> 'But God, who is rich in mercy, because of the great love he had for us, even when we were dead in our transgressions, brought us to life with Christ, raised us up with him, and seated us with him in the heavens in Christ Jesus, that in the ages to come he might show the immeasurable riches of his grace in his kindness to us in Christ Jesus. For by grace you have been saved through faith, and this is not from you; it is the gift of God; it is not from works, so no one may boast. For we are his handiwork, created in Christ Jesus for the good works that God has prepared in advance, that we should live in them.' (Eph 2:4-10)

Are we not uplifted, encouraged?

Faith takes over when our eyes fail us. These are not new words. They are certainly appropriate for us who believe the words of the priest when he raises the consecrated wine and bread and says: "Behold the Lamb of God. Behold Him Who takes away the sins of the world."

Trust in those words allows us to believe in Jesus' Body and Blood, Soul and Divinity, God and Man, all the events and words of His life on earth, *all that He is, truly present* in the Sacred Host and Precious Blood. Trust in the words of Jesus allows us to accept the statement He made to His listeners two thousand years ago:

> 'I am the living bread that came down from heaven; whoever eats this bread will live forever; and the bread that I will give is my flesh for the life of the world." (Jn 6:51)

> "Jesus said to them, Amen, Amen I say to you, unless you eat the flesh of the Son of Man and drink his blood, you do not have life within you. Whoever eats my flesh and drinks my blood has eternal life, and I will raise him up on the last day. For my flesh is true food, and my blood is true drink. Whoever eats my flesh and drinks my blood remains in me and I in him." (Jn 6:54-56)

No wonder many of his followers were incredulous and no longer accompanied him. Without faith and enormous trust, the command to eat Jesus' flesh and blood is an impossible one to believe. The very fact that the true Presence of Jesus in the Eucharist is being attacked today speaks to a loss of faith, a faith crisis resulting in pure heresy.

Whenever we too are attacked, we can say with the apostle, "Lord I believe, help my unbelief." (Mk 9:24)

Just because we trust in the fact that we are children of God and heirs of heaven; just because we believe that we can remain in the love of God and be His friends by keeping His Commandments; just because we have faith in the promise of Jesus that He has conquered the world; doesn't mean we will never have trouble in the world. He has warned us about this too, but we can take courage (Jn 16:33), if we trust.

Jesus told Blessed Faustina Kowalska, "Mankind will have no peace until it turns with trust to My Mercy."

The essence of Divine Mercy and the message of mercy is trust in Jesus. In trust, we allow Jesus to transform our lives and give us New Life in Him. We become a *living message* of Divine Mercy.

Mercy is the gift through which sinners are forgiven, the blind recover sight, the oppressed are set free, the captive is released, the good news is preached to the poor. [4]

Mercy demands that we give mercy to others as a condition for us to receive it. "Blessed are the merciful, for they shall obtain mercy." What greater incentive to have trust in the mercy and promises of Jesus: to enable that mercy to set us free to share that gift with others.

I remember a poem I had recently read:

> 'Trust Him when dark doubts assail you. Trust
> Him when your strength is small.
>
> Trust Him when to simply trust Him seems the
> hardest thing of all.
>
> Trust Him, He is ever faithful. Trust Him, for His
> Will is best.
>
> Trust Him, for the Heart of Jesus is the only place
> to rest.
>
> Trust Him. Then, through doubts and sunshine
> all your cares are cast upon Him, until the
> storm of life is over and the trusting days are
> past.' [5]

I was brought from my reflection back to the sound of another ringing telephone and put down my work for the day.

Walking toward the phone, I was brought up sharply by the view which greeted me through the vast expanse of the window in the front of our house. Ignoring the phone, I opened the outer door in the foyer and stood gazing at a nationally famous phenomenon: the Arizona sunset.

---

[4] *Rich in Mercy*, Encyclical of Pope John Paul II.

[5] *Cenacles of Divine Mercy Newsletter*, January, 1994, Arizona.

Palm trees across many yards were in silhouette to the blazing sky. Neat rows of tiny clouds marched across the heavens dressed in red and purple, toward the setting giant. The sun itself, falling behind Camelback mountain, sent its rays to higher clouds, turning them pink and grey.

The mountain, shamelessly masquerading as a camel, contains a rock formation that looks exactly like a monk on his knees. Hence, the name 'Praying Monk.' He was in sharp relief to the golden glow, as though his prayer were causing a mighty response.

I smiled and sighed. What a sight! Having seen pictures of a sunset upon our arrival to the Valley of the Sun thirteen years ago, I thought them exaggerated, touched up. Now I knew the truth. Now I knew the origin of mauve! Turning finally, I walked slowly toward the kitchen to answer yet another ringing telephone.

Chapter Eleven

Perseverance

"I will meditate on your precepts and consider your ways. In your statutes, I will delight, I will not forget your words." (Ps 119:16)

Life is difficult, with hardships of every kind. Especially we struggle against our human nature. But our Lord Jesus and His holy Mother come to sustain us in these *end times,* these times of great *tribulation, purification* and *preparation.* For these special days of grace and mercy, They ask in my heart that I share Their words with you:

Blessed Mother: *'There is no grace, no joy without struggle, and each must experience this in order to be strengthened to do my Son's work.' (8/22/92)*

Jesus: *'Stay close to My Mother, wrapped in her Mantle. You will be strengthened and protected there. Trust that all I have told you is true and that all will go well.' (8/22/92)*

Jesus: *'You are safe in the silence of My Presence, and I promise to heal you quickly if you will allow Me the opportunity.' (9/2/92)*

Blessed Mother: *'The war is fierce as Satan attacks my dear ones relentlessly. He wishes to defeat me and destroy the souls of all those who love me. You will see more of that hatred very soon and must pray fiercely to combat these attacks. Many will turn from me thinking to save themselves. You must believe that no harm can come to you, although it will seem at times, to be the end of everything. Only by allowing Us to lead and guide you will you complete this arduous journey.'* (9/2/92)

Jesus: *'Have confidence in your Jesus. Trust your Mother and Me.'* (9/4/92)

Blessed Mother: *'Fear is not a productive attitude and can cause further negative thoughts to develop.'* (9/4/92)

Jesus: *'Happy the life which bears the marks of My sufferings and joins in a union with Me that will never end. Happy the one whose trust is in the Lord and whose journey is tied to the pattern of My life.'* (9/8/92)

Jesus: *'The days are about to turn into darkness of mind and heart for all My children, even those who love Me. They will be like lost sheep who wander in the streets looking for shelter. Rally around Me and My Mother. Be assured, My children, of My love and My Mother's love and Our continued presence with you.*

When the hour seems darkest, bring My people to Me. Assure them of safety and protection, and promise them salvation in My Name.

When you are weary, seek rest in My Sacred Heart.

When you are lonely, seek comfort in My arms.

When you feel empty, take courage and be filled by My Presence in the Blessed Sacrament.

When all looks bleak and overwhelming, come to My Mother and Me, and We will refresh you with Our words for your understanding.

As you listen and trust in Our words, your faith will increase and be a strong beacon for all.' (9/16/92)

Jesus: 'Do not be concerned about defending yourself. I, your Lord, God, will defend you at the proper time, on the Day of Salvation.' (10/2/92)

Jesus: 'Be of good cheer. Persevere and have faith, and know that you are not alone and that I hear every single word you say and think. I know everything and will stand by your side until evil is conquered in the world.' (10/31/92)

Blessed Mother: 'The days to come will see many temptations and attacks from the evil one. He is joyful when you are down and discouraged. Please, just focus on my Son, Jesus, and be comforted by the love He has for you. The time is coming now for all that I have told you to be fulfilled. Peace will seem like a lost notion in the days to come. Chaos will reign in the streets and violence will be commonplace. All will be fearful and afraid to venture from their homes. People must be prepared for these days to come, for a time when safety is no longer possible in the streets. It will be too dangerous to leave your homes, and a state of emergency will exist throughout the land.

When all looks lost, I will continue to save you, protect you from evil and harm. Believe in these words, for they will help you to prepare for the time ahead. It is most serious of which I speak. People need to be convinced of the dangers that will exist. Tell my people they must prepare to fight evil with the weapons of prayer and penance and fasting. Be at peace, My children, no matter what occurs.' (11/15/92)

Jesus: 'In these days, stay close to My Mother and to My Sacred Heart. Call upon My Mother to assist you in perseverance. Call upon the Angels to strengthen you and all the Saints to come to your aid. There will be nothing *you cannot do for Us when We ask it of you if you have faith, believe and trust.' (11/23/92)*

Blessed Mother: *'Hear my Son, children, and take His words to your heart. Ponder them and be filled with the truth and power of the gifts He offers you.* (His power, His peace, His strength, His love, His mercy, His forgiveness). *Stand by me and hold my hand in the days to come. You will be unable to continue without Our help and a constant reliance and dependence on these promises.' (11/23/92)*

Jesus: *'Know that all will be accomplished and will go well for those who trust in My words.' (12/8/92)*

Blessed Mother: *'Satan is wreaking his havoc now, and must be stopped through the prayer and sacrifices of my faithful ones. Call out to them and tell them of Our love and the safety which can be found in my arms.'*

Jesus: *'Be humble and obedient children, trusting in My help, My strength.' (1/5/93)*

Blessed Mother: *'Do not worry about anything. Just go forward, trusting and trying to do all the things that have been asked of you. Daughter, my heart breaks at the sight of all the sin and suffering in the world. Nothing but the Father's wrath will reach Our people now. They only listen to violence, and are completely insensitive to real love.*

No longer can people hear Our plea because of their own fear and pain. The Father will do what is necessary to cleanse the earth and its people. We know that He only wills what is best for us. Remember this, as fire and destruction rain down upon the earth and its inhabitants.

Praise God for His mercy and generosity. Thank Him for giving you the means to be saved and to return to Him, though there is no one on earth found worthy of His

grace. It is a great gift of the Father, given with uncondi-
tional love and mercy. Surrender to Him and His Will for
you. Accept whatever He sends you and say, Amen.' (1/93)

Blessed Mother: *'Hold tightly to my hands, my dear*
ones, relying on the strength my Jesus and I have to give
you. Count on your Mother to be ever-present with you,
and be aware of this. Strengthen yourselves with the
knowledge and faith you have in my Son and myself.
More graces will be available to those who heed the call to
return immediately to the House of God and raise their
hands and hearts in supplication for their sins.' (1/11/93)

Jesus: *'In times of war, the enemy is everywhere. When*
your battlements are built on a solid foundation, all will
be well. There is nothing to fear for those who trust in Me.

Please, remember that you are never alone, as I am con-
stantly at your side and in your heart. Know and trust
that each problem you encounter makes you that much
stronger, more able to defend with determination My
plans for all of you. When doubts and challenges arise,
they cause those involved to think more clearly; to or-
ganize what needs to be and to prepare more diligently
and in a more concise manner what will best reach My
people. The Father's Will will be done.' (3/22/93)

Blessed Mother: *'Please, take each event as it comes, in*
peace and with complete resignation as God's Will for
you. You all must learn more patience and trust in the
Father's Providence. Remember, My dear ones, He has
been caring for His people since the dawn of their creation
and always does what is best for you at that moment.'
(3/22/93)

Jesus: *'Trust totally in My power to defend and protect.*
Do not let yourself be overcome with fear or a lack of hope.
We will give you all the strength and courage you will

need to stand against the evil one. He will wear many faces and be as subtle and cunning as the lowest serpent. Be docile and quiet, and prepare for the events which are about to begin and will lead my people to the Day of the Lord.' (3/27/93)

Jesus: 'The Holy Spirit is with you, My child, inspiring and leading you in the necessary direction you must take. It is Love which brings you to the new path of My Light. It is Love which shows you the elements of truth that will touch others and quickly bring them to a new understanding of the mysteries of God, the truth of His Holiness.

As you prepare, remember the One Who sends you, Who walks with you, Who loves you and will never leave you. Never, for an instant, are you left alone or unprotected.' (5/16/93)

Blessed Mother: 'It is a matter of seconds now before war begins, and one disaster after another renders your country vulnerable to those who plot against it. Now is the time. We must be brave and only look to the coming of my Son Who will bring renewed life to this earth and begin to fulfill the Father's plan of salvation for His world. Maranatha! (this means, Come, Lord Jesus.) Be brave and trusting children. I am always at your side.' (5/17/93)

Jesus: 'This is a combination of trust and surrender which, of course, goes together. Child, your ability to change is only a matter of openness to the gifts We wish to give you.

In the quiet of doing nothing, strength is built up.

In the quiet of listening, obedience is developed.

In the quiet of just being, Love will flood your hearts because We have the chance to love each other and be further united.' (7/2/93)

Jesus: *'Please, trust in Our help and remain ever recollected with Us in your ministering. We are by your side and in your heart, My people.'* (9/10/93)

There is an age-old controversy we learned in Psychology 101. Roughly, it has to do with an argument between those who believe that a person's behavior is affected and formed mostly by their genes (therefore, predetermined at birth) and those who believe that the environment and experiences mold a person into what they become. This is referred to as the Nature/Nurture debate.

Most of us believe, of course, that the answer lies somewhere in between, a combination of the two sides. What is certain is that we do become like a person with whom we spend large amounts of time, especially in our younger, more impressionable, formative years. Most of us become a lot like our parents. We take in everything they do and say, all their mannerisms, without even being aware of it.

It is said that imitation is the highest form of flattery. Little girls play house in reflection of Mommy. Boys carry around hammers. Small basketball sets hang in the dining room. Lots of conversation begins with, 'when I grow up, I'm gonna be just like . . .'

You must know children who not only strongly resemble one of their parents, but speak, gesture and laugh exactly the same. We absorb a lot of the characteristics of a person who is nearby because we are made that way, and this seems to continue throughout our lives.

We are made in the image and likeness of God (our spiritual genes).

When we 'hang around' Jesus in the Blessed Sacrament daily, as He is inviting us to do, we spend more and more time in His company. If we do this in a spirit of openness, listening to His words in Scripture or within our hearts, we are going to subconsciously absorb His thoughts, His way of doing things, His gentleness with people, His total acceptance of others.

The Virgin Mary has invited us to reject our worldly spirits and disposition and ask for *hers*. We are shown that we can reject our own lack of virtue and seek hers. Our unloving hearts, full of coldness, can be *'turned in'*, replaced by hers. We will be better able to *love Jesus* with *her love*.

We need to do this over and over since we never *get it* completely or *keep it* for long because of our fractured humanity. (Makes me think of the story of the little girl who was praying to Jesus to fill her heart with love. He said to her, 'I just did that yesterday.' She replied, 'I know, Jesus, but I leaks!')

When we are born, we are a completely blank page, without any social and few motor skills. I used to think of our children as uncivilized, actually. A child needs to be taught how to act; what behavior is expected; the results of rebellion; how to love by being loved. As it grows, it hopefully develops new skills constantly, in a routine patterned way. Pretty predictable, but also very much with the mannerisms of their parents, or teachers.

A great amount of trust is needed by the child for the parent. Trust tells us it's safe to be with a certain person, our parents, in our own house; that we can believe what that person says. The tragedy of child abuse is the destruction of trust within that small person. It never really gets a chance to develop. Without trust, where do we go, who do we believe, what do we believe in?

Our spiritual lives are like that. When we are reborn, we are not quite a blank slate, but there are many behaviors we must spend time rejecting, unlearning, before we can proceed with new patterns of living. We bring knowledge of our past behavior as a modifier and that's called *prudence*. We're not sure yet, what to do, but we sure know already what we cannot do.

The more time we spend with the person teaching us, the more quickly we will learn and the more we are apt to pick up a lot of that person's habits, ways of doing things, personality.

Soooo, don't you just bet one of the reasons we are being called to all of this new behavior that includes reading Scripture; being made aware that we are living minute to minute in the Presence of Jesus and Mary; asked to pray (any conversation with God) with other people who are being formed in the same way, is significant? Then we're invited to develop an intimate relationship with Jesus by spending time in front of the Blessed Sacrament, getting to know Him personally, modelling ourselves after Him. Just *being* with Jesus heals us by emptying out the old stuff and making room for the new, the peace that only He can give.

In trust and hope and joy we believe we are becoming more who we were created to be, children of God ... more like Jesus and Mary: meek and humble of heart, suffering servants, trusting that the Will of the Father is right for us and accepting His decisions in our lives, on His timetable. We will become more like our spiritual Mother and our Creator, Savior, Redeemer and Brother when we spend more and more time listening to them, and without even realizing it, absorbing their essence.

In "I Am Your Jesus of Mercy, Volume I", inspirations from Jesus are quoted, explaining that the first step to having faith is surrendering with *trust*. We must not, He says, confuse faith with feelings. Faith, to believe, is a decision, an act of the will much like loving and forgiving. It has nothing to do with how we feel on a particular day. Faith is trusting in the truth...the truth that He will save us and care for us.

God gives us the invitation to come to Him and trust, the promise that we *can* trust Him, even though there may not be one trustworthy person in our lives. '*Come to My Mother and Me,*' He says, '*and We will protect you.*'

He knows how difficult this is because of the countless betrayals and disappointments we experience. People continue to let each other down.

And if we get discouraged or think we can't change, can't open up to new ideas or new possibilities, we might pray to Abraham's wife, Sarah. Imagine being 102 and keeping up with your two year old!

Chapter Twelve

Surrender

"Your attitude must be that of Christ: Though he was in the form of God, he did not deem equality with God something to be grasped at. Rather, he emptied himself and took the form of a slave, being born in the likeness of man." (Phil 2:5-7)

The four of us were sitting, once again, in the living room of our home. We had caught up on news and begun sipping more cool drinks. The mood was serene and filled with expectation for the further information about to be shared.

"As we were saying, Theo, your parents have been dealing with trust and mistrust for a long time. The longer we live, the more of life we experience, and the easier it is to become disillusioned, discouraged, depressed if we aren't supported by an active faith in God and a rich prayer life.

It won't surprise you, I think, that we are going from the subject of trust to that of surrender. We have a fair understanding of the fact that surrender means accepting the Will of God for our lives. 'More like Jesus, more like Mary.' We see that dying to ourselves is the key to the whole dynamic of abandoning ourselves to Him.

Would you three do me the great pleasure of allowing me to listen to you take turns reading the messages to my heart from Jesus and Mary? I have recorded in my journal all these months. It would make them come alive in a new way. Reading aloud is a great enhancement to any text, as is listening to them in that way."

The papers were shuffled amongst them and we settled down once more. Thomas began in his perfect-for-Jesus voice. That was good because many of the beginning words were His.

We said a prayer to the Holy Spirit to open our hearts and minds to enable us to truly listen and hear the deepest meaning of these words to us. Then Thomas cleared his throat and began:

> Jesus: *'You are doing My Will when you pray often and come to visit Me in My Blessed Sacrament. The more time you spend in quiet and listen, then will your heart be stilled and your mind quieted for the communication I wish to give you.' (7/22/92)*

> Jesus: *'I wish for you to abandon yourself to Me more completely so that I can work My Will in you.' (8/17/92)*

> Jesus: *'Seek to be hidden in the heart and arms of My Mother. She will care for you and be with you every step of the way.' (7/29/92)*

> Jesus: *'Complete freedom is necessary for you to accomplish My plan for you.' (8/23/92)*

> Jesus: *'The time for My Father's hand to fall upon this earth is now, I tell you. The day is not important. Just be totally prepared at all times to live a long time or a short time. When you are prepared, it is all the same. When you are united with Me and serving Me here on earth, it is no different than doing the same in Heaven. The discomfort you will experience here will be dulled by the joy of loving Me and serving Me. All will be accomplished smoothly and easily if you abandon yourself and trust in your Lord Jesus.' (8/27/92)*

Jesus: 'Your mind will be purified and your heart healed the more you spend time just being in My Presence. Empty your heart out to Me, your weary heart, and I will soothe and heal you forever. This can be done, My child, and I desire for you to be at peace and emptied of harmful residue of the past. Remember that no one work is greater than another, and you will be humble and tender and small like My Mother, eager to remain hidden in constant prayer and listening.' (8/28/92)

Jesus: 'Focus on Me and all that is about to unfold. Remain as quiet and recollected as possible. You must be emptied of all that holds you bound so that I can heal your ills and free you to serve Me and My people. Please, child, avoid all that would disturb your spirit for your own sake and dwell in My Sacred Heart. Only by allowing Us to lead and guide you will you complete this arduous journey. As you are emptied, more of My grace and love can flow through you to them.' (9/2/92)

Jesus: 'Please, My children, continue to come to Me and just rest and be with Me in comfort and quiet.' (9/4/92)

Jesus: 'Happy the one whose trust is in the Lord and whose journey is tied to the pattern of My Life. When all looks bleak and overwhelming, come to My mother and Me, and We will refresh you with Our words for your understanding.' (9/8/92)

Thomas read slowly and between each one there was the silence of deep thought and reflection before he began again:

Jesus: 'Waiting is difficult, but it is good for the soul and purifies the heart.' (10/31/92)

Jesus: 'Be open to the Will of the Spirit, and this will help you to know what to say and how to help each person We send to you. It is important to pray constantly to My Spirit that He will give you the guidance you need.' (11/6/92)

Jesus: *'The need for obedience and acceptance of God's Will in the lives of all is a necessary ingredient in the plan to enlist the co-operation of Our people. Please, continue to invite Me to pray with you, and I will constantly be at your side, fighting with you in the battle for men's souls.'* (11/28/92)

He nodded to Theo who continued to read with much emotion in his voice, for these were powerful words we were hearing.

Blessed Mother: *'Hold my hand at all times and remain close to Me. I love you.'* (11/28/92)

Blessed Mother: *'Continue to work and plan and go forward with the tasks you are performing for Us. Continue as though nothing were in your way or causing an interruption. If you do not allow yourself to be distracted, no distraction will slow you down or impede progress.*

Pray much and surrender all, while at the same time, working hard. You will see a quick resolution and completion of all that I am asking of you. Offer each step to my Son to bless and purify.' (3/22/93)

Jesus: *'Each moment of the day, seek to be united with Me and do not question Me about things which only serve to distract you. You are trying to figure out too many things and I, your Lord, need for you to come in total freedom, complete simplicity, and just BE! This is very difficult for you, but you will be able to do this if you come often and persist.'*

Theo looked up at me. "Sounds like you were having a rough time, Carol."

I only smiled and nodded, but sat there thinking back to several weeks in April of last year when many of us were confused and perplexed. It was a time of pain and darkness. The feeling of no-peace was a sure sign something was wrong, that we were not listening properly, patiently waiting on the Lord and His agenda. Theo continued:

'If you will come without thought or agenda, only seeking Me, you will see what I mean.

If you will allow Me to lead you, then you will learn to truly follow.

If you will seek My Will and My thoughts and My ideas, they will be given to you to be shared with all the world.

Continue to seek My help and that of My Mother. You can become the instrument of hope for My people if you allow Me to work through you. Please, allow Me. Come to Me.

Abandon all of who you are and receive all of Who I am. Take My gifts and use them for My people. You will learn quickly if you begin. Begin now, child. There is no more time.' (3/29/93)

Jesus: *'Come to My waiting arms and find there the love you seek. Come and be refreshed in spirit and join your heart to Mine. Please child, desire to spend every spare moment with Me. Think of nothing else save being with Me, walking in My love and sharing My thoughts and feelings.*

Walk with Me, daughter. Carry My Cross with Me. Fall with Me and rise to continue to the Hill of Shame. Come now, and be lifted up with Me. Hang on My Cross and die with Me in perfect union with My Will for you. Stay close to Me. Lean on Me, for I am strong.' (4/4/93)

Blessed Mother: *'Surrender to Him and His Will for you. Accept whatever He sends you and say, Amen.'* (4/93)

Jesus: *'Our Holy Spirit will arrange each step you will take. You have only to say, 'yes' each day and be open to*

My demands on you. These will be accompanied by all the help necessary to carry out these requests. Your faith in Me will enable you to do what I ask of you.' (4/93)

Blessed Mother: 'If you will surrender yourself totally to the Father's design for your life, you will feel total peace and constantly praise Him Who has created you and knows what is best for you. Give thanks to the Father for all that is, and you will be filled with joy and a surrender you have not experienced before.

You know the meaning of these words, but it is time to put them into practice. Please, know and accept where you are with grace and patience. Be meek and humble with your God and wait patiently for Him to move in your life. All will be accomplished and all will be as it should be.' (4/30/93)

Listening to this one, it came to me that Our Lady must have been rather sad because of my anxiety over the slow progress of my soul. She didn't say this, but all I heard was. . . ego, ego, ego!

Jesus: 'Ask for the direction and help of the Holy Spirit for any endeavor and place yourself in His hands.' (6/16/93)

Jesus: 'Practice silence and humility all the while praying for sincerity and joy. Your ability to change is only a matter of openness to the gifts We wish to give you.

In the quiet of doing nothing, strength is built up.

In the quiet of listening, obedience is developed.

In the quiet of just being, love will flood your hearts because We have the chance to love each other and be further united.

In these days, the graces are ten-fold because you are required to wait on My Will for you and bow to My commands. The understanding will come only after you *acquiesce to My Will and desires for your time and energy.*

Is it not peaceful, just knowing you are in My Presence and doing My Will? The particulars of My Will become more apparent when My Holy Spirit works to show you what is needed for a particular time.' (7/2/93)

How simple He makes it sound. Why can't I do that? The quiet was an indication that each of us had the same thought.

Jesus: *'In the near future, events will occur which change the face of this country and the lives of millions even more drastically. It will become obvious to many more that all of Our words are coming to pass, and that the Father in Heaven has unleashed His wrath upon them. If you will recall all that I have told you, you will be filled with peace and a sense of direction that will not be shaken.' (7/30/93)*

We all stopped and looked at each other. Taking a drink of the cool liquid and without a word, each reached for our Rosaries, and began to pray together for the difficult times which would soon arrive. We finished and this time Judith began to read.

Blessed Mother: *'Praise the Father, and all focus will remain away from yourself and your concerns. We worry and mistrust when we are too self-absorbed.*

If you will just praise and thank Him at each moment, you will notice a return of peace and be much more able to make progress in your work. The love My Son and I have for you is meant to strengthen you and allow you to rise above these temptations to doubt and worry. Don't you know that all has been accomplished already, and you have only to co-operate with each event, each request, for it to be fulfilled in you?

The overwhelming times in which you live and all that is being requested would be too much to handle if it were not for the fact that these are all gifts of the Father to His people. Please, concentrate on the goodness of God, Our Father, and believe that He will gift you with all the help you need because He loves you and because He has given Us to you.

Each time you feel panic begin to invade your being, stop. Refocus on my Son Jesus and myself. Ask to be reunited to Our Hearts and be allowed to concentrate again on truth and the reality of all that is.' (7/31/93)

God the Father: *'Your place in this plan of Mine, in My Divine Will, has been in place since before you were born. It was purchased and assured for you by the death of My Beloved Son.' (8/5/93)*

There was a long pause and my friends looked at each other in a questioning manner.

"Good heavens!" said Judith, "do you suppose He is referring to all of us when He says that?"

"He most certainly is," I assured her. The confidence in that fact nearly lifted me off the chair. "It's amazing how words can change you, fill you with a firm resolve, if we allow them to work that way," I said.

"There's one more," said Judith. "Would you like me to continue?"

"Well of course we would, Judith. What makes you even ask? However, let's plan to call it a day, then. This is a lot to think about, good food for meditation. You know, Jude, you really sound like Jesus' Mother might have. Very nice."

Blessed Mother: 'I was little and hidden in the tiny village of Nazareth.

It was there I taught my Jesus the things He needed to learn as He became a man and prepared to do the Father's Will.

It was there that I spent hours in silent communion with the Holy Spirit, listening to the words I would share with Our Beloved Son.

It was there that I learned what was meant for the future of my Son and what was in store for Him.

I explained the value of suffering and true obedience to my Jesus.

My daughter, obedience is what is needed for each step of the way, if you are to allow Us to guide you. Never look back to the life behind you. Never allow anything or anyone to hamper you in your response to God's Will.

We will be at your side at each moment, holding your hand, guiding your words, molding your actions. It will be a process of listening that will be most necessary for you, child. Do not be frightened or dismayed. All can be accomplished according to the Will of God if you only trust in my Son and me.

Remain in constant communion with me, wrapped in my Mantle and listening of my works. This is a serious time of preparation, and I wish for you to come to me often in prayer. Pray, walk, write, listen. All will be accomplished.' (7/20/92)

Speaking in a rather hushed voice, Theo said, "Could I make a copy of these, Carol? I think we'd all like to read them many more times and absorb the contents."

"Of course you may, Theo. I just might sit here awhile myself and let it sink in a little more. If we don't take the time to do that, the powerful words can't be as effective as possible, can they? Let's meet here in three days. Would that work for you? Good." They rose, walked to the door and left quickly.

Sitting back down, thoughts and feelings invaded me. What would make the *whole world* listen and take seriously the words I had just heard read in this room? How could the maximum number of people be reached in the minimum amount of time that was left? I heard again in my mind:

> 'Do not be frightened or dismayed. All can be accomplished according to the Will of God if only you trust in my Son and me.'

I knew that our Lady didn't mean it was only up to me to trust. She meant for each of us to pray that the mercy of the Father would be released for all the inhabitants of the earth, and that it *could* happen.

It dawned on me that the prospect of dying to myself was something I had not given much time. No one wanted to think about dying, no matter how we might long for the joys and gifts of Paradise. It wasn't dying that was the problem, but how to die to oneself and still live? 'More like Jesus, more like Mary.' That has always been the challenge for the Christian. Now the need for swift action was paramount.

Dying to self means many things: complete detachment from people and things in order to be freed up to love and serve God. As we say, *'It reads easy in the script. It plays hard on the stage.'*

Recorded in my journal in June of 1992, Jesus chided me,

> 'You must let go of your concern for your children so that you can be free to respond to Me. This does not mean you do not care about them, but that you trust completely in My care for them, according to their needs and My Will.' (6/17/92)

Have you ever spent weeks, months, even years thinking you had let go of everything and everyone? Do you struggle with letting go and taking back again? Of course. We all do. It's very discouraging to find out how many times Jesus has needed to beg us to trust Him. Imagine *His* discouragement.

Allowing ourselves to be emptied was the only solution that would work when you look at it from every angle. We are not able to do that for ourselves. Scripture must be talking about that sort of action of the Spirit when it talks about the potter breaking and remaking the clay.

Thinking about that made me feel like a lump of clay alright. How many times do you get put back on the potter's wheel? How many times does a new shape, subtler shading and new function need to be given to us? This is the stuff of purification; doing all we can to empty ourselves, be rid of the habits that cling, attachment to people and their opinions, for example.

The possibility of making a list came to mind. What could I let go of that would bring me to a state of surrender and emptiness so that He could fill me with all that goodness He talks about? I took out pen and paper and began to write.

SURRENDER LIST

> Abandon my will, my energy, the gifts He has given to me, my whole self to the Father's Will.

> Forgoing opportunities to justify myself, explain, change someone's opinion, when I think it's unfair or untrue.

> Allowing humiliation, misunderstanding, rejection, ridicule.

> Attachments to things, possessions, house, clothes, even children and too much control.

> Judgmentalism, criticism, gossip.

> Expectations, emotions, being right. Having the last word. Impatience, pride, vanity, selfishness, self-centeredness.

> Arguing, competition, irritability. That one will take a long while. (Think of all the people who make me irritable. Not good.)

> My opinions, the importance of other's opinions of me; righteousness.

My own agenda, priorities, my integrity and good
  name. (It's just possible the Lord might ask that
  of each of us.)

Dishonesty, the support and understanding of
  loved ones. (This could get pretty lonesome
  without Jesus and Mary.)

Self-absorption, anxiety, fear, control, anger, all
  the un-virtues. My false independence, making
  decisions without God.

Wanting a quick fix. (. . . take away all my sins,
  Lord, now.)

That was enough for one day. The Holy Spirit was obviously working too hard here. Maybe it would be a good idea
for everyone to make a list like this.

Integrity was a major part of surrender, that was certain,
consistency too.

To nourish ourselves with Scripture, community
  and prayer.

To live one day at a time in honesty, no matter
  what it takes.

To be authentic, sincere, trustworthy, without
  guile.

To understand obedience and attempt to focus on
  Jesus.

To become a child by growing up.

To become independent by becoming dependent
  on God.

To know that accepting responsibility increases
  our 'response ability', our ability to answer yes
  to the call for more; believe that I can and must
  change.

To live without fear, filled with conviction and
  trust.

To shed my false self and die in order to live.

To know my faith, share it and be ready to defend it.

To look beyond the barriers and see Jesus in every person.

To see the games I play; withholding love or lashing out, just to get my way.

A scene played across my mind. When she was only four years old, our granddaughter Ashley had asked me a particular question. Hearing a rather lengthy answer, she tilted her head to one side. "Grandma, how do you know that?" she asked me solemnly. Well, Ashley, I said just as seriously, "I'm very smart."

Shaking her head and placing tiny hands on her hips, she said sadly, "Get real, grandma!"

Jesus is telling us to be serious about His warnings and promises; to stop playing a worldly role and 'get real,' be authentic and sincere.

Will we join the rest of Mary's children and come forward to gather about our Holy Mother, to march in the battle on the Great Day of the Lord? I opened scripture once more to a favorite place.

'Put on then, as God's chosen holy ones, holy and beloved, heartfelt compassion, kindness, humility, gentleness, and patience, bearing with one another and forgiving one another, if one has a grievance against another; as the Lord has forgiven you, so must you also do. And over all these put on love, that is, the bond of perfection. And let the peace of Christ control your hearts, the peace into which you were also called in one body. And be thankful. Let the word of Christ dwell in your richly, as in all wisdom you teach and admonish one another . . . do everything in the name of the Lord Jesus, giving thanks to God the Father through him (Col 3:12).

Chapter Thirteen

Mercy

"Go and learn the meaning of the word, 'It is mercy I desire and not sacrifice.' I have come to call, not the self righteous, but sinners." (Mt 9:13)

Several more weeks went by before the Dunne family checked in again. Meanwhile, a copious amount of work just writing and rewriting took up my time. Rereading the material took me back to the beginnings of the young adult prayer group, and I thought about how at first, everyone gathered in the church on and around the altar steps.

It was marvelous for me to be praying with all of these great young people right at the foot of the Tabernacle. In those days, Jesus and Mary would answer prayer requests immediately through Gianna or Stephanie in the form of external locutions. There is a time at the end of the formal prayer when everyone mentions petitions aloud.

One night quite early in the life of the group, someone prayed aloud to Blessed Mother for his Aunt who had just had an abortion and was not doing so well, feeling terrible about what she'd done.

Our Lady's response came immediately to his heart:

'My dear child, she needs to know that he (the baby) *is with me. He has forgiven his mother and is praying for her. All my young ones need to know that their babies are*

with me. They have forgiven their mothers and are pray-
ing for them, and waiting for the day to greet their
mother when she comes to heaven and to introduce her to
the Father.'

There was a long, long silence, and not a dry eye. It was not that Our Lady was condoning or making less of the seriousness of abortion, of course not. She was offering comfort and urging all young women to seek the opportunity to reconcile with God by confessing that sin. In those few words, she offered so much hope. In a short period of time, the understanding was given that each mother was already forgiven by her child who also prayed for her. She could be encouraged by this fact to forgive herself and seek healing from the deep spiritual wounds left by the act of abortion.

Leafing through pages, each reflection filled me again with the warmth of our Mother's love and concern for her children. The gifts showered by Jesus to this group have filled all with an awe and wonder. One night through Gianna, Jesus prayed for his children gathered around Him and offered them to His Father. He began, *'Dear Father, I offer these beloved ones to you,'* and then continued in Hebrew or Aramaic.

It's true I'm not a student of those languages, but certainly recognize them. It sounded like that kind of dialect to me. It happened another time while Jesus was praying to the Father (through Gianna) over an extremely ill gentleman. The person has since recovered, slowly but surely, and he was on a respirator and nearly dead at the time of the prayers. The same marvel flooded my brain now, and swept my entire body. "The Mighty One has done great things for me and holy is His Name," (Lk 1:49) comes to mind.

Such compassion we are shown, such forgiveness, such mercy. I marvelled again. And the key word is unconditional. It's all there for the taking. We just need to ask. Oh, our pride and lack of humility get in the way, but after a while, we're obviously just abusing ourselves by rejecting such opportunities to be healed.

Such mercy we are offered. The pictures of Thursday prayer nights came flooding across my mind in rapid succession.

Ave Maria, gratia plena, dominus tecum benedicta tu!

Gianna and Annie dropping to their knees with a precision that couldn't be practiced in a million drills, and looking up to the same spot in front of the statue of Our Lady of the Americas to the left side of the altar: their faces different from each other, one happy, one serious; one head nodding in animation, the other tilted to one side and listening intently.

Father Jack walking to the bottom altar step and lowering his head, pausing a minute and then, a deeper or lighter voice of either Jesus or His Mother speaking to us. When Jesus speaks, He usually ends by raising his (Fr. Jack's) arms and saying something like, 'this night I give you My peace, or My mercy, or My love, My strength, or My courage, My gifts, My virtue . . .' That image will never leave my brain.

It became obvious that Jesus was not just showering us with all this goodness and, *bam!*, we were fixed. Listening to His explanations, we gradually understood that it was up to us to actively, consciously *accept* these gifts. We had to *allow* Jesus to give them to us and then *receive* them with an open heart, with the determination to *use* them, practice using them, anyway. The personal responsibility was to give them away. They were not bestowed upon us to keep, but to share with all those whom 'They' would send into our lives.

This pattern is a major part of the Plan, the plan to reach and change others, not by preaching, but by showing them we had changed. If they could see and feel the difference in us, they would become convinced that there is something to this grace and mercy stuff. They would become curious and want to investigate. The Holy Spirit takes over the minute the seed is sewn.

It was very good news that we were not expected to convert the world, but that this was the Holy Spirit's area of expertise. One particular night I recalled, Jesus was reminding us that *He is not a distant God.* It must be extremely important for us to understand that, I mused, since it's a recurring theme with Him.

'I am as present in the tabernacle of your heart,' He said, raising His arm and pointing toward the altar, *'as I am in the Tabernacle of this altar, if you will allow Me to be.'*

Many nights we believe that Mary or Jesus explain to our hearts that the Divine mercy they are here to teach was not just a matter of God's mercy to us (the unconditional love and forgiveness), but the fact that we would become *instruments of mercy* for Them to Their people. If we denied mercy to someone, Jesus said, it was His mercy we were withholding. If we showed mercy to another person, it was His mercy we were allowing to flow through us. That certainly made acting in a merciful way a lot more interesting and personally impor-tant. The feeling of co-operating with God can really grow in a person who desires to serve in this way. And Jesus has made it very clear that there is no mercy for us if we do not trust Him; that we do not truly love Him and His mother Mary, if we do not completely trust them.

Being a selfish person, I always want to know what's in it for me. Well, it turns out that the more I act with mercy, the more I will become like the merciful and gentle One I am allowing to love and work through me. That *is* good news.

It hasn't been easy. Children of Mary all over the world are struggling to *love, forgive* and *forget,* be gracious and kind, live in ways we should always have been living and weren't.

This message, these teachings are not just for the people in Scottsdale, but for everyone in the world who will accept them.

Jesus and Mary humble us with gifts, cleanse us by Their presence, heal us with Their love.

You can hear a pin drop when the messages of Mary and her beloved Son are spoken through Fr. Jack. He is as vulnerable as it gets, standing up there completely surrendered, resigned to God's Will. These gifts and heavenly happenings have not been accepted by his brother priests for the most part. A prophet is not accepted in his own country, indeed (Lk 4:24). All the priests in the world, especially those who are responding to our Lady's call, are in great need of our support, love and many prayers.

All of this remains as a vivid picture: color, sounds, awe, the thrill of the spoken words from heaven still fresh.

I reached for my own messages, filled with such love and warnings to repent and live now, more than ever, in a merciful way. Some of them would be frightening without the gentle assurance of our Savior and His Mother that there is no need to fear, that all is well for those who fear the Lord.

Jesus: *'Do not worry about the patience and meekness you need. Just call upon My Mother each time you feel a need for a particular help.'* (7/19/92)

Jesus: *'It is necessary for all to welcome the many who will be lost, and in need, in My Name and show them the love in your heart, My love.'* (9/10/92)

Blessed Mother: *'All of the things we do, child, are a result of God's gifts to us. He allows us to then serve Him and each other by using these same gifts. All that we have has been given us by God and, without His presence at every moment, we would have nothing and be nothing.'* (9/10/92)

Jesus: *'Be of good cheer, always, and receive each one with a smile and kind word. These times are difficult for all, as each person struggles with their own purification.'* (10/2/92)

Blessed Mother: *'Know that I suffer with you when you are sad or disappointed or hurt. Just focus on My Son,*

Jesus, and be comforted by the love He has for you.'
(11/15/92)

Jesus: *'It is only a short time before all the things that have been foretold by My Mother begin, and you must be ready to succor* (give assistance in time of need) *My poor lost ones, as they wander aimlessly in search of food and shelter.*

Feed them with Me, daughter, the source of all life. Shelter them in My arms and hide them in My Mother's Mantle. Lead them to the Father through Me.' *(1/10/93)*

Blessed Mother: *'Before time runs out, so much needs to happen to fulfill Scripture and prepare the way for my Son's return.*

In the olden times, men spent much time fasting and preparing for the coming of the Messiah. They lived in joyful anticipation of this event.

Today, no one wants to spend time being still in prayer and fasting in order to be purified and prepared for my Son's return. The feast days are forgotten, or barely given attention.

People do not rejoice as they once did and prefer, instead, to revel and go to parties and drink to excess. The emphasis on religious observances has disappeared and, instead, is replaced by an emphasis on the goals of this world and having more.

I say these things again about an ungrateful world because I wish for all to understand why the punishment to come will be so severe. It has been delayed so many times and awaits only the command of the Father to be accomplished.

My own sadness is nearly unbearable. The pain and grief of a suffering humanity is felt in its entirety by me in me heart.

I tell you, child, my heart is heavy with grief. I am in the pangs of labor as I give birth each moment to a new grief and a new child of sorrow, carried in my heart for these many years.

As the wrath of Our Father is poured out, my anguish will continue, although it will end in the dawn of a new creation, a new earth.' (1/10/93)

Jesus: *'In the coming days, it will be love which reaches My people worn with exhaustion, fear and loss. They will be so cold and empty, and only My love, given through My chosen ones, will reignite the flame of life which once burned in their hearts. How sad they will be, daughter, and desperate for comfort.*

You must begin each day asking Me for a greater capacity to love; to heal; to reach out and touch the hearts of My beloved lost ones who themselves will be nearly dead from grief.

As the light dims in the world, you must shine as a beacon of truth. The only way to men's hearts is to touch them with love, Our love.' (1/15/93)

Blessed Mother: *'Allow the graces to flow through you to each one you see. It is time to shine with love and conviction. Work diligently for the Second Coming of My Son and the Triumph of Our Two Hearts.'* (1/15/93)

Jesus: *'All the splendor of heaven awaits those who will listen and act. All of the treasures of My Father's House await those who come and see.*

Follow Me, My people.

Come to the banquet of grace.

Come to the House of My Father.

Belong to the Family of God.

Please, My beloved ones, don't you see Me? Can you not hear Me? I love you and wish to gift you with Myself, with My solace, with My healing. You must come and be opened, be emptied and then, be still, so that you may be filled.' (3/12/93)

Jesus: 'It is with great longing that I view the plight of all My children. I long to hold each of them in My arms and soothe their heartaches and pain.' (3/19/93)

Blessed Mother: 'Be of stout heart and good cheer. Lead my children back to me, that I may also prepare them and see them cleansed in preparation for this Great Day.

Pray that many more will hear the call of their Lord and His Mother before it is too late.' (3/19/93)

Blessed Mother: 'It is with a persistence that I continue to come to call to all to listen and come back to my Jesus. It is with a certain joy that my heart contemplates the purification of this world, as it will render many more able to receive my Son at His Second Coming.' (5/6/93)

Blessed Mother: 'Please, practice tenderness and thoughtfulness. Allow the words you speak to all to reflect Our love and concern, Our tenderness and peace. It is a logical and natural progression that you would become more soft-spoken in your journey back to the Father. Trying to constantly live in His Will for you, you will become more introspective and quiet.' (5/14/93)

Blessed Mother: 'The love We have for you is boundless, children. Please, allow this love to flow through you and out to all you meet. It is not easy to look beyond the feelings and attitudes of others, but you must learn this important lesson and practice unconditional love and gentleness.

It is only love which can melt the hardness of Our children's hearts. You can do this. I know it."

Pray to the Angels to help you and remind you each moment to offer all to me, and I will purify each thought, each act, and carry your pleas to my Son Who awaits your love and service with great eagerness.' (6/9/93)

Blessed Mother: 'The only way to men's hearts is to touch them with Our love.

My heart is filled with such longing to save my people. It is such a joy to see those who work for the coming of the Kingdom, and such a sorrow to see the many, many who do not listen.

It is a human heart that beats in my breast, and you know how heavy and sorrowful that can be.

I would not continue to hope without my faithful children of the world. I could not continue to plead with God, Our Father for His mercy to be extended.

When the first events occur, all those who wait to 'see' will be convinced of the truth of my words and come quickly to me for the protection of my Mantle. This protection is real. It works. Please, My dear ones, know that I am praying constantly for you to persevere and continue to pray more and more.' (6/23/93)

Blessed Mother: 'You must not be discouraged by the struggle still necessary to change within yourself. There will always be this residue of sin which clings, which allows each of God's children to find some small or even large smudges, signs of sin to be cleansed. The important thing is to continue to try to discover the roots of personal sin and bring them to My Son in the Sacrament of Reconciliation.' (3/6/94)

Jesus: 'The days are quickly running towards the completion of My Father's plans for His people. It is an instant before the next event which causes Our people to groan under the hardships of a mighty destruction. Please, child, pray harder for all of My dear ones that they *will welcome their Risen Lord after walking with Him the bitter Passion of the Cross.' (3/10/94)*

Jesus: *'Remember the great acts of mercy in your own life and have faith and trust in the continuing love and mercy for each of Our poor lost ones who will wander in confusion. Turn only to Me with the help and in the presence of My dear Mother. Stay as close to her as if your life depended upon her. It does.' (3/13/94)*

Jesus: *'How My Mother prays for her little ones who desire to serve her. How she pleads with Our Father to pour His mercy and gifts upon each of you to make you stronger and more able to persevere in the coming darkness. You have no idea how difficult this will be, as the enemy gains strong footholds on every side. The degree of success he will enjoy will seem totally out of proportion to all We have told you, and you must simply trust that We shall overcome his forces at the proper time. Were you to know all that is to befall the earth, you would flee in terror and refuse to believe that you will be able to handle each difficulty that will come your way. Please believe that all you have heard will come to pass. It is not a matter of being worthy, but a matter of being prepared.*

It is only through following up with your actions that a promise of the heart can be proven and developed. Mere words are empty when not followed by actions which help you to live out these promises.' (3/27/94)

The door bell rang and there stood all three of the three newest people in my life. We hugged and Thomas, Jude and Theo quickly got settled. This time we sat in the family room which faced a patio. Subtle reds of flag stone glowed from the warm, ever present sun. The world's bluest sky could be viewed through many clerestory windows, and gave added color to the nearly all white room. We smiled at each other in the warmth of the early morning sun and a new friendship. This was to be our last 'session' for a while and expectation filled the air.

"Well, Carol," boomed Thomas, "do you have a plan for us today? We couldn't wait to get back to learn more and perhaps pray again. That was just lovely a few weeks ago. Didn't we say so, Jude?"

"We certainly did, dear. And we're just happy to be sitting here with our son, too. What with his new schedule at ASU and all the homework and prayers he's added to his life, he's never home anymore. Never thought we'd all be attending a prayer group together once a week, and then Theo would go to an extra one," Judith chuckled.

"I'm grateful to be meeting so many people, too. Thanks Carol, for the intro on Friday," Theo chimed in. "I find myself just waiting all week for Thursday to roll around and then Friday, too. I'd feel like a nut, but after sharing that with a couple of new people I met Friday night, they said they do the same thing. Boy, was I relieved."

I laughed and said I'd forgotten how that does happen for everyone at first, and then just mellows into a joyous routine.

"It only gets worse, Theo," I told him. "You change as many plans as possible to get some daily time in for that rosary and a visit to Jesus in the Blessed Sacrament. Not too shabby."

"Shall we begin?" I said, and looked at each dear face. The format we might use is for each to read a message . . . rather long ones at first. Then we'll say a rosary for all of Jesus and Mary's intentions. After that, we'll close this session with all the joyful, hope-filled things we can find to remind ourselves what our focus needs to be. How's that with everybody? Good. Judith, why don't you read first."

She took the pages from me and read to herself for a few moments. Then with a deep sigh she began.

Blessed Mother: *'The days grow so short before the coming of my Son. The time is coming when you will see only darkness before the dawn of a new world, cleansed and renewed by the power of God and the presence of my Son.*

Count on your Mother to be ever-present with you and be aware of this, child. Strengthen yourself with the knowledge and faith you have in my Son and myself.' (6/16/93)

Jesus: *'The time approaches, please believe Me. I appeal to all of your good sense and the wisdom you have received to accept the reality of My words. Watch and pray. Listen and lament the fate of all those who will not watch and pray and listen.'* (8/19/93)

Blessed Mother: *'My dear child, I, your Mother, love you. Nothing can cause your heart to expand and fill with more love than the service one performs for my Son and me. This union of purpose and action is cleansing and purifying. It will heal you quickly of all superfluous activity and desires.*

The sun continues to set upon the world. The rays carry less warmth, as darkness falls and obscures the view of the Light of the world.

Please, continue to pray that graces and mercy will be released for each person on the earth until the last possible moment.

The future is completely in the hands of God, Our Father. Peace and joy are about to disappear from the land.

You must find the joy and hope in your store of treasures that you have hidden where moisture cannot creep in, nor moth destroy.

Wherever your treasure is, your heart and mine will be. Share your treasure, child, with all who will accept it. Go now in peace to be renewed.' (8/22/93)

We sat quietly for a minute, allowing her last words to sink in and fill us with peace. Then Thomas nodded and began:

Jesus: *'Oh child, I weep for sorrow at the senseless loss, the grate waste and carnage that occurs daily. Plans are being made at this very moment to destroy more of My babies, My Father's gifts and His holy ones. There will be so much bloodshed that weeping will be heard throughout the land. Just continue to work and pray and come to Me, and I shall accomplish all.'* (1/12/93)

Jesus: *'The battle has begun. The lines are drawn. The trumpet has sounded. The charge begins.*

Ride with Me at My side and feel the heat of the battle, and know the smell of death and the flush of defeat.

Victory will be ours, but not until the last possible moment.

I realize it is hard to believe these words, as nothing is obvious to you yet, but soon you will see and recognize all I speak of. You will know the saving power of God, as He rides next to you now and for the rest of your life on earth. Never will He leave you, child, or abandon you to the wiles of the enemy.' (5/2/93)

Jesus: *'The time is very short now before grave events take place in your world.*

A war is beginning to take shape which will take so many lives and ultimately engage the entire world. It is a sorrow which will touch all, and those who are called to fight and die defending truth and justice and the rights of My children will come quickly to heaven to be with Me forever.

So many of Our chosen ones have not remained completely faithful to the purity of their first response, and

We must count, more than ever now, on those who are striving to be faithful to all that We are asking of them.' (5/2/93)

Blessed Mother: 'It is a matter of seconds now before war begins and one disaster after another renders your country vulnerable to those who plot against it. Now is the time, child. We must be brave and only look beyond the destruction to the Coming of my Son Who will bring renewed life to this earth and begin to fulfill the Father's plan of salvation for His world. Maranatha. Be brave and trusting, child, I am always at your side.' (5/2/93)

Blessed Mother: 'The hour grows so late on the Eternal clock. The events beginning to unfold will continue to rock the earth. This country must see so much destruction, child. Most of my time is spent weeping at the things to come. All of heaven joins me in sadness at the commencement of grave events.

Know that the mystery of the Father's Will is tinged with sorrow at the suffering allowed and given to His dear ones in order to perfect them. This has always been the dynamic of struggle. Suffering will allow you to let go more completely of all the things that hold you bound to the earth. After being cleansed of everything superfluous, the soul is able to rest more easily in her Lord; to be at peace with all that occurs and to acquiesce more completely to the Holy Will.

The Father, remember my dear one, knows what is best for each of His children; what will prepare them most quickly to receive His Will in the future. He enables each one to most completely live in His Will by experiencing the events which are allowed to occur. Please pray to accept His Will for you in complete docility and love. Please remember that I am with you and praying for you at every moment.' (2/4/94)

Blessed Mother: *'The end of a day is such a beautiful time to spend here with Us as you love and adore My Son. Be renewed, my child, by His Presence, His Holiness, His perfect obedience. Think of all that He is, and be uplifted and strengthened. Continue to thank Him for all He does for you as He goes before you to smooth the way.'* (2/8/94)

Jesus: *'These days of waiting in My service are difficult for all My children who desire to serve Me in a greater way. Happy is she who waits on her Lord in peace and tenderness of heart. Happy is she who does not need to know, but content to wait in trust for the next step of Our Plan.'* (2/19/94)

Jesus: *'It is with sorrow that all of heaven spends itself praying for the world. The terrible events already occurring are but a shadow of the future and life in your own country. What sadness you will feel seeing the destruction of the great beauty of your cities and so much of the land.*

Sin is rampant and has brought corruption to hearts in every corner of the land. I am bringing many into eternity already, where they will be given an opportunity to learn about Me and choose My Kingdom. Every soul will be given this chance at salvation.

Purgatory will be filled with souls groaning and suffering with remorse at the sinful lives they have led. The hearts of those that repent and seek Me will be led to My Father and learn of His Divine Will. It is these requests that will allow them to be saved.

Pray that more will listen and return to Me. Believe and take seriously every single word We have told you.

Time runs out. There will be no more delays and all will begin now to unfold in your own life. The time of preparation of My warriors has come to an end.' (4/20/94)

Blessed Mother: *'The days go by quickly. Please, do all in your power to pray constantly for mercy on your world. The recent events show even more clearly the deception which is taking place on the earth. Death is everywhere and no one will lift a finger to help. Only the prayers of My beloved ease the ache in My Heart and effect great graces for those who are dying. Please, continue to plead their cause to the Father through Our intercession.*

Even in your imagination you could not come close to the reality all will suffer. It is not necessary to worry about being properly prepared. Just continue to pray, collect what provisions you can and wait in joy and hope for the coming of My Beloved Son.

The seriousness of the times can only be born by a complete trust in all We have told to the world. It is a blink of the eye before more direct tribulation and suffering is experienced.

For those who take my words to heart, nothing more is needed now. You will be led to the many people who need to hear you speak for Us, and they will be led to you.

In many ways will Our children have further opportunities to be healed and turn back to God. This period of grace will be short, however, so all must work without ceasing, expending all your strength on those who come. It will be like the new church when many thousands are converted on one day.

The Holy Spirit will pour out His increased power upon the earth and upon all those who work for the Kingdom.

The grace and peace of the Triune God be with you.'
(4/20/94)

Jesus: *'Time is so short before a new day dawns for the world. There will be so many times when all will seem lost, and you must remember My words to you and be encouraged.*

My remnant church will survive, and be able to greet Me when I come again. Although the danger will be great, believe that you are protected by My Mother and Her Angels.

The beginning of tribulations in your country is about to unfold. All will suffer to some degree as a result of these events. Your country will become weaker in the coming months, and this will be according to plans laid by world governments to subdue the world.' (4/30/94)

We had listened to that before, but the clear picture was a good way to prepare us to pray for all those who would be involved in the events to come. We prayed a rosary quietly, sat in silence once again, and then continued.

"Theo, it's your turn now, okay?"

"Ready," he said.

Jesus: *'Think, child, of all the wonderful gifts of mercy I can give to Our lost children. Think of all the poor lost souls that will be healed and saved. Think of the joy when I can bring them home to Me and present them to My Father. We will be able to do all of this because of the great love of My Mother for all her children.'* (9/4/92)

Jesus: *'Rejoice, daughter, in the Queenship of Mary, My Mother, who loves you with a Mother's love and cares so much for you as her daughter. Follow her; listen closely to her, for she will bring you to My Sacred Heart each moment of the day.*

Be united with her in prayer and love. Allow her to be your teacher and guide. Stand by her in the dark days to come. Be a beacon of truth for all who will seek Me.' (9/8/92)

Jesus: *'Happy are the pure of heart, for they shall see Me in each incident, in each person that comes to them.'* (10/2/92)

Blessed Mother: *'Praise be to God Who is and was and always will be.'* (10/13/92)

Jesus: *'It will be a time for such rejoicing as you cannot imagine, and all sadness will be wiped away by the joy of your first sight of Me.*

On that day, the world and all of Heaven will explode with the joy of victory, and the Triumph of the Sacred and Immaculate Hearts.

On that day, all tears will be wiped away and you will see the glory of God shining upon the faces of all His creatures. His children shall be the olive branches at His table. The feast will be filled with merrymaking, and the Light of Christ shall fill your hearts and beings forever.

Remember this, children, and be filled with eager anticipation for all to be accomplished, as I Am.' (10/31/92)

Blessed Mother: *'Be at peace no matter what occurs. It is with great excitement that I contemplate the Coming of my Son into a purified Kingdom on earth.*

Oh children, think of this day and pray and long for it to appear. There will be many hardships and sorrows first, but a concentration on the happy events to come will pull you through and enable you to strengthen others and give them courage from a knowledge of the happy times to come.' (11/16/92)

Jesus: *'Ask Our Holy Spirit to help you to wait in joyful hope for the coming of the Kingdom.'* (11/23/92)

Blessed Mother: *'Praised be the God and Father of us all. To Him be dominion and honor and glory forever.*

Praise Him constantly, child, and continuously give Him thanks for His great gift of mercy which has been extended so many times now. Live only in the moment with what you are doing and do not worry.' (1/2/93)

Blessed Mother: *'Wait in joyful anticipation for the Coming of the Lord. It will be a glorious time, child, and the thought of this is often the only thing that keeps my heart from breaking completely, as I see the sin and corruption in the world and watch my children continue to reject me and my Son.*

A new day will dawn, child, for all those who love the Lord, their God.' (1/5/93)

Jesus: *'Prepare for the events which are about to begin and will lead My people to the Day of the Lord. On that day, My child, you will see the Glory of Heaven coming on a cloud, and your heart will rejoice and sing Hosannas!*

The lion and the lamb will dance in victory over the defeat of the evil one.' (3/27/93)

Jesus: *'All will continue to be right and good for those who truly love Me.'* (3/31/93)

Blessed Mother: *'Each trial is a treasure being stored in heaven for your return. Persist in love and truth and know again of my constant love and protection. I am your loving Mother.'* (6/9/93)

We took a deep breath and sat back in our chairs momentarily. I then asked if I might read the last one to them. They smiled in agreement. Taking up the remaining pages, I began slowly and clearly.

Jesus: *'The great battle on the Day of the Lord will occur between the forces of evil and My own chosen people. Then I will come on a cloud with My Angels surrounding Me, and We will defeat Satan and His cohorts, and they will be chained in the bowels of Hell for a very, very, very long time.*

Then will I live and reign with you among My people in the beauty of the world, as the Father intended it to be.

There will be no pain, and joy and laughter will echo throughout the land. Already I am writing My Name on the foreheads of My beloved ones who will live with Me in a purified world. Then we will see and live out all that Scripture has foretold, the promises of Yahweh and the promises given by Me.

All who live will see the saving power of their God.

All who dwell on this earth will see My Coming in Glory on that Great Day.

I am anxious for this, daughter, as I have waited for time to reach its fullness, and a new time, a new era of peace and happiness will begin.

Happy they will be who remain faithful to Me during this time of purification. They will be too few, child, and you will struggle for Me, work with Me, fight for My cause and the ultimate victory over evil.

I put My trust and hope in all of you. Please, put your trust and hope in Me.' (1/11/93)

As I finished, the phone rang and we all laughed. I let it ring. We stood up, exchanged hugs again and made plans for them to come to dinner two weeks later. As they opened the door to leave, the phone rang again. I laughed and gave up.

"Oh well, I guess it's time. See you in church."

"Many have undertaken to compile a narrative of the events which have been fulfilled in our midst, precisely as those events were transmitted to us by the original eyewitnesses and ministers of the word. I too have carefully traced the whole sequence of events from the beginning, and have decided to set it in writing for you, Theophilus, so that Your Excellency may see how reliable the instruction was that you received." (Lk 1:1-4)

As We Wait in Joyful Hope

A Continuation

By now many, many more people worldwide believe the fact that fourteen years ago the Blessed Virgin Mary appeared to six young people in Medjugorje, Bosnia-Herzegovnia, and continues to appear to four of them daily wherever they happen to be. Since then, she has appeared all over the world and in every state in the United States.

The basic message is the same everywhere, for all people: Pray daily with your heart, principally the Rosary, not just reciting words with your lips, but sincerely attempting to mean every word. Fast, do penance. RECONCILE...with God, with everyone in our lives, with ourselves!

Hopefully, we have learned by now that the place to begin any spiritual preparation and renewal is with reconciliation...wipe the slate clean, tidy the house, throw out the unsightly and fill up with Beauty.

The most practical element of this journey has become the way we treat each other: our honesty, sincerity and mercy; unconditional love and forgiveness lived out in attitudes, words and actions. These are impossible things to achieve alone. What's more, Our Lady tells us that Satan is busier than ever, more powerful than before, affecting our weaknesses and brokenness (how quickly and easily we fall without the help of grace from Jesus through the heart of His Mother). He is, to all outward appearances, gaining ground every day, and we will need to hold tightly to Our Lady's hand, pray and trust and fight the power of evil until the very last moment before Jesus comes again because that's what this renewal and preparation is all about.

Jesus has sent His Number One Prophet, His Mother, to get the attention of every person in the world. Many have discovered the joy of coming to know her as friend, teacher, intercessor, source of the love that softens our hearts and, most of all, our own dear mother. She wishes to guide us on the path of all the virtues and right conduct. She desires to increase an awareness of our need to receive these gifts and then give, BE these gifts to others, especially those closest to us. We must learn the difference between discerning and judgmental, constructive conversation and gossip, escape and surrender!

We are led to understand that the choice must be made now for all of Mary's requests which lead us to that focus on Jesus, Alone. There simply isn't any more time to harbor anger, resentment, bitterness and unforgiveness in our hearts, but only to become people of mercy. We are not meant, however, to respond to these requests because of worry or fear for ourselves, friends and loved ones. We are meant to spend time in prayer, in an intimate relationship with Mary and her Son, because we have grown to love Them so much and wish to be their instruments of mercy, to plead for God's love and forgiveness for ALL.

Prayer is not enough. We are called to change, to turn back to God and acknowledge Him as our Creator and Giver of all things, to then live in gratitude and praise for all of His gifts. Those who are Catholic Christians must, when possible, attend Mass and receive Jesus in the Eucharist every day. We are invited to spend some time daily with Jesus in the Blessed Sacrament, seeking to be healed by our Divine Physician, to develop an authentic love relationship with Him, one which only develops as we accept Love through trust. Fasting and penance are no longer an option for people who profess membership in the army of those answering the call of our Heavenly Mother. Other religions will be able to practice reconciliation, fasting, penance, prayer with the Rosary, and a return to God through His Son, Jesus. Above all for our times, each person is requested to accept Mary, Jesus' Mother, as their own and the truth of Mary as the Mother of God (a priority in His Plan).

The world has never been in such danger from the effects of sin. According to many prophesies by the Blessed Virgin Mary, the world is going to experience severe tribulations, cleansing and purifying by God, the Father, in order to render those, who will then live in it, worthy to reclaim their inheritance as children of God. All over the world Mary, the Mother of Jesus, is begging everyone to allow her to guide us to her Son. Both will then lead us to the Father Who waits to gift us with Himself and all the graces prepared for us since before we were born.

We are being transformed by the love and mercy and forgiveness of God in order to live in a purified, transformed world. In this renewed life, we will exist in complete joy and surrender to the Will of Our Heavenly Father, as we were always meant to be (before the fall of mankind through the sin of disobedience). The Father does not wish to destroy us, but to heal us, to return to us our original identity as child made in His Image and Likeness, and return the world to the beauty of His original creation. It is our hearts which must be healed and emptied of all pride and possessions, all hatred, envy and jealousy in order to be filled with Jesus and His peace, which is the Kingdom of God. (Rom.14:17).

In all of this, Satan is fighting for our very souls, to take them with him to hell for all eternity. We aid him in this endeavor by espousing the 'world' which is the domain of the evil one, the prince of lies. We are being called to seriously answer the requests of Mary, the Mother of all people ever created, in order to allow her to defeat Satan, as is promised in Scripture, (Genesis 3:15) This call is for everyone in the world, (not just one particular religion) to return to God, their Creator.

It is important and essential for us to have a knowledge of the major points being given by Mary and Jesus to so many of their messengers that we might incorporate them into our behavior. These messages, when authentic, always lead us to Jesus and speak of prayer and humility, forgiveness and mercy, and surrender to the Divine Will of the Father with joy and docility. They offer us the opportunity to recover from the effects of the Original sin of pride, of resisting God and living a false independence, evidenced by our cold, hard hearts. They are not meant to replace Scripture, only to echo and remind, reflect and call us back to basic gospel teachings.

We need help. We need reminders. We need to know and believe that we are loved and appreciated, that we are not alone...not ever. That the Triune God, Who resides deep within our hearts, and our Mother, Mary, are always with us and we will NEVER be abandoned for a moment. All we have to do is accept these facts, and go on to share our gifts and love with our brothers and sisters. We can learn to celebrate and appreciate each other!

There are several truths which can serve to guide us. Jesus died and obtained our salvation. We were born without our consent, our personal agreement. We will NOT be saved without our consent, our individual agreement. The decisions we make, a result of the gift of free will, determine our future. Holding Mary's hand makes decisions easier.

We have been given the opportunity to experience suffering and believe that it can be redemptive to others, to continue the sufferings of Christ that we may also reign with Him (2Tim2:12). We process in our lives what it means to be 'saved'; to live as a child of God, a redeemed person; to consciously accept everything involved in this dynamic, so that whatever we do, we do for the glory of God (1Cor. 10:31). We remember Jesus' life with our own.

We have been in a period of preparation that might remind us of basic training. Now, it seems we have entered what might be considered combat training! The suggestion has been made by Our Lord that we relate to each other not only as community, but as a fighting team. Acting upon that image He then continues to give us teachings that will enable us to be more perfectly ready (combat ready!) to serve the people He has been talking about for so long, those who will come to us after significant events in this country and periods of great trials, as well.

These people will be lost, heartbroken and, in many cases, outraged at the tremendous devastation that has occurred. It will be up to the people (who agree to help), to give them clothing, food, and shelter where possible. Most of all, we can answer questions and guide them toward priests for the Sacrament of Reconciliation and an understanding of the fact that all of this is in preparation for the Second Coming of Jesus.

For those who have lost patience, lost interest, lost faith in the words and warnings of Our Lady, we need to reflect that God does not play with our minds, he tugs at our hearts. It takes a long time for people to change. Also, the Father responds to our prayers for mercy on the world and effects delays in His plans to accommodate as many lost sheep as possible to return to the fold. He gives us time to convert and practice this new way of being.

The Potter breaks and remolds the vessel many times before it is emptied and able to hold His truth, His timetable, His love, His Will. We are being re-formed in order to wait with patience, and be purified by this waiting, for the prophecies of Jesus and Mary to be realized, (when the appointed time known only to the Father reaches its fullness). Until then we have the opportunity, with the help of Mary and her Son, to support and love, sustain and strengthen each other.

Presented here is simply an update of teachings, words of hope and encouragement for our further preparation. They are continued from the last message contained in the book "AS WE WAIT IN JOYFUL HOPE" until the present time. They are received by me during prayer when Jesus or Mary or God, the Father, allegedly speaks to my heart that these be might be shared with all of you. They are meant to strengthen, not frighten us. They are built on what we already know and has been mentioned earlier. We are invited to be God's instruments/vehicles of mercy by practicing corporal and spiritual works of mercy in thought, word, deed, prayer and attitude. We are urged toward constant prayer of praise, love and gratitude to the Triune God; daily study of Scripture (even small bits); prayer to the Holy Spirit for guidance. We are invited to ask Mary, the Mother of Jesus and our Heavenly Mother, the Angels and Saints to pray with us in order to multiply our prayers. Reminded to live life as a child.

May I suggest that these be read in small segments, followed by repeated readings and reflection. There is so much presented here that, after awhile, it all runs together, and we can miss the richness and power of Their words and meaning.

Carol Ameche March 1, 1995

Jesus....."My remnant church will survive, child, and be able to greet Me when I come again. Although the danger will be great, believe that you are protected by My Mother and her Angels. Time is so short before a new day dawns for the world. The beginning of tribulations in your country is about to unfold. All will suffer to some degree as a result of these events. Be of stout heart, child. Have no fear. Be completely at peace about everything! (4/30/94)

◆

Jesus..."the hour grows late on the Eternal clock! How quickly have the years fled by My people, absorbed in themselves and their merrymaking. How quickly it is all coming to an end.

The influence of My Mother causes you to wish to spend more time in front of Me in this Sacrament, daughter, and urges you on to more and more study and preparation. The hour is upon the world and yet, it sleeps. I, your Lord and God, speak now to share with you all of My sadness and concern for the people of My world who hurry by Me each day, too busy to seek My company in the quiet of their churches. Soon I will no longer be present in these churches, child. Soon the enemies of My Mother and Myself will gain seeming control of the world and all that is allowed to occur.

These events take place to fulfill Scripture before My return. You have seen Our words beginning to be fulfilled. Beyond all that has ever befallen mankind, 'My Father is about to allow His justice to be visited upon the earth. It is only His mercy pouring forth upon the earth to cleanse it before My return.

Child, there is nothing to be done, save prayer for the salvation of all souls. It is My only desire, that as many souls as possible be snatched back from the Pit and turned toward the love and grace offered by My Father Who loves His children beyond all telling.

In the beginning of creation, the evil one was always waiting for an opportunity to corrupt the beauty created by My Father. It is still thus, only so much more so. It is difficult

1

for you to imagine such hatred as exists in the heart of Lucifer. Remember that, please child, and be guided by an effort to defeat that hatred which constantly wars against the goodness of a loving and merciful God.

Satan does not wish to receive mercy, nor does he desire to experience forgiveness and remorse. Although you are protected in My arms and within the Mantle of My Mother, you must remember that Satan is always working to deceive and trick you. You must be constantly on guard against his subtle machinations and defeat him with prayer and the love in your heart. He is powerless against pure love, since God is love. While he has been given the power to tempt Our beloved children, he will never measure up to the power of God Who is the Creator and Lord of Lucifer and his cohorts. This spiritual battle has been waged since time began. It is reaching new heights as the amount of evil in the world only adds to Satan's power and, in turn, results in more evil being loosed upon the world.

These are most serious times, as is any time of war. The battle being waged by Lucifer is the ultimate battle for souls. It is the true belief of his henchmen that they will be victorious in this attempt to win souls for the cause of the world. Power corrupts like nothing else. The lure of money is a blinding force, and mankind is unable to think in a rational way. When I say darkness is descending upon your world, I mean a darkening of the intellect, the reasoning powers of the mind, the ability of the soul to choose for good.

Man is so steeped in corruption, he is unable to see truth; to make rational decisions; to see the difference between good and evil. In the darkness, everything looks the same. The dim outline of reality is further clouded by the heightened senses gratified at every turn by whatever pleases the spirit at that moment. If a person is blind, he cannot see the difference between choices and so, chooses what is most pleasing, most gratifying and stimulating to his senses. Lust is at the core of most of the choices of My people. It has completely defeated the ability they had been given to make decisions for a noble cause, for the good of another, for the common good.

To live in community, at peace with the rest, is only possible for a soul guided by motives of love and mercy. It is for this reason that My beloved chosen ones will live in this fashion to protect themselves from the chaos of the world.

Death and violence will exist everywhere. Only in a hidden environment, removed from the violence of the streets and the violence in men's hearts, will it be possible to live in union with My Mother and Me. We will be there with you, although even this fact will be partially obscured because of the amount of evil in the very atmosphere. Your faith and perseverance will be tested to the last ounce of your strength. You will fight to the very end and the last moment before My Coming. From now on, everything will be more and more difficult, as Satan attempts to defeat you and the work you will do for Me.

Just remember all We have told you. Keep Our words and ponder them in your heart. Allow them to be an occasion of Our peace and presence, Our strength and Our love. Break open these words each day and nourish yourself with them. We are always here with you. You will never be alone. Just focus on Me in the present moment as though no danger exists. This will often be your defense and the only means of saving yourself from fear.

The armor of truth will be your greatest strength. The cunning and wiles of the enemy can never prevail against truth. The truth will set you free on every occasion! Take refuge in My truth and be comforted by it when there is no other comfort to be found.

All the ends of the earth will see the saving power of God. And you shall see Me descending in the company of countless Angels, as I return to claim My inheritance. Be comforted, daughter, by the belief that you will never be overcome, although at times seemingly defeated.

There only remains for you to live out each day listening for My voice, the voice of My Holy Spirit and the Will of My Father. Be solemn, My children, about the awesome task ahead of you. Remember that each obstacle will be overcome because we are together, and all of My strength and power are behind your own actions." (5/10/94)

3

Blessed Mother (same night)....."Dear one, please be always acutely aware of the greatness of God and His humility in sharing Himself with you. We can never comprehend the enormity of His gifts, but we can praise and thank Him constantly and, thus, enable even more gifts to be given. As the days go by, each task, each event will be filled with more difficulty as the evil one attempts to discourage you and turn you away toward an easier path. Remember, the easier, more comfortable way is not the path to My Son. It is not the Way of the Cross where true unity is only accomplished by constantly embracing the difficulties and pain of your own cross.

Children, you are in the company of many Saints and Angels when you walk the path of My Son. It is only in the quiet of being alone with Us that you are able to perceive Our presence. The more time you spend in Our company, the more time you will wish to spend. With My Son there is hard work and fatigue, many times tasting defeat and rejection. As you live out this Way of serving, you will be transformed from a creature of the flesh into a creature of the spirit, able to do more of the things reserved for those who live more united to the Spirit. You will see much accomplished by your hard work and perseverance. It will not be without the rewards of seeing others gifted with conversions and healings.

Remember to stay close to me and hidden in my Mantle. The evil one knows well your weaknesses and will attack your pride at every opportunity. Remember, the occasion of sin for each person is different and must be avoided as soon as it is recognized. Continue to pray to the Holy Spirit to help you to recognize these occasions. You will need all of your strength just to carry out the Father's Will for you. Do not dilute that strength with anything other than His desires for you. You are safe in My Immaculate Heart. (5/10/94)

✧

Blessed Mother.....Continue to listen, My child, to the voice of My Beloved Spouse. His Wisdom is all you need to take into the Battle as a shield of protection, a weapon with which to meet the enemy and defend all that you believe and know to be true.

4

The truth of Christ is the ultimate weapon of defense against all the powers of hell. The love of Jesus is the adornment for your soul which dresses it for battle and sustains you in attacks of the evil one.

The light of My Son will shine forth as a beacon to light the Way for all those seeking Him as a refuge. In the coming days, your preparedness will be the source of preparedness for all My children. They can then, in turn, prepare others. When the stone enters the pond, its ripples reach ultimately to the farthest shore. The action of the Holy Spirit, initiated by your reaching out to others, will go on and on until it eventually returns to nurture even yourself once again!

The love and grace of My Jesus never stops overflowing onto all those who seek it and receive it with an eager heart. Continue to work and persevere in fidelity to this cause of salvation for the world. The Sacred Heart and My Immaculate Heart are your refuge, your home, your comfort, the place of renewal in times of need and renewal. All danger will be overcome when you flee to Our Hearts and receive the love and protection waiting for you there. Continue, child of My Heart, to study and pray in preparation for the Second Coming of My Jesus." (5/23/94)

❖

Jesus.....My dear one, I, your Lord, need to speak to your heart. It is too long now since we have spent time like this (Adoration of Blessed Sacrament) and there is no time to waste in other ways. The days left grow shorter as the days grow longer. (This was just before June 21, the longest day of summer!) Soon, a rumble will be heard across the land which will tear it in two. Soon, cries of anguish will fill the air, and all who are willing must come to the aid of their brother.

There will be much panic and chaos and terror because, following certain events, a state of fear and mayhem will prevail. There will be no safety in the streets, as people fight and loot and further destroy each other in fear and panic. This will truly happen, My dear one, and you must be ready to calm the fears of those around you.

Rally the forces around you into a team of people ready to minister to those who come, who survive this time. Encourage all to reach out to all in need with all you have. The food and supplies will not last long and will give way to conditions of famine. An extremely difficult time is ahead of everyone. Not only will there be chaos and bloodshed, but this nation will be crippled by one disaster after another. The powers of your country will be defeated by the overwhelming destruction and turn to other nations for help.

It will be at this time that the enemies of freedom will come in and take over the control of your government. It will be then that the forces of evil will gain a foothold on the people and will force them into submission. This will be so subtle at first, as to deceive all who receive help. It will seem like the answer to economic woes and physical destruction.

During these times, My people, My faithful ones, will band together so as to lend strength and courage and aid to each other. This will also set up the time when you will be living apart from the rest of the country, growing your own food, living in virtual hiding from the powers that will overwhelm the land.

In the days to come, drought and famine will deplete stores and decimate families. The government which controls your country will force men into labor and women and children into detention areas as a means of controlling the people. You may believe all of this, although it will be a small while yet before all becomes a reality. I tell you these things, My beloved daughter, by way of further preparation for you. We will not leave you unprepared or wondering what to expect. Just continue to wait and pray and study.

Events will also come to pass that will shepherd My faithful ones and keep you safe for further events. In the meantime, child, continue to work and trust. Spread My Mercy to all who will receive it. Be My beacon, My trumpet, My song which calls all to the truth of My Father. No more will we sit in quiet and rest. From now on, plans for battle will escalate and break over the people like a series of bombardments, explosions that will rock the land and split the firmament.

The darkness which has developed is beyond description.

You know nothing of this kind of evil and hatred. Stay close to Love and prepare to suffer for Love's sake. Holiness is only achieved through suffering the Way, the Path to Holiness." (6/3/94)

Blessed Mother....."My dear child, I, your Mother, will speak to your heart for your further instruction and grace. You are invited this night to spend every spare minute from now on adoring like this My Precious Son in His Blessed Sacrament. Destruction is imminent, child. No matter how much you prepare, only the grace of God, Our Father, will be sufficient to allow you to be sustained and to support others. The strength, which will come to you from Us, will only be as available as you are willing to be emptied and opened more to receive it!

Each one must be a living Tabernacle which carries the Presence of My Son to those who seek Him. Before leading, you must know the Way so well that even darkness will not confuse you and cause you to leave the Path. For not much longer will you have the opportunity to spend golden hours of peace and praise, love and adoration of the Triune God united in the Blessed Sacrament of My Son. When we realize we are losing something precious, it is only natural to want to spend as much time in that presence as possible. If more of My chosen ones would focus on My Jesus, they would not become lukewarm. Pray, child, pray with all your heart and soul and might." (6/8/94)

Jesus....."I, your Lord, will speak to your heart this day. Great is the plan of Our Father for the salvation of His people. My chosen ones must be ready to have mercy in their hearts for all those to whom His mercy is given. Please, continue to pray, as you are, for the poor lost ones of this world who wander in pain and darkness. Their plight is heart breaking to behold for all those with love to share. Great will be the opportunity to show love to the suffering poor who will come.

Please, act always with the understanding that all of time is short, and there is none to waste on a delay of their response to a Merciful God Who calls to them to come back in repentance to know, love and answer His call to them to become His heirs forever in His Kingdom.

The seriousness now present in your heart keeps your focus where it belongs and keeps your face and heart turned towards My Mother and Me. Yes, it is tragic, what continues to occur in the world, but this is only a preface, a forerunner of the events which will engulf the world. At the present time, leaders of the world are in full agreement about all that is playing out for the rest of you to see. Great deception marks each public event. Diabolical scheming is present behind the dubious events being presented by the media throughout the world.

In the meantime, innocent people continue to suffer and die. My church around the globe is the focal point of all wars and destruction, despite news to the contrary. It is this deception which allows enemies to continue to persecute those who follow Me. My Mother's enemies are everywhere and know the great power she has been given against Satan. That is why they continue to down play her role in My Church and will not cooperate with her requests throughout the world. It is a sad time to see. It is a reason by itself to cleanse the world. But they shall see evil defeated and all of their plans brought to ashes.

You must be totally committed to the Father's Will for you, My child. Continue to pray and be with Me each day in order to allow the grace of Our Spirit to work within you what yet needs to be accomplished. Persevere, child, and persist in prayer." (6/15/94)

❖

The Father....."there is nothing greater than love which can unite us. Even suffering, if done with joy and love and surrender, is the unity that is accomplished only when two people love each other. That is only possible when My grace is received by a person who puts all of My needs, all of My desires before her/his own. The more you surrender your will

8

to Mine, the more you will be in peace and contentment.

A warrior must nurture the gentleness of My Mother in her soul in order to have the strength of the Creator and Redeemer. A perfect balance of strength and gentleness will serve you on the battlefield and allow you to face any sort of situation. The days to come will present the need for great inner strength in order to persevere, but at the same time, the gentleness and compassion and patience to deal with the heartbroken survivors who seek help.

I am a God of Mercy Who wishes only the best for My people. I have called to them since the beginning of their creation, yet the lure of the senses clouds the reality of My Beauty and Goodness. The excitement of the moment befuddles the mind and causes My children to lose the Way. These, daughter, are problems of faith. These, child, are the results of sin and turning away from Me. Do not think that it has ever been different. The pain in the lives of My people has always been so great because of the resistance offered by them to My simplicity, My good judgement on their behalf.

The ability of My people to resist Me is given greater strength by the presence of evil in their lives. Those who indulge each whim, each desire, will never be in My peace until their own needs are not first, their own desires do not consume them. Their own fury rages and destroys that peace which I long to give them.

Again I say to you that gratitude is a means of overcoming doubt and inexperience. The ability to dwell in thankfulness for the moment, no matter what the occasion, will allow My children to overcome their struggle and gain the freedom necessary to allow My Will more completely.

(Then I had the feeling that He was speaking in a more general way to everyone, so have put in single quotations.)

'Do not be fooled by your own understanding of Me. Seek only the gifts of Understanding and Wisdom of My Spirit. Sit before Me in silence and ask for these gifts if you would seek to truly know Who I Am. Allow My Spirit to direct you more completely, more fully. Practice this, My people, for it is a knowledge you need, if you are to learn to love Me and not your own concepts of Me. When you are truly humble before Me and bring a repentant heart for Me to heal, I cannot resist you, nor deny your requests.

Oh, My dear people, how I long to reveal Myself more fully to you, if you will only allow it. You must come in simplicity, and seek My Kingdom in simplicity, and wait in simplicity, and be grateful at every moment for what has been and will be. I promise you My love forever.

I need for you to desire to love and know Me and then to serve Me, all in a greater way. I am waiting for you to seek Me, My dear children, in total simplicity and openness. Please, My dearest ones, desire Me as I desire you. Seek Me as I am seeking you. Pour yourselves out in praise and love and gratitude, as I pour Myself out for you. Let us begin now to walk arm in arm in peace and simplicity so that My joy may be yours and your joy may be complete.'

Child of My Heart, remain in My love and in readiness for the next need of any of My people, for the next act of My Will on your behalf. This waiting builds your strength and perseverance to a greater degree.

Anyone who wishes to serve Me must be willing to wait in peace for Me to act in their lives. My Spirit will let you know when these times of action are to occur. The benevolence of a loving Father always acts for the very best interests of His child. Always, live in the faith and trust that I am performing good for My world, for My people. I am your Lord and your God Who is and was and will always be." (6/22/94)

❖

Jesus....."My dear one, please write. It is I, your Lord, Who comes to you this night to speak to your heart. Many are the times you will long for this to happen and it will not be given, for soon the Will of My Father will decree that no more conversations between Us and Our special messengers will occur.

The time for quiet reflection is nearly over, and action will fill the lives of My faithful ones. You will be busy at all hours of the day and night, daughter. It will seem like one very long day interspersed with short periods of rest. All will finally come to pass, as We have been telling you, child. The waiting has been long and difficult, and you have handled this time period with courage and obedience. It is never easy to wait without a sure knowledge of what is to come. The days seem longer and time seems to drag.

My daughter, when you see the destruction of the earth, (not total destruction He refers to), you will be glad for all of the delays and will understand the reasons for My Father's actions. The world is about to become so very open in its disobedience and sinfulness. Yes, the Cairo Conference is a primary example of the blatant lack of love and respect for human life. The fact that so many countries support these ideas for population control should be a warning to all of the dangerous state of affairs. If no support is given to certain age groups, soon it will come to pass that all age groups are at risk, who stand in the way of the progressive forces in the world.

Please come and pray before Me for your country. It will be many years before there is a return of peace, and the world will be decimated by then to an incredible degree. The hearts of My beloved followers will be broken and you must gather them into your arms and assure them of Our love. It will be a huge endeavor to convince them of this in the face of so much chaos and ruin. Only patient love will reach through their sorrow and, in many cases, outrage.

The Angels and Saints and all in heaven pray for you constantly and for all My chosen ones who wait for the hand of My Father to move upon the earth to cleanse it. I need all of you to pray for each other and be united in love and deed. I need for you to think of each other often in prayer and love and unity.

The clock is striking the hour which begins the Day of the Lord. Stay near to Us, as My Mother and I guide you on the path to victory. Continue to study and pray, as you are, and spend every moment you can in My Presence in My Blessed Sacrament. The time will be here soon enough when you do not see Me or have Me on your altars. In preparation for that time, daughter, fortify yourself with My strength and beauty contained in this great gift of My Father. Thank Him, child.

11

Praise Him and adore His majesty as we wait together for the hour to strike. All is in readiness. Spend all your time in the light, while time and light remain." (7/3/94)

◈

Jesus....."It is later, still, My daughter, for the time goes by relentlessly as the days march toward the beginning of My Father's actions on your behalf. The beauty of your country and the peace your country enjoys are about to be altered by a mighty event. Even though there are new delays in some of His plans, the timetable of other events will remain as it is. You will see the results of this and weep. You will see My heartbroken people and be moved to many tears on their behalf.

There is much that can be done for them simply by the love and compassion in your hearts. There will always be the possibility of healing, as long as My dear ones seek it. The doubt present in many hearts will vanish as these events are viewed. Please remember, daughter, that all will be well because all is according to My Father's Will and meant for the good of His people.

Think of all the souls who will be saved by your prayers and waiting in obedience. Allow those thoughts to move you to pray and wait more and with greater joy. In love and peace, stay near to Me, pray with Me, comfort Me. In joy and happiness of heart, bring My love and mercy and gentleness to all you meet. Be filled with joy and praise and gratitude, daughter. The Kingdom is at hand." (7/13/94)

◈

Blessed Mother..... (same night) "My daughter, I your Mother, am speaking to your heart. In the days to come, please remember to call upon me at each moment, to include me in all of your endeavors, to ask me for help and guidance for the dear ones who come for help and guidance. Please, listen to the voice of My Spouse speak to your heart. He will give you the strength on absolutely every occasion you defer to Us with irritabilities and frustration. These are human reactions

12

and can be turned into enormous strengths, if you will continue to give them to My Son and to call on me for help.

If those who pray and attempt to follow my requests are confused, think of the state of mind of all those who will come here not knowing me at all! What patience it will take to allow their stories and then attempt to get them to listen to Our words and act upon them. Remember to consecrate these dear ones and hold them and their words up to My Son for healing. Be aware of the Angels and Saints and their prayers. As the light dims, you will need to remain even closer to the Light of Christ in order to see the truth and live it."

❖

Jesus....."The understanding of each human on earth is limited by many things. Especially, the mind is confined by what it can perceive. To understand a mystery more fully, one needs to enter into it more fully. Therefore, the more you are united to Me, the more fully you have surrendered yourself to Me, the more you will know Who I Am and understand how things happen in our relationship. The mystery of oneness can only be explained once it is experienced and, even then, it is a matter of degrees and increases.

The growth into becoming Me, united to My Heart, more like Me, is a matter of death, death to yourself and your heart's desires and your personhood. Your whole person will become more divinized, more Christlike, the more you spend time in My Presence, commune with Me, love Me and be loved by Me. To study My actions and words while I lived, even those I have spoken to you all of this time, will give you a certain knowledge, examples to follow in order to be My follower. But to become one with Me is only accomplished by the two of us being alone in order to absorb each other's being, presence, essence: the true Knowledge of My Selfhood perceived by gazing, listening, contemplating and reflecting.

This is what you are constantly invited to: to absorb the essence of Me in the closest proximity of the Eucharist, in the company of My Sacred Heart displayed in My Blessed Sacrament. There is no other way to gain the union of our wills that you seek and which I offer to you.

13

Ponder the depth of these words, child, and then see how your priorities might differ. If is so important for you to be totally united in the oneness of My Father. Come and rest in My arms for the rest of eternity. There is nothing you will miss, nothing that you will be avoiding, nothing that you cannot do without. The victory, the outcome of our endeavors, depends upon the degree of unity, of oneness, that we share. Take advantage of all of Me. Take My strength and gifts to use as your own. Take the power of the Trinity which is possible to those who dwell within Our oneness. If you will only begin to surrender more fully, you will see all accomplished without much effort on your part. If you will allow Me, I will accomplish for you in a twinkling all that needs to happen in the days to come. Surrender more to Me, dear one. Allow your Jesus to be your all in all. Peace to you, child. Come!" (7/19/94)

✧

Jesus...(8/8/94) "My child, it is I, your Jesus. You are weary with chores that you continue to do. Please surrender more to the peace and silence of My company, the ardor of My Heart, the burden of My tasks, My Will for you.

Breathe deeply, child, the odor of My sanctity, the sweetness of My Presence, the air of mystery which surrounds this Sacred Place, this Blessed Sacrament of Mine.

Ponder again the greatness of My Father's love and gifts and mercy for you. It is the way to holiness. It is the means to the perseverance you desire, my dearest one.

The ability to serve faithfully does not happen, is not given all at once. It is built, develops day by day. In looking back to remember God's gifts, you will be filled with more gratitude which, in turn, will feed the desire to continue to serve Him in fidelity. Remember, My child, that GRATITUDE IS THE KEY TO THE HEART OF THE FATHER.

The morning of each day sees the world renewed for whatever comes. Let each morning be a new beginning of your own preparation for the Will of My Father. Thank Him first, child, and then listen for His whisperings of love. This is the way you will avoid being devastated by all who reject you. They do not know what they are doing now, just as they did not know in My day. Persist in Our Will, in Our words, in Our love."

❖

Jesus..(8/13/94), ..."the answer to your ultimate preparation for what is to come is to spend every waking moment in My Presence! Please, children, seek to build up now the secret well of grace and strength deep within yourself, so that you might dip into this refreshing treasure trove, and be renewed and strengthened.

There will always be chaos around those who serve Me, but as long as you stay united to My Heart and wrapped in My Mother's Mantle of love and protection, you will be filled with peace. These opportunities will seem even more special because of the terrible conditions that will exist everywhere.

The contrast between the chaos in the world and the quiet and peace of My Presence will itself draw people to Me through all of My chosen ones who seek to bring My lost children back to Us.

Sitting in silence will be the vehicle of emptying all of your own neediness and lack of peace so that you may be filled with the remaining patience and strength needed to serve My people. Just continue to be and to surrender all of yourselves to My Father. Be the supple flowers blowing in the breeze of Our Spirit.

The Light of the World will soon shine only from within the hearts of My faithful ones. Allow yourselves to be emptied more and more and be filled with My Presence that My Light may shine upon all."

Jesus...(8/17/94) ..."Prayer is the only weapon against the inroads already made by Satan against My children. The mercy of My Father is moved by the pleadings of His chosen ones, and more will continue to convert and come back to Him.

15

All that has been foretold is coming to pass. Please, assure all of Our loved ones of this fact. It has not really been as long and difficult a time of preparation as all of you think.

Our children in other countries and parts of your own are suffering terribly at the hands of My enemies and the natural events occurring in various places. You must continue to offer up the waiting and reflect upon the differences between your lives and theirs.

You have all been greatly blessed here who have remained faithful, and will continue to be held close to Our Two Hearts."

❖

Blessed Mother, (8/25/94)....."My dear one, it is I, your Mother, who speaks to you. Please, listen attentively to my words. The days are quickly running towards the completion of this Age. It is difficult for you to understand or imagine what this will be like. Just know that the times can only be lived out in prayer, day by day, filling your lives with the duties which present themselves.

It is only a matter of minutes now on the Eternal Clock before more chaos erupts in the streets of your country. Events will occur so quickly once they begin. Do not give any time or thought to what may or may not happen.

THE GOOD NEWS OF THE KINGDOM IS ABOUT TO BE PROCLAIMED TO EACH INDIVIDUAL ON EARTH. EACH WILL HAVE A CHANCE TO CHOOSE AGAIN FOR THE GIFTS AND INHERITANCE OFFERED BY THE FATHER TO HIS CHILDREN. EACH WILL KNOW WHAT IS BEING OFFERED. WITHOUT THE ACCEPTANCE OF THE GRACE THAT WILL BE OFFERED, MANKIND WILL BE UNABLE TO ACCEPT THE OTHER GIFTS THAT WILL BE PRESENTED!

Please pray that many more will choose the Kingdom before this period of grace and mercy is withdrawn. The grace of God will flow upon all who seek His healing and forgiveness. Continue, little ones, to pray for them and for your children."

Jesus...(9/2/94) "My dear one, please write My words. The only focus of your life must be My Father's Will now, My daughter. Do not think of anything else. The days of only prayer and preparedness are ending so very soon. Do not worry any more about anything. Living in trust and abandonment is such a freedom of soul and mind. Your spirit waits only for the Will of Our Father, the requests of My Mother and Myself.

Please continue to pray as much as possible. This is not to burden My children, but to free you from the world, to help you withdraw from every occupation that is not helpful to your own spiritual health and, in fact, may be harmful!

The outcome of prayer and obedience is holiness. The fruits of virtue are born by the spirit of those who dwell in the Garden of My Father's Will. Here, all is peaceful and each action is fruitful. Here, the effects of your response are completely united to My Heart and the Heart of My Mother, and are totally able to affect the lives of all Our children. They are in such need of My Mercy, daughter. You see more clearly how much I need you and all My chosen ones as vehicles of this mercy.

Without it, My children will be lost forever. The world rushes headlong into destruction with each new decision to regulate the control of who lives and who dies. The seriousness of these decisions cannot be measured in human terms. They are a result of the hatred of Satan for My Father and all of His creatures and creation.

Join My Mother and Her Angels with all My Triumphant ones in heaven to beg and plead with My Father that these terrible decisions for wholesale death of the innocent will be defeated.

Encourage all to pray constantly. Put on the armor of trust and love, and fight this new battle of the forces of darkness and death against the decency and love of My Father for His children. Please, do all you can as we ride into the battle this night."

❖

Jesus.....(9/7/94)... "The love of My Father for His children knows no bounds. Therefore, His mercy will be unconditional and freely given if only Our poor children of this world will seek it. The coming days will see increased hardships, My dear one. You will need to rely on all of Our promises and the words of hope and love We have given to you. Be emptied now of everything other than the Will of My Father and the love of the Triune God and that of Our Mother.

Days are nothing to consider. Time is nothing to be concerned with from now on. Only the Divine Will for you and the needs of Our people. More freedom is gained by the soul who responds in joy and patience to each request that is given it. A simple approach to all We ask of each one is, 'Yes Lord, Thy Kingdom Come'."

❖

Blessed Mother...(9/9/94) "There is so much evil in the world now, dear child. We must continue night and day to beg for God's mercy upon the world. What good is prayer if it is not said for the welfare of souls according to His Will? Only God could defeat the evil one with His love and mercy. It has always been decreed that the world would suffer in this way, as it waits for the return of My Son."

❖

Jesus...(same night).."It is such a small time now until the enlightenment of each one's heart. This grace, this mercy of My Father, will act as a catalyst to bring so many back to Me. This time of grace will last for yet a small while, as those who choose to return to Me are given the opportunity to do so.

Praise the Father, My dear ones, for all His grace and mercy. The time for these gifts grows shorter as darkness clouds the minds and hearts of the world. The evil one will rejoice at the seeming victories he will enjoy. IT WILL BE NECESSARY FOR ALL TO HAVE THE GREATEST FAITH IN ALL OF OUR PROMISES. THE POWER OF MY FATHER TO SAVE HIS WORLD AND HIS PEOPLE IS ABSOLUTE AND WILL NOT BE OVERCOME BY ANY OTHER POWER.

The time allowed the evil in this world to increase has been allotted by My Father to cleanse the earth and hearts of all. When the amount of evil has reached the appointed measure, the love of My Sacred Heart, the power given to My mother, will burst upon the world to defeat all who stand in the way of the Triumph of Our Two Hearts. Until then, all will need all of the strength and grace We have to give you in order to persevere."

✦

Jesus...(9/13/94) .."My daughter, new plans for the world are escalating the Father's justice in order to cleanse His people. The evil and slavery intended for this country is most appalling. The harm which will be visited by the enemies of the Church and freedom can only be lived and withstood with the help of My Mother and Myself, with all the Angels and Saints to rally around you in prayer and protection.

Please, tell Our people to be aware of the opportunities for this protection. TELL THEM TO ASK FOR HELP AT EVERY MOMENT. This is the only way all of you will survive and continue to persevere through the dark, dreadful times ahead. All that We have revealed to you will come to pass.

THE DELAYS ARE MEANT TO STRENGTHEN YOU AND TEST YOUR RESOLVE, YOUR COMMITMENT AND LOVE FOR US. THE TRINITY OF GOD IS GIVEN GLORY, HONOR AND PRAISE EACH TIME YOU ARE OBEDIENT, EACH TIME YOU DEFER TO THE WILL OF THE FATHER, EACH TIME YOU GRACIOUSLY AGREE TO WAIT JUST A LITTLE LONGER FOR HIS WILL TO BE DONE IN YOUR LIFE.

My Heart and the Heart of My Mother are soothed by love and patience. These gifts can only develop in your soul by being exercised, and they will be sorely needed in the days to come. The store of treasures, the well of grace will be there for you whenever you need them.

When all is done in union with Us, there can be no failure to Us, to Our beloved little ones whom We send, or to yourself. The successes will be hard-won and, in many cases, short lived. Have confidence in the promise that each will have another opportunity to return to Me and be saved."

Jesus...(9/15/94) "How blessed you are to use this time to sit in My Presence in silence, to rest and heal your spirit, and to study and become one with Me and all of Our words to you. This will further enable perseverance, patience and endurance during this period of waiting.

Do you ever wonder what it was like for Me in the days before going up to Jerusalem to begin My Passion and ultimate death? I had no true support other than My Mother who understood completely what must occur. It was her love and encouragement that allowed Me to wait, to continue one day, one step at a time the Path to Calvary.

Being human, I was assailed by temptations to flee, to escape, to impatience, to despair. Flee to My Mother, dear ones. Escape into her Immaculate Heart. Bring your impatience and thoughts of discouragement to leave with her, as you hide from the hatred of the world within the safety of her Mantle. I tell you, this is the only behavior which brought Me the strength and courage to follow that Path, but more importantly, to wait for the actual day, decreed by My Father, for it to begin.

Follow the same footsteps I trod, My sweet ones. Walk by My side. Hold the hand of My Mother and allow her to console you, encourage you, strengthen your resolve. From the Cross, We will descend into the depths of hell and free the captives held bound there within their own hearts. But first, continue to announce the good news of My return. The cycle is repeated with each person you will meet."

✛

Blessed Mother..(9/23/94)..."When you proceed in trust and courage, you proceed to victory in the final battle against evil. It will be a long campaign with many bitter moments. Only total trust will see you conquer those moments because you will never be alone or without Our assistance.

Continue to focus on the goal. The Second Coming of My Son will be the only way to renew the earth and save it from the evil one who will have conquered nearly all of it at that time. Please, believe in all We have told you. THE LONGER A PERIOD OF WAITING FOR THESE EVENTS, THE SHORTER WILL BE THE PERIOD OF TIME SPENT EXPERIENCING THEM. The Father hears your prayers and is moved with pity and mercy for those who suffer so terribly in the world."

❖

Blessed Mother..(9/27/94)..."The love of My Son is too much for most people to resist. When it is time for them to respond in a deeper way, the Father allows that love and goodness to touch those hearts to bring life back into them, the supernatural life of grace. Encourage each other, love each other, pray together for all and for each other. The bell tolls the beginning of the Day of Justice throughout the land. The harvest of souls will be great, as the Father's Plan for His people in enacted!"

❖

Jesus...(10/18/94).."The days, child, will not see much change in the daily routine of all Our chosen ones and then, suddenly, the great miracle of My Father's mercy will be upon the whole world. Each will see the state of sinfulness existing in their soul. Each will know exactly where they stand with God.

In order to prepare for this great event, please implore all to pray and fast and do penance as much as possible. My Mother and I will give you all the help you desire, if you will request it through the Holy Spirit. My Father will be moved with great pity for all sinners by these increased appeasements and by this approach.

His Will for His children will always include the desire for all to pray and do penance for each other. What greater way to be your brother's keeper?"

❖

Blessed Mother...(10/25/94).."The days are filled with anguish throughout the world for those who suffer from war and the greed of their brothers. You would not believe all of the secret plans that are in place to dominate the world by those who are enemies of God and His Church.

In the coming weeks, there will be an escalation of warfare in many new spots on the globe which will further dilute

21

your own protection in this country. This is all by design to weaken your government at home.

The warning which the Heavenly Father will give the world will be scoffed at and laughed off as a trick by those who do not believe in God, and plan to overtake all of mankind. These final graces will do nothing to help those hearts already filled with so much hatred.

My Son and I grieve as never before to behold the atrocities being committed against Our beloved children everywhere. This cannot continue to go unchecked by the justice of God Who will only be acting to protect His chosen people from the crimes of the evil one and his cohorts, his instruments of destruction on the earth.

Meanwhile, you can all continue to pray and watch and stay close to My Immaculate Heart. You can see that there is nothing else to be done now. The threat of the powers of evil is too enormous to combat in any other way. You must trust and wait in peace and hope, loving and praying for each other until the obvious battles begin in your own lives. All will occur as We have told you, My daughter.

Each of you, who has been faithful, has nothing to fear, for protection is yours within my mantle. The golden age of peace and purity, that is about to become a reality during the Triumph of Our Two Hearts, will be filled with those who persevere to the end.

The salvation of all My faithful children of my Army has been assured! It will be they who lead all Our lost ones back to the one flock and one Shepherd. The gifts the Father will give to affirm His faithful ones will be stunning to all who behold them, and a source of grace and conversion. The Father has so many wonderful gifts to shower upon all of you. Continue, My dearest ones, to wait in peace, believing that all will be accomplished when you least expect it."

◈

Blessed Mother...(11/1/94).."The Holy Spirit is able to speak to your heart when you are quiet. Your own knowledge of the importance of obedience will greatly help all to understand with clarity how much this virtue is necessary to salvation. Without obedience to the Will of God, Our people are like loose bearings in a machine. It runs this way and that without proper control and often ends in a crash.

The spiritual 'accidents' of God's children can be avoided. The deadness in hearts, the lack of direction, of purpose, can be avoided if only Our dear ones would become more obedient to the Commandments, the Beatitudes, the Mercy that is being set before them daily.

TO BE A CHILD OF GOD, ONE MUST PRACTICE BEING CHILDLIKE AND DEPENDENT ON THE FATHER'S CARE. ONE MUST TRUST THAT HE WILL PROVIDE ALL THAT IS NEEDED IN THAT LIFE, ALL THE WHILE PRAISING AND THANKING AND LISTENING TO THE FATHER.

The lives of Our people have become much too complicated. While progress is a good thing, they were not meant to move at such speed, to focus on their own abilities the way it happens today. Your world has become consumed by noise and motion and a false idea of freedom. The evil one has enticed too many of Our youth with the glitter and 'possibilities' of a corrupt world.

There is nothing that will work like the Father's Plan for His people. First, the glitter and corruption must be destroyed. An appreciation of His gifts must return to the deepest core of individuals. This can only happen when they are deprived of any comforts and excesses. The Father's Plan includes many bitter lessons which must be learned. But Our people must also learn the peace and joy of living in simplicity and in the love of their Creator.

These next years will see continued opportunities to return to God, but will also witness the Apostasy within the Church of My Son and the bloodshed of millions more innocents and those who remain faithful to the Magisterium.

Despite an unprecedented number of signs and miracles worldwide, Satan maintains his stronghold on the minds and hearts of too many of Our beloved people. Before he is defeated entirely, total destruction will have occurred. There will be a greatly reduced number of people left on the earth. You will all be exhausted from your perseverance throughout the chastisements. Only my words and assistance and that of My Jesus will give you the peace and patience required from now on. Be little, my children. Be one with my heart. Be attentive to my words. Be at peace."

✣

Jesus.....(11/7/94) "My dear one, please write. It has been a lot of days since you have felt strong and well. Sometimes, we need this kind of thing to deal with in order not to be overwhelmed by the waiting. Imagine what it must be like to be in a prison or suffering from famine or the helplessness of poverty. Please, unite any discomforts with all of My beloved ones who suffer from these afflictions.

Now the ravages of winter are descending upon many places on earth. Please, dearest ones, keep these people in mind and prayer constantly. Identify with them. Share their days and lend them your strength and love. They will feel your prayers and good wishes for them despite the distance which exists between you. The trials of My people are increasing now, as events near the time to occur.

The time truly is near, dear one, for the illumination of all people's souls. What a great gift and revelation this will prove to be. Some will not survive this time. Many will return quickly to My Father. Whatever happens, please just say, 'Amen' and 'Hosanna' and continue in peace to live out each event in your life with perfect trust.

YOU SAVE YOURSELF SO MUCH GRIEF AND ANXIETY BY REFUSING TO SPECULATE ON EVENTS AND THE TIMES OF THEIR FULFILLMENT."

✣

Jesus...(11/13/94).."Nothing can affect your own journey like the surrender, the reception of My Father's desire and plans. This peace, My peace, is a reflection of Paradise.

When the water is still, one can see more deeply into the pool. The shapes within are more clearly defined. Your own reflection is less ruffled on a calm surface. The days are

24

reflected in the beauty of nature arrayed in all of the colors of the Father's Will. Keep this image in mind and dwell in it as a safeguard against all the ugliness and brutality about to descend upon the earth. No, you cannot imagine it now. Just trust in these words and continue to stay ever closer and united to the Heart of My Mother. Persevere. The Kingdom is about to unfold before you."

❖

Jesus...(11/21/94).."My child, it is I, your Lord, here with you. Child, these days only seem long because you are focusing upon them instead of upon Me(!) My Mother has reminded her children so many times that the focus must remain upon My Face, My desires for you and all that We have requested of you.

You are concerned about many things when the only thing you need to do is surrender more. The events about to happen will set the stage for many more to be open to My mercy. Just please, continue to trust and prepare for this time which will occur so shortly. Only when My people desire to listen, will all of the information and material be of any use to anyone. The obvious problems for any ministry are always involved with the means of exciting interest and need in the hearts of those who should be listening.

In these days of so much evil, great signs are required to obtain the attention of My people. These WILL BE GIVEN in enough time for those who are prepared to spread My mercy, to do so. Until then, please continue in prayer for those who will need all each one has to give them from Us.

A concert pianist must practice many years in order to be prepared. Know that you can never be overly prepared to minister to the many who will be sent to all those who wish to serve.

The time of giving is at hand. The time of preparation for My Birth Day is here. The time of listening, waiting and watching is upon the world as, once again, a celebration of My Birth will fill you with joy and peace. THE HEARTS OF MY PEOPLE ARE TOO FILLED WITH THEMSELVES TO EVER BE THE EMPTY MANGER INTO WHICH I MUST BE LAID."

Blessed Mother...(12/2/94).."The future of the human race still hangs in question, waiting to see the outcome, the response to the next event which occurs. Please, continue to spend more and more time in prayer for all, that they may choose for God and the gifts He is offering.

The ability of each one to respond varies greatly, depending upon many things. Most of all, there is great hatred in the world among and within Our people. To save souls is the only reason We plead constantly, to all those who will listen, to pray unceasingly."

✦

Jesus...(12/5/94)..."The gift of Our Warning to the world will signal the time for the enemies of Our Church to swing into greater action. There will be rage and fury among those who hate Me and My Precious Mother. It has been a long wait for all and now, there will be retribution for all those who turned their backs on My Mother and Myself.

There is great excitement in heaven to welcome so many into the ranks of the chosen beloved of God who will serve the Father and praise Him for the rest of their lives here and in Eternity. Their future has been secured by the love of God, the action of Our Spirit and the prayers of My Mother on behalf of all of you. The clock strikes the hour of the Day of the Lord. Please, explain what a great gift is the Illumination of their sins, deigned to assure their salvation when they then return to Our waiting arms.

Think of the numbers that will swell the ranks of My Church, even if only briefly, as this new faith will immediately be challenged by the powers of Satan and his cohorts. Please, try to convince all to remain calm and believing in spite of the events which will follow. A focus on My Face, a trust in the love and protection of My Mother is all each one needs to live through the trying times about to unfold."

✦

Jesus.....(12/15/94) "It is difficult for you, and all My chosen ones, to believe how much you are loved and how I long

26

for you to spend time with Me in loving communion (during Adoration). The time left for these visits to My Blessed Sacrament is truly so short. You cannot imagine the chaos about to erupt, as the Father's gift of enlightenment for each soul will unleash the forces of hell against My Church and all who attempt to return to Me. This waiting for the Father's action in the world is bringing together more of those faithful who anxiously seek to serve Our people.

There is nothing different to do than what you are doing. A new appreciation of events about to occur fills your beings. The pull of the world and the evil one can be overcome more and more easily, as you simply turn away from trivial pastimes. The strength to do this is there within each of you.

It is so important that you stay as united as possible, in purpose and deed, to My Mother and Myself. The world does not know the shock it is about to receive. So many will not understand what has happened to them. It will be up to My chosen ones to explain the course of action which will bring them back to Me. The confusion which follows will need to be guided by all of you to the priests who remain faithful and available to them.

Once a person has come back to seek forgiveness and reconciliation, that person will need further help and support. All will unfold precisely, according to My Father's Plan for His children. There is absolutely nothing to fear or be concerned about. EVERYTHING IS IN THE HANDS OF MY FATHER, and will occur according to His Will. Trust that all will be well, that your lives will be protected and directed according to these plans, My dear ones.

Allow yourself to be filled with anticipation at the commencement of all these promises. It is difficult to believe all of these things will finally take place. It seems to you like a long wait when, in fact, it has only been a snap of the eternal fingers.

THE MORNING DAWNS ACCORDING TO THE ANCIENT PLAN. THE PLAN OF MY FATHER WILL OCCUR JUST AS SURELY AS THE DAY DAWNS...EXACTLY ON SCHEDULE...WITHOUT FAIL."

27

Blessed Mother...(12/19/94)..."Our messengers and chosen ones must be as prepared as possible to serve the throngs that will be sent to them. All of you will know and understand better when you are in the midst of all We have foretold, and appreciate the strength and fortitude that will be present within you.

The days before the celebration of My Son's birth are such a perfect time to prepare for all that is about to occur in the world. All of heaven prays in anticipation of the next great gift of Our Father to His people. The chaos will be apparent immediately, dear ones. You will all be galvanized into action by the arrival of so many.

Just continue, please, to love each day as you are, content in the knowledge that all is in the hands of the Father for the good of all His people.

Ride with Joseph and myself and the Babe on the wearisome trip to Bethlehem. Feel the cold and the discomfort of the ride, but feel also, the nearness of My Infant Son Who kicks and moves against the confinement of my womb. It is time for Him to arrive and begin the journey toward His Mission for the Father.

He is already aware of all He must suffer, and so am I. The long months of waiting have seen Him grow within my womb, but also, have been a time of pondering and listening on my part. The Scriptures have taken on a whole new life, now that the journey of the Messiah into the world has begun. I read them as if brand new, and in wonderment and awe.

Each step of this poor beast of labor takes us through the final Scripture stories right up to the coming of My Son. And so it will be for all of you. Each step you take brings the world that much closer to the coming back of My Jesus into a world that rejects Him. Before His arrival, hearts are already closed and hardened to the possibility of His Second Coming.

Continue to believe, My daughter, and to encourage all you meet. These days are blessed and oh-so-holy. Please, walk by My side with Our Beloved Joseph now. Allow him to tell you about this journey. He has great love for all who love and serve me, and he will give you all his love and support in the coming days. Be filled with peace and contentment."

❖

Blessed Mother..(12/25/94)..

"I adore My Infant Son with all of the Angelic Choir this holy day. I invite you to come with Joseph and Myself and adore Him, too.

Do you know the joy which filled My heart at the first sight of this Holy Babe? Can you imagine the delight and joy and gratitude that lifted me above the ground to behold this miracle Who was truly My Son, yet truly the Son of the Most High?

Little time passed before the Shepherds arrived to pay Him homage. They were speechless and full of wonder at the sight of this Infant bathed in light and surrounded by Angelic Choirs singing hosannas to the Highest. We all simply gazed in amazement, transfixed with joy at the sight of this miracle.

I was overcome with happiness and gratitude and humility. Joseph wept continuously, as he did everything humanly possible to make that lowly stable into a setting worthy for a King.

In a second, it seemed as though all of Heaven had been loosed upon earth. The Angelic music continued without ceasing the whole night long. Joseph was overcome with strong emotions, as he waited for our slightest need. The time was not without its discomfort, and we both attempted to keep our child warm. Often, we were overcome by the realization of all that had just occurred and wept together, clinging to each other in joy and awe.

The Shepherds adored without uttering a word, leaving what extra clothing they had to add to our comfort. Days passed in this way and gave way to conditions of routine. We continued in this manner, not knowing what each new day would bring, but content in the absolute belief and understanding that the promised Messiah had come into the world and been entrusted to our care. This knowledge left us with nothing but trust and gratitude. We knew for certain that God would provide for us and, most especially, for this tiny Son of His.

You may believe in this way also, My dearest child. The world continues to ignore Our signs and pleadings. The cup of the Father's wrath for the rejection of His children has overflowed all boundaries. Men have tried His patience far beyond limits ever attained before.

Child, the Father and Creator of us all has reached the end of His own endurance. The children of this Age have exceeded any behavior practiced in the past which rejected their God. Tragedy after tragedy fails to move Our people's hearts. The focus of each one is strictly upon personal gain and the success of the world's standards.

Come with me and await this great miracle. Prepare yourself for everything that is to come. More and more, you will find yourself ready to burst with the fullness of My Jesus. The waiting for childbirth causes a pressure, an anxiety to be delivered from the confinement. The presence of the Babe is heavy within, waiting to burst forth at just the right moment for all to see and benefit by. This holy scene is enacted again and again in the lives of those who love and serve Us. You wait for the birth of all of the promises of God in your life. It is only natural that you would become anxious for this event to occur, and begin a time of greater service in your life. You know well that the child cannot be born before the proper time!

Kneel now and adore. My love and gratitude are with your efforts to love and serve My Infant Child. Persist. Just take each event in stride as a gift of the Father and thank Him for it."

❖

Jesus.....(12/29/94)..."My dear one, please write. The hour grows late on your own clock, but also on Mine. You know that all will be well because We have told you so many times that this will be the truth of your experience. I, your Lord, am with you now to lead you to the peace that only I can give to

30

you. Please remember that you will need all of your strength in order to hold on to My strength and courage for all who come to you. Surrender is the word. The hour of total abandonment is here in which you must let go now and allow the Father's Will to completely reign in your life and all of your loved ones'.

I am the Lord, your God, Who was and Who is and Who will always be. I am your sweet Jesus of Mercy Who loves you beyond telling, Who will lead you into battle with the powers of hell and Who will triumph over them. Be assured, child, of the truth of these words. Be immersed in My love forever more. Be one with My Heart, with My Spirit, with the Will of Our Father in heaven. Dear child, be at peace and be secure in Our love."

✠

Blessed Mother..(1/4/95).."My dearest one, please write My words for your refreshment. I, your Mother, am here to soothe your troubled spirit. The hours spent like this (in prayer with people visiting here), are food for your soul. It is only in communion with Us that you can continue to be prepared. All of the delays have been given to the world in order to perfect more of those who will serve. The Father continues to grace the world, even as it continues to reject Him. No one can imagine the immense amount of love He has for His people. Human ability to love and forgive and tolerate each other's behavior is barely a shadow of the Father's ability to do so. But this has also given way to a complacency in the hearts of all; a false understanding and taking for granted the continued forgiveness as a license to sin, to put off changing and living life as a child of God.

It is this condition, a scheme of the evil one, which has lulled the world into an illusion of reality. Nothing of the world reflects the goodness of the Creator as it was meant to. Now, that beauty is about to disappear. The love and longing for His people's love is about to force the Father's Will into action. He will, once again, do what is necessary to reach the dull minds and hearts of all who sleep in the false security of the world.

31

Little time remains before events of the greatest magnitude send the world into an abyss of suffering and slavery. You can see already how many parts of the world are consumed with hatred, trying to dominate and destroy each other. You can see how necessary it is to rearrange the minds and hearts of the inhabitants of earth. This understanding will be so necessary in the days to follow. Each person who serves Our plan will need to continually remind the poor lost ones, who will roam the earth looking for shelter and warmth, that the Father is returning beauty to the world by first destroying all that is ugly, all that is not of Him, all the reminders of the evil one! The amount of love and grace and mercy being poured upon the inhabitants of the earth is a thousandfold.

The chaos which exists now as a result of the power of the evil one and his cohorts is nearly equal to that which existed at the creation of the world. The darkness descending is an attempt by Satan to return the world to that hate-filled time when only demons roared in the abyss.

Great beauty and peace will be the final result of all that is about to occur. It has been the Father's Plan at work all along for the preparation of as many of His children as will respond to Him.

It is love and healing and mercy and forgiveness and new life He offers to a tired world nearly dead already in sin and debauchery. You know the joy of a purified heart, My daughter. Continue to pray for this for all, as we wait now...together."

❖

Jesus...(1/6/95).."You know that this has been a long and difficult journey and yet, now the end of this phase is near and there will be no peace again until My Return. Please trust that all will be provided for so that My Father's Will can be accomplished. This will be the work of Our Spirit, and you will marvel at all that will occur.

To dwell with Us in the present moment is the answer to being faithful and persevering. A focus on My Mother and Myself, present with each of Our chosen ones, will serve to bring you through impossible trials. These times and trials are necessary to accomplish all My Father has planned for His people. Trust is the only answer for all of you. Many more of your number have come to realize the truth of that fact, and are living in this way.

The days are truly about to change forever. The interim time before My Return will be lived in a totally different way which will incorporate all of the things We have told you already. It is good to come to Me in your need, daughter of My Heart. Do not ever hesitate to do so while you still have the opportunity to record My words. Yes, it is a great and awesome gift that I, your Lord, have been allowed to speak to so many of My special messengers.

All of those who wait and wonder will have their questions answered. It will now be a time of great cohesion among the members of My Mother's Army. A new appreciation will fill the hearts of all of you as you view the gifts given to each other. Praise the Father Who loves His people with great tenderness and love."

❖

Jesus...(1/11/95)..."The mood of many is to doubt. The evil one casts aspersions (a damaging or disparaging remark, slander or innuendo: Webster.) upon My messengers and chosen ones. The Heart of My Mother breaks at the lack of support each of them receives, as people worry about their own needs and their own intentions.

The focus must be on Me, child. You have been told this so often, and you can see the destruction brought about when one listens to what everyone is saying. When you are focused on Me, there is no time for other opinions and other things people are saying, which is really only gossip! There must be no place in you life, My dear one, for idle chatter and wonderings. The time left is too precious to waste on idleness and selfish chatter.

To be united to My Heart and Will, you must be quiet enough and close enough at all times in order to hear what it is I or My Spirit are saying to you. Praise My Father now,

33

daughter. Thank Him for all that is and for His wonderful plans to save His people. Go in My peace."

❖

Blessed Mother...(1/15/95).."The bells ring the hour of battle, child. The world is poised on the brink of disaster and goes about uncaring and unthinking. Without enough people to convert back to God, there will certainly be all of the devastation ever mentioned to all of My special messengers.

You must continue to pray for the salvation of all souls until the very end. Without people who persevere in prayer, many will not have a chance at conversion. Dearest children, listen closely all day to the voice of the Holy Spirit. Without His direction, you will be uncertain on too many occasions. He will be very active and present in the near future, when no more messages and apparitions are allowed.

This is in accordance with the Father's Will. Each one's faith will be tried to the fullest. Please, remind Our beloved ones who cry out that MUCH FAITH IS NEEDED TO JUSTIFY THE MANY WHO WILL RETURN TO US AT THE VERY LAST MOMENT. You can see how you will all be victims for their sakes, and must accept this with joy, if you truly wish to serve your brothers and sisters. They will have no one else and no other way to have the graces reserved for them released."

❖

Jesus..(1/19/95).."You are in great discomfort this day, yet come to be with Me and, I tell you, I am grateful. The time for comfort has fled the world, but especially for those who serve Me. You must unite your sufferings with all of those in the world who are experiencing pain and hardships because of natural disasters, wars and poverty. Your prayers for them will release more graces at this time when they are most needed.

Yes, the added time after a promise of the warning brought a sobriety of thought and action to many of Our people. This is so necessary for all of you who hope to serve. A complete reliance on Us to care for you, a total peace with all

34

that does or does not happen is needed from now on, and many have now made this adjustment.

You see conditions in the world escalating towards further events of even greater magnitude. If you are waiting in silence with Me, then we can perform all the deeds, survive all the battles that present themselves along this journey toward the final battle with the powers of evil."

◈

The Father.....(1/28/95) ....."Daughter, the hour is nearly gone which sees My world as it is this moment. Events are being unleashed, as I speak to your heart, which will alter forever the face of the earth. You will understand shortly so many more of the words that have been given to you. My wisdom has been poured out upon you tonight, as you pray and await My words. My commands to you are to continue in this joyful pattern of praise and acceptance.

The Day of the Lord is upon the world in all its fury. Events will escalate rapidly now, dear one. Your history is about to be even more directly guided by Me for the good and salvation of all mankind. Gone will be all vestiges of normalcy. Gone will be the familiar ways of being and doing.

Please continue to pray and come constantly to My Son and Our Mother. We are in a holy company of Apostles and Martyrs, Saints and Angels, all who dwell in Heaven with the Triune God. Persevere in holiness before the throne of your Father Who loves you into life."

Jesus...(3/1/95) "To believe in Our words, you must be willing to pray more. A preparation can only be made thru a complete surrender of your time and gifts. Come to Me now and bring your heart's longings. Tell Me again of all that troubles and pains you and ask Me to take it from you. You must be free of anything that would hinder a nimble climb on the path that is ascending sharply now.

The time for leisure is long past and only serious endeavors must occupy your time. The work that you will do for us will require you to be extraordinarily brave. You can only adhere to the needs of all, and Our requests, by allowing the Angels and Saints, My Mother and I to help you at every moment.

Continue to prepare as though all will occur tomorrow. There <u>will</u> come a time when that very thing will happen. The waiting will end and the harvest will begin. Great will be the industry of all My people for their Lord."

Blessed Mother...(3/13/95) "Whatever needs doing must be completed. If there is a period without activity, you must offer that as a means of building more patience and trust. These are days of waiting for everyone, and you can pray for each other's patience and perseverance better as you experience these needs yourself.

It is such a healing for your own hearts and such a balm for Ours when you spend your days in greater union with Our two hearts and the Father's Will for you. Much wisdom is being poured out by the Holy Spirit upon all those who will accept it!

Many special signs are being given to Our faithful ones everywhere. The world waits for the Father to act in specific ways and often misses the signs he is actually giving.

Be aware of your brothers and sisters everywhere who suffer greatly and have far less of the world's goods to give them any comfort. The love that fills your heart, Our love that makes your heart swell and your spirit sing, can never be taken from you, even though you one day may lose all other possessions.

Just continue to be at peace with what is, to accept everything that occurs in your lives as God's Will for you.

Great will be the peace and protection for all those who live in this manner. This is living in the Father's Will, child. This is surrender, the abandonment of all you hold dear for the Lord's sake, for His honor and glory and the good of all the people in the world.

The focus in your mind and heart will help to keep you grounded. Live as though nothing else existed now, save Our Presence with all the Angels and Saints, for that is truly living in the Kingdom.

Life always continues after a person dies. However, that person continues to live and grow and learn and develop in new ways. That person continues an association with others, but in a whole new way of being and interacting.

You will do this as you more and more surrender to being more deeply committed to God's Will each step of the way. Living in this world in this manner is to be an instrument in the hands of My Son. You have been molded into a fighting team with all those you know and love from many different areas of this land.

You will all serve Us in a far greater capacity, as events become more dangerous. After the enlightenment of men's minds to the state of their souls, and the destruction that ensues, the people of the world will be vastly changed. Transformations will be an everyday occurrence for a period of time.

As all of you continue to watch these events unfold, you will be guided by the Spirit in a greater way. You will know what to do and how to proceed if you listen intently for His voice. The love in your hearts will continue to grow. Please always believe in the fact that you will be protected in My Mantle of love."

Jesus...(4/25/95) "Be grateful for the opportunity to perform service for all your brothers and sisters and to unite yourself to the Body more closely in this way. Be assured that many opportunities to serve Our people await you in the future.

Please continue to offer all to Me for purification and every hardship to the Will of My Father. The Way of the Cross is full of hardships and, sometimes, danger for those who serve Me. The darkness through which you walk only reflects the condition of the world, and is a means to build your faith."

◈

Blessed Mother...(4/31/95) "The days are moving so quickly now, and all of Heaven waits for the next move of the Father's hand. In the coming days, I wish for you to be in deeper prayer. I know that you desire to serve Us and Our desires to the best of your ability and so, I remind you again of how little time remains.

The time is truly upon the world, My dear one. It is difficult to overcome the effects of delays in your heart and with your will. We will never leave you without the strength necessary to overcome your own inclinations to be lazy (!) or put off a certain task. I am in your heart at every moment with My beloved Jesus to sustain and strengthen you.

Dear one, do not give a minute's notice to doubt or despair. When you look back, you will see that you have needed all the extra time you have been given to finish each chore. The needs of Our loved ones will be so great, and you must be ready to serve them to the best of your ability.

Every promise, every phase of the Father's plan is still in place for all His chosen ones. Remember, the Babe must be ready to be born at just the right time, in order to benefit the greatest numbers. No one could possibly know this time like the Father Who sees all!

Be filled with courage and new hope for every gift of the Father to be given."

◈

Jesus...(5/7/95) "Your heart is full of the energy of love. A desire to serve and be faithful to the Father's Will is the fuel of industry in every instance. So many times you will think you are without the strength to continue, and a simple reflection in My Presence, a reliance on Our strength will grant the renewal needed for you to continue.

The time grows even more chaotic in your world, My

38

child. You will see terrible events soon, even more terrible than before, occurring in the troubled warring nations.

Satan is gathering many more to his camp and filling them with assurances of power and victory. These beliefs incite men to even greater acts of rebellion against authority. The teachings of Our beloved Pope John Paul II will be more openly ridiculed and rejected in the coming months. Please, continue to pray for his strength and safety.

In the future, many bishops and priests will openly demand his resignation and break away from him. This will cause terrible hardships for all of you and signal the beginning of difficult times for all who attempt to remain faithful.

It will be a time of much confusion, as Our people wonder what is truth and which way to turn. The ability of those who attempt to lead will be greatly impeded by the power of evil present in the world and especially within My Church.

My Mother weeps constantly at all the destruction about to occur. You will all need each other, as the plan of My Father escalates and causes more pressure to be exerted on those who pray and follow My Mother.

Concentrate now as though the battle were about to erupt in your life. It is, child! There is not a moment to waste. Be encouraged, daughter. Be filled with trust and My peace for all that will be. The day of the Lord has begun and all of Scripture is being fulfilled as it was written."

Blessed Mother...(5/21/95) "You are cooperating with the Holy Spirit by remaining open to Him. Please, continue to listen to Him and His gentle nudgings. The day is coming, child. It IS coming for all to unfold and be revealed. Go in the peace of My Son, Jesus. Never, for an instant, let go of My hand and your great desire to be loved by and more perfectly united to My Son."

Jesus...(5/26/95) "Please be at peace. Do not worry about your ability to prepare or your place on the road to My Father's Will for you. The impetus to pray and prepare is a sign of grace and favor!

Our Spirit of Wisdom and Truth will come to your aid

every time you call upon Him. You may believe this and count on His Help completely. We will never leave you without the help you need to succeed on behalf of Our loved ones who come to you.

The ability to retain knowledge and facts is the result of hard work, but also the gift of Our Spirit. He will not let you down, I promise. It is His nature to be Wisdom and Light to all who call upon His Help.

There is still much within you that needs quieting and healing. Your own welfare is important to the welfare of all Our needy children who will come to you in very great numbers.

TRUST WILL SEE YOU THROUGH ABSOLUTELY EVERY TRIAL AND OBSTACLE. The more you rely on Us to help you, the easier it will be to trust. This is a wonderful spiral reaching up to the heavens that will lift YOU up!

As you travel the rest of this journey, the path is steep. Trust will give strength to your steps and elevate you quickly. The climb will seem less difficult when you allow Us to carry you on the wings of trust. Absolute confidence will be needed by the one who climbs to such heights amid dangerous winds and rocks and storms.

Wrapped in the Mantle of My Mother, trust and confidence will be the climate protecting you from the storms. The enemy will lie in wait for you and appear when you least expect it! You have only to call upon the power of My Name to deal with him. The attacks of the evil one will result in greater strength for the time period that will follow them.

All has been arranged and is in place for everything to occur in your experience of it. This living out of My Father's plan will continue to require only your 'yes' and on-going cooperation. It is only for you to go along in joy and peace with each step that unfolds for you.

JUST DWELL IN A DEEP CONVICTION OF MY LOVE AND CARE FOR YOU. This will be your peace. This will give you victory at every turn. This will fulfill the Father's Will for you and for His people. Live in My peace, child. Live immersed in My love."

Jesus...(6/1/95) "I, your sweet Jesus of Mercy, come this night to fill your heart with My sweetness and a firm resolve. The minutes are running out in the time before My Father's plan to gift His people with the enlightenment of their souls will begin.

To see clearly the state of sinfulness existing in each soul will cause many of Our loved ones to panic. Our people are simply not aware of the sinful patterns in their lives. This revelation will be a source of bitterness and great sorrow to many of Our chosen ones, as well. Calm the frightened hearts of My faithful ones, as well as those who will come here seeking help and comfort.

The time of waiting is not much longer. This I promise you, My daughter. My Father has accomplished so much good in His faithful ones by delaying His hand. You are all so much better prepared to meet the dangers that will be everywhere.

You cannot imagine how bad the situation in your country will be. The police are more aware of the organized activity of gangs everywhere (!) They do not report these facts for fear of inciting panic among the people. All We have told you will soon begin to be manifest in the streets. Please, child, be prepared to stay within your homes for safety's sake. Your husband will be forced to stay away from his work and other places of routine and the economy will begin to falter.

The earth will soon tremble violently in your area and throughout the entire land of this great country. Be prepared for anything on an emergency basis. The need for calm will be great.

It is with such sadness that all of Heaven expect and await these days of pain for the people of the earth. Great upheaval will be the norm for all of you. Please, be prepared for events to begin at any moment. Confess your sins and stay in My grace as close to My Mother and Me as you can.

Everything that has been revealed will begin to occur. Time is so very short now, My dear one, and all of the soldiers in My Mother's army will be called upon to march for the good of their brothers and sisters who are so lost in the world.

You may believe that I, your Lord, am speaking these words to you. I, who love and adore My Father in Heaven, tell you this is truth. You may prepare to act on all you have ever heard Me tell you. You must simply wait in readiness now to act at any moment. You will not be surprised when the action of My Father does begin in this country because you are prepared for it.

Stay quiet, daughter, and even closer to Our two Hearts. Please, child, thank Our Father for gifting you so as to render you battle-ready! The trumpets are sounding the charge, once again. The battle in your streets will soon erupt for all to see. Encourage all, who will listen, to be ready to defend their homes and souls against the powers of darkness. YOUR WEAPONS MUST BE PRAYER AND TRUST AND MERCY. The peace you all need will remain ever present in your hearts as My grace pours out to sustain you."

Jesus...(6/4/95) "The missions given to each of Our chosen messengers are in place, are complete, are prepared for by each one involved. All is definitely in readiness now for My Father's Will to begin. As I have told you, just please be ready for anything at any time.

The illumination of men's minds will be the ultimate act of mercy before the justice of God will be visited upon the earth. All of the plans shared with Our children will become a reality. Soon is not a vague time period now, child. Be assured that all will begin before you realize what has occurred.

The need to prepare physically is important. Your children will be totally convinced of the need to join you here after viewing the enormous effects of these events. You know well, My daughter, how much I long to bring all of you home to Me. This will be occurring at different intervals throughout the entire plan of My Father. In His wisdom, He plans what is best for each one. It will be easier to accept whatever happens because you believe this fact.

You trust what the Father desires to be part of His wisdom and knowledge of what is best. The idea that you will all be returning to Heaven will be a cause of rejoicing in your heart. Think of all you will see unfolding for the rest of your life on earth! Truly, you are all most blessed to be living at this time."

Jesus...(6/19/95) "I am your Lord and God, Jesus Christ Who reigns forever. My flesh is given for the life of the world. When you see the Abomination of Desecration on My altar, know that all will be accomplished very quickly to the end of this era.

Time has run out for all delays of My Father's plan. Please spend what time is left with Me, your Supreme Commander and Chief. The Army of Heaven marches to the battle in legions for the great confrontation between good and evil. The forces of Heaven will win, but the struggle will be fierce.

All of My Mother's army waits for the first sign to be given to galvanize into action. The Day of the Lord, child, is here for all to behold. You will see now each thing we have told you begin to unfold. You are aware of how quickly the years have fled and are a bit dismayed at the enormity about to break over the heads of all.

I speak these words to you, My loved ones, to calm your heart so that when events begin, you will be strong and calm in the face of so much chaos. Please continue to pray as much as you can this week. You see how quickly time goes by and how easy it is to allow prayer to remain unsaid.

Human weaknesses play right into Satan's hands and render you more vulnerable than ever to his wicked schemes. Please! Be on guard! Confess your sins each week. Stay recollected in Our Presence with the Angels and Saints. These are your companions for the remainder of the journey. Call on them, thank them, love them and know that this love is deeply felt and returned by all of them. Rejoice. The Kingdom comes!"

Blessed Mother...(Same Night) "Be at peace about each event that occurs, child. These must happen in order for My Son to return to the earth and claim His inheritance. Thank the Father, too, for the enormity of His gifts and love for all of His children, who are held tightly to My Heart."

Jesus...(6/26/95) "I, your Lord, speak for your comfort. You are filled with sadness today and I beg you to surrender all of these feelings to Me. Please remember, child, that you need to fly above doubts and fears on the wings of trust in your Lord Who loves you so much.

These words are all you need for now, child. Please ponder them and seek rest for now. The Day of the Lord is here. All is being accomplished. All will see My saving power amid incredible destruction.

Be of stout heart! Trust in Me and ride by My side into the battle against the forces of darkness. Please do not fear. Be at peace."

###

Jesus...(7/1/95) "I, your Jesus of Mercy, come to you with joy. Your preparedness brings you more and more near to the moment when My Father's hand reaches out to cleanse the inhabitants of the earth.

Soon a new dawn will break over the sleeping inhabitants of the land. They will awake to the reality of life lived as God calls them to see. No misunderstanding can exist for those who accept God's call to come back to Him for healing and forgiveness. The beauty can be restored to mankind only after the ugliness is removed.

The laws of My Father for His people will be reinstated in hearts emptied of sin. The graces He wishes to shower upon them will flower in the renewed soil and cause beautiful blossoms to bloom, once again, in the Garden of His Will.

Please remain in simplicity and humility, waiting for My Father's Will to act on behalf of the world. NOTHING will happen until He decrees it. But all will occur, as you have been promised repeatedly.

The waiting is nearly over, daughter. Believe and persevere. Be filled with peace and Our love. Be one with the Will of My Father."

###

Jesus...(7/8/95) "Please take these words. I am your Jesus Who loves you and longs to hold all My children forever in

My eternal embrace. This waiting, this longing in your heart is strengthening you beyond your understanding. There is no way to arrive at the new wisdom flooding your heart than to seek to be open to the voice of Our Spirit.

No, dear one, I cannot tell you more or when, but I can tell you why you should be filled with wonder and gratitude at all that will transpire in your life.

Please understand that you ALL have needed every spare moment to PREPARE better and to SURRENDER more. What more can be said by way of explanation?

As you let go of expectations and fears and excitement, you learn to just be in joy and peace and hope in My Father's Will, accepting whatever happens or doesn't!

It is absolutely necessary for you to be able to live like this in order to live in total union with Me. It was like that for My Mother waiting for all to be accomplished when she knew all of the details beforehand.

It was a matter of PATIENT WAITING FOR ME, as I traveled the hill country around Jerusalem waiting for the exact time to be revealed to Me.

You know how things must unfold in My Father's plan. It will always be this way, since it is only Our Father's Will that is being fulfilled.

Please allow yourself to relax and just be here with Me before My Blessed Sacrament, to be nurtured by the peace and silence of My Presence.

Do you not feel My love? Can you not see My face smile tenderly at you? You must not worry ever again! You must not be concerned with anything, but only surrender and be at peace.

The days will pass quickly if you will allow Me to grace you with this peace. My Mother will continue to bring you through this trying time of waiting. Call on her at every moment, but especially when you feel a return of anxiety.

Please, daughter, believe and persevere."

Blessed Mother...(7/24/95) "Dear child, I wish to speak to your heart...Faith must be built be following whatever the

Will of God appears to be at the moment without hesitation and without conditions.

Know that the Father's time is not yours, no matter what is said! Know that your docility and obedience to all that does or does not occur is central to your growth into His Divine Will.

The only thing necessary for you to say at each moment is 'yes' and 'Amen'. If you are upset by anything, do not be alarmed, daughter. You are very human! When you bring your emotions to Jesus and to Me, We can heal you more and calm your inner turmoil.

Daughter, trials are just that. They leave one feeling inadequate and puzzled and helpless. They are designed to place the focus on God and His power and show us our own lack of it!

When we are completely dependent on God for all things, we will experience this in a huge way, so that we cannot miss the fact that He is God and will provide for everything. Nothing that happens in your life is not being completely guided by the hand of the Father.

In the future, action will fill your days. I know that you anxiously await this time, as I do. Be assured that all you do for Us during this time of waiting is just as important as your future actions will be.

Please, go in my peace. I am your Mother."

Jesus...(8/7/95) "Daughter of My Heart, do not be sad that weakness continues to plague you. It is this which shall continue to humble you and lead to sanctification.

The Kingdom of Heaven is worth any sacrifice, any suffering in order to render one ready to approach the gate. I am the Gate, child; I am the Narrow Path. I am your All, your only means to salvation through the Heart of My Mother and power of My Spirit.

Your heart is consecrated and dedicated to Me in the Holy Trinity. If you will retreat and renew yourself, you will find all the strength you need waiting in My arms. The power of grace to overcome temptation and struggle is victorious every time you ask for it. Come to Me more often.

You can know the battle is accelerating when the fight becomes more difficult. The struggle against evil can be nearly overwhelming and frightening, too. You see why trust in My Mother's protection and My strength is so important. Your heart and mind are filled with conviction about all We have ever said to you.

Just remain in the shadow of My Cross, resting now in My arms; lean on My Mother. Wait in peace and joy that you will be in the right place at the right time to receive all My Father's gifts, to serve Him and Our people faithfully and powerfully.

Be renewed and refreshed now, daughter, in My love for you."

Blessed Mother...(same day) "My daughter, I your Mother of Sorrows, come to be with you this day to pray and build you up again. You are proceeding properly child, in this latest test of your endurance. Be assured of My constant prayers and presence with you. These days are fraught with danger in many disguises. Be constantly on guard, but at the same time, at peace about everything.

You must be ready to fight the evil one by My side. Together, we are going to face every subtle trick he has to trap Our poor unsuspecting little ones. Absolute humility and dependence on God is necessary to respond to the needs of all.

47

Please, just stay closer to Me than ever, relying on My protection and help and prayers. You are strong, daughter, and filled with great wisdom from the Father. Use all of your gifts now to tend to yourself and your own healing and renewal."

Jesus...(9/1/95) "The times of fulfillment are so near. The preparedness you have worked so hard to develop is a breastplate of strength for your heart. When you feel weary, take the time to rest! Recover from all of your struggles with My help and in My arms. Loneliness is meant to bring you into My Presence, accepting all the love I wish to give you.

Vulnerable is a condition that can change when one's motives are humbled and purified. All can be tempered by penance and fasting. When you offer all things with joy, great strength, (My strength), will take their place in your heart.

Weakness, child, is meant to alert you to the need and areas of healing that must be offered to Me and then requested in trust. The Divine Will of the Father is that you and all of His children be purified. You hesitate to surrender to the death you must endure to all that is of this earth. Please, daughter, rest in My embrace and heal. I am your Lord and Savior Who waits with great eagerness for the fulfillment of all Our promises to you."

Jesus...(9/19/95) "My child, it is I, your Lord. Thank you for coming to Me again. Your visits are so important to both of Us.

Truly, daughter, you are ready to go out to all Our loved ones who need encouragement and support at this time. Know that your efforts are doubled and tripled many times over by the graces accompanying Our words. It is hardly a moment now before momentous events rock the lives of all who wait.

The lives of those who do not know Our words of warning will be desolate at the emptiness they find in their hearts. Pray for them, daughter, that they will respond to the graces being offered to them.

Persevere and believe. Hang on to all you have learned. Learn more deeply about all the beauty and love in My Father's Kingdom. Tell Our people of the immense peace and love waiting for them. Be a channel of that love and peace, little one. Never forget how much you are loved."

Blessed Mother...(9/27/95) "My dear child, I your Mother, am here to speak words of strength and comfort. Do not be alarmed at any trials you are experiencing. Trust in My protection and prayers. Daughter, your heart is so full of all of Our words. You are straining to begin the final journey toward the Day of My Son's Coming back to the world.

The portals of Heaven stand open. The inhabitants of Eternity have engaged in prayer and readiness to fight by the side of Our faithful ones.

Please, tell Our people to remember the added strength available at this time through the Presence of the Angels and Saints. This is real, daughter. All must call constantly for the help available. The Father's Plan would never allow His beloved to suffer these times without the help each requires.

This does not mean that all will be saved from suffering and dying for their faith. Incredible hardships will begin any moment, and I beg you to remain in constant prayer that each will receive the graces offered. Your children will ultimately find their way to this area. The darkness will be immediately obvious. The persecution of all the faithful will forcefully cause people to make the choice for God.

Each one will realize that their decision will depend only upon the individual (themselves). The knowledge that God has written on each heart prepares a person to accept the graces offered. It is a choice we make alone, devoid of the influence of others, and that must then be lived out in spite of the choices of others or their future decisions.

The excitement to begin the great Harvest and Shepherding of God's people is shared by all who wait. Each one has been brought to the straining point of endurance!!

The added supplies you need should be tended to immediately. Think of the extra ones you may be looking after, but be assured of Our care and protection for yourself. Please, receive the Sacrament of Reconciliation as though you might not have the opportunity again. Give your attention to My Son and Myself. Live now in Our midst and count on all the help you will ever need.

Know that these words are true and you may believe that I am here with you speaking. I am the Immaculate Virgin Mary who waits eagerly, as well, to begin the final battles. Much will be accomplished and then again lost.

Perseverance is the gift all of you must offer to the Father during these times. As you are more purified, the conviction will become stronger to remain faithful. And as you pray and serve, your purification will become greater!

Please remain in readiness for all We have told you to commence. Be filled with joy. No more delays will cause your heart to grieve. Be filled with courage and love and the peace of Jesus, My Beloved Son. I, your Mother, give My blessings of perseverance to all gathered in this place."

Jesus...(10/27/95) "...The time, child, is so near to an unparalleled event. You will be galvanized into action for the rest of your life. Continue to make notes on all that comes to you from Our Spirit.

You will see miracles soon, performed by many of you who wait in trust and mercy. My Heart overflows with love for all of you here who pray and wait with diligence. The Father's Heart is full of gratitude toward each of you. The clock has reached the Hour for My Father to act.

There are no new words. You have all of the information you need. Your own waiting is shared in the same way by all Our special messengers.

Continue to believe and endure each day in total abandonment. Go forward as you have been. Your gathering (new prayer group at my house), will be a further bonding for all who attend and will receive My special blessing for all. Each time you pray together, a new link is forged in the living rosary of My Mother's children. The community spirit you work for is being strengthened, and will bring all of you through many trying times.

Please, offer boredom and routine to Me for the purification of your own souls. You cannot imagine how much good is being done by the patient obedience of all Our dear ones in Scottsdale.

The week-end is bringing many special graces to your entire area. It will be protected for as long as it is necessary for you to remain there. You are right to believe that I will shepherd all of you at just the right moment to just the right place. The alarm has been sounded for the world. It will catch so many unaware, when My Father's hand lands upon the earth in His merciful judgement.

Please, tell Our people that time has evaporated. It no longer has meaning, nor does anything other than Our Will have any importance in your lives. Each will know what this means for them and must be waiting to act on behalf of millions of Our dear lost ones who will come here.

All has been set into motion. My Father bids you be of good cheer and <u>do not waste the precious time that remains.</u> He is blessing and smiling upon you at this very moment. The strength of the Tribune God courses through your veins. You will have and be all that will be needed for the future. Continue to live and believe in My Love and My Words. I come!"

※

Jesus...(11/15/95) "My dear one, you may write My words, given for the strength and benefit of your heart.

Each person is truly helpless on their own and needs to realize how much you can depend upon Our assistance. We will always be available to all of you. There will be no danger you cannot overcome or withstand when you accept Our help and protection. Flee in prayer to My Mother and plead her assistance. Remember that you are always in Our Presence with the Angels and Saints, and react accordingly.

Please remember that you will be protected with all the help you will ever need. Each one's weakness will be the target of ongoing attacks by the evil one. Each one of Our soldiers will be subjected to many trials to prepare you for future trials.

The escalation of My Father's plan has begun. You see signs all over the world. Do not ever believe that each major event now occurring is not a sign from My Father. He is attempting to alert and prepare the world for warfare and economic hardships. Ruin faces your nation this very day. Hardships of every kind will follow. You are indeed ready now for any happening to unfold.

Each of you brings a smile to the Face of My Father and to all of Us in Heaven. You are trying so hard to do His Will. You are all loved and appreciated, My dearest daughter. You will all be strengthened as you desire. That is Our desire, too! Be at peace now for this gifted journey."

Jesus...(12/4/95) "Dearest one, your concerns are well placed about all the unrest within My people. Satan will play upon the pride of each one as best he can with all his subtle cunning. There are not enough words to warn you all to prepare to be bombarded with his attacks.

Above all, these are allowed by My Father to strengthen you by pointing out your particular areas of weakness. He can bring good out of every situation and therefore, will allow you all to be tried in particular ways so that you might learn important lessons. These new understandings gird you for the future when temptations will be greater and graces less available to all.

The darkness of the soul will invade all of you, and choices will seem more and more difficult. It will be then that a focus on My Face and all you know to be true and holy will be the only means of defense against the forces of evil.

Do not be alarmed by this news. It would have to be this way in a spiritual battle. As you attempt to hold out, please remember the ultimate goal of Heaven for all Eternity. Remember that you are never fighting without the aid and actual Presence of the Angels and Saints. Recall all the times we have promised you Our strength and protection. Believe in this, My child.

Remind each one that you are never alone for a moment, that trials will be the stepping stones into Heaven, that each step has been smoothed first by Our footsteps walking before

52

you.

The feelings of love and comfort and joy will seem to lessen for a time, also. This is so you will all struggle to remember and have faith in all Our words. To have this kind of trust will bring light into your souls and be the sounding board for all Our dear lost ones who come to tell their stories.

Your own trust and hope will be a beacon, an impetus for the faith of all who seek. There will be little light left in the world ... only from within the hearts of My faithful ones in order to show others the way back to My Father.

I will be that Light, My Dear one. I will be the Answer to all the questions ever posed to you. I am the Way, the Truth and the Light. I will be your salvation at every turn. I will be the One Who saves on every occasion. Do not fear to hope in complete protection at every moment. Do not fail to count on all We have told you to occur. The adversary has no power like that of his Creator. He has no ability to defeat Our purposes or the Will of My Father in Heaven.

Even though all will seem lost, you may trust against all odds, all appearances, that We will be victorious at just the right moment of the fullness of time.

Prepare with the Angels and Saints on high to celebrate My Birth with My dearest Mother and Joseph. Listen to the sounds of Angels singing their songs of welcome as I am ushered into the world. The plan of My Father nears completion for the world.

Soon, the many signs and wonders will be darkened by the overabundance of evil in your world. Remember that all must occur according to His Plan to fulfill the words of the Prophets before My Return. Dwell in Me, daughter, in joy and great anticipation for the great Day of My Coming back to you. You will see and do all you hope for, daughter, and more, I tell you. You will be astounded at the great plans My Father will unfold for all to see.

Rejoice, child, the Kingdom is about to be revealed for all to see and choose. These times are like no other, and will convince so many of the truth of all the words spoken by My Mother all over the world.

The Triumph of Our Two Hearts has begun and will be more apparent as the darkness falls. Be My Beacon and live

My love and My Words for all.

◆

God, the Father...(12/22/95) "My child, I am your Father in Heaven Who graces you this night with My words. The time remaining for My promises and plans to be fulfilled has arrived. Hurry to be in waiting every second now, always re-collected to My Will for you. Nothing else must fill your days as you live out this Will of Mine for your endeavors.

Ask what you will, child, and it will be given according to what is best for your soul. The souls of all My dear faithful ones are as gold gleaming in the Light of My Son, the Christ and Savior I have sent into the world.

As you prepare to celebrate His birth, please remember all I have told you. Please stay recollected with Me now as you view these events. Imagine My delight as I watched each one transpire. Imagine the joy in My Own Heart to see the perfect obedience of this Holy Family.

Only My Wisdom, daughter, can determine the proper moment for the commencement of My Plan. So many things play an important part in the decision to begin My cleansing action of the earth and its inhabitants. These are My people! These are My creation, and I act with the greatest love and mercy to prepare everything and everyone for the return of My Son.

It is with great anticipation for His return that I begin even more to send special signs and wonders to the world. It could not be a better time to begin than when the hearts of My people are most prepared by celebrating the Birth of Jesus.

Be filled with longing for Me, child. Be filled with grati-tude for My love for you, and go in the peace of My Will. Daughter, I Am."

◆

Blessed Mother...(1/8/96) "Oh, my child, please write these words given out of the Father's love. I, your Mother of Sorrows, come this night to share my grief with all my chil-dren who will listen and pray.

These days are running so quickly to the completion of this Age. It is no wonder that so many do not believe in this fact. They have not listened deeply enough to my words about all that is to occur before the end of this century.

The bell tolls the passage of enormous events. It calls all to come and see, to watch and listen and hear truth proclaimed. If the heart is too full of other things, it cannot hear the tolling, the call to gather around the square to listen and learn, to be prepared for the battle before the enemy arrives in full force. The enemy, child, is at the Gate in all its fury, waiting to devour innocent members of the town, who stand idly about the square, engaged in foolish pastimes.

The trumpets are sounding the charge, My daughter. Yet, many do not hear. Too often, laughter and idle chatter consume the minds and hearts of Our children.

It is with such great sadness that I view this plight of My little lost ones. They do not hear the Mother's voice above the noisy din of the crowd. They cannot hear My voice call out to them to come to Me and to be saved within the protection of My Holy Mantle.

Daughter, please pray with Me this night that yet more will listen to My voice and heed My words. Such great atrocities await humanity.

Satan is not human, therefore, he has no merciful qualities. He is chaos and ruin. He does not wish forgiveness or mercy. He only desires the ruin of God's people. He waits at every turn to trick each one into a complacency that makes one put off the prayer and reconciliation that must happen now in the hearts and lives of each one of Our little ones.

Continue, My child, to attempt to convince all of the need to accept the forgiveness of God, Our Father. I am His Daughter. He is My Father, too, and I know Him better than anyone who has ever lived on the earth.

Please, work with all your might to convince Our children of the Tender Heart, the Loving Mercy which awaits all who seek it: the love and forgiveness they so ardently need.

The dwindling days cause a rush of terror to My own Heart when I think of how many still need to listen and return to their first love, their first response to My call.

So very few have remained faithful, daughter of My

Sorrowful Heart. You know what it is like to be misunder-stood, to be cast aside as foolish and out of date. You know the sorrow of a heart filled with loving concern for the good of her children.

Please daughter, spend all the remaining time joined with Me in prayer for the children of this Age which is about to end.

There are many great and sorrowful events about to begin. Please, believe that nothing can prepare My people like the prayers of the few who are willing to sacrifice them-selves and the time remaining for the salvation of all.

Daughter, I beg, I weep, I call, I plead for as many prayers as can now be said on behalf of the little lost souls around the world. They are as surely a part of you, each of you, as the members of your own families.

Peace is an outmoded concept which is used as a politi-cal tool to set the world into an even greater position of col-lapse in the coming days. The world is fooled by all the mil-itary and governmental answers that fall so easily from the mouths of your leaders. Your leaders, My dear one, are tak-ing the world into a condition of slavery that will be more apparent with each passing month.

Please, My daughter, be ready to live out all We have told you. This time, there will be no delays, as time has run out.

The evangelization of the Americas must take place. The plans of the Father must be fulfilled by those who wish to serve. You will each serve by praying and being a beacon of light and truth to all who will come, who will seek, who will need all of you to lead them to Us.

All of your desires to serve will be fulfilled. Please tell My precious leaders and messengers and workers they will have great opportunities to fulfill the longing in their hearts. The events will continue to unfold and lead to the possibilities for which you pray and prepare.

Do not worry, My faithful soldiers, about what you are to do and how you are to do it. All is about to become very obvi-ous. The directions you seek will be apparent to all and you will spend the rest of your days teaching and leading and caring for the souls I send to each of you.

I love you all with a Mother's faith and delight. You have been faithful and strong throughout this long period of waiting.

Blessed are you who hope in the Lord and all His promises to you. They will now be fulfilled beyond your greatest hopes, with the strength and power of the Lord, Himself, leading the way to victory.

My Heart overflows with sorrow, daughter, at the coming events. My Heart also fills with joy at the commencement of the magnificent Plan of the Father to save His children.

Pray with Me now, My little one, with all the love in your heart. I am your loving Mother who will never leave your side."

Jesus...(1/16/96) "I thank you, daughter, for coming before Me in My Blessed Sacrament today. My desires for you will always include time spent like this, here in quiet and greater unity with Me.

My child, I am your Jesus. I am your Savior and your God. I was present always in your life and I am always present now. You are doing well to be in touch with My Presence, little one. This will take you far up the path of My Mountain. The Way is winding, and you would be weary without My strength to sustain you.

Be assured that this strength will always renew you in the days to come. A simple visit with Me will suffice to return to you the vigor and energy required to continue to serve My little ones who wait to see you. Together with My Holy Mother, we will serve the lost ones who seek Me.

My Father watches with delight all those who continue to pray and spend time with Me. Do you think all of this is a coincidence, daughter, that you are able to spend this time and have the freedom to prepare? Each of you here will benefit by realizing how your lives have been arranged according to your needs.

Please continue to offer all your feelings and thoughts to Me, and I will continue to sustain you. Each one of My warriors is ready to enter into the battle which erupts soon. Each of you will serve with honor!! The strength that is required is as near to all of you as I am!

Do not plan heavy attachments to busyness. Prepare as best you can, child, but reread and study and ponder all of Our words. This alone is needed now. You must spend the remaining time in prayer and study.

All who desire to serve shall have their desires fulfilled. All are in the palm of My Hand. All are poised on the brink of battle, but also on the edge of a new era, a new dawning of grace.

Pray, daughter, all of you here, pray for the world, My poor, poor lost ones. Love them, My dearest one, as I love you."

Jesus...(1/30/96) "I am grateful for your presence here with Me these special days in this very special place. You are filled with more of My Strength and Wisdom. You are ready to go forth into the battle.

So many of My people are confused, and this confusion will only grow.

My Father desires to clear the hearts and minds of His children so that nothing but His Will can dominate. This idea of domination is one which requires total surrender on the part of His people. When a leader takes His soldiers into battle, they must be of one mind and heart, ready to fight at any moment.

A spiritual battle is no different. All must be in a state of readiness to stop every activity and fight for the protection of the weak. You have been fighting to build up your own strength and obedience to lead those who wish to follow Me.

At different times throughout the history of My people, it has been necessary to cleanse them and lead them to a new land, one that has been promised to them in order to begin anew.

The land flowing with milk and honey has been described throughout Scripture. If ever there was a need for a new land, a new world cleansed of evil, it is now, My child.

There is no one able to fight Satan and his cohorts without the strength of God, Our Heavenly Father. It is He Who has created all. It is to My Name that every knee must bend. It is a new beginning My people need in order to return to the understanding of Truth as it has always been revealed and accepted by Our chosen people.

There are many phases of this Plan to be worked out and lived through. It is not a Plan that will fail, although that will seem to be the way it will go.

I cannot tell you how difficult it will be to persevere in spite of appearances, in the midst of seeming defeat and certain doom. No one who fights a battle could have the strength to endure without a strong leader to guide them.

MY FATHER, OUR SPIRIT AND I WILL BE WITH EACH OF YOU AT EVERY MOMENT. Yet, My little ones of this world will need leaders to encourage and convince them to persevere until the end.

I cannot tell you how important will be your own ability to trust in all the words We have given you. You have been given special gifts to enable you to withstand the attacks of many of the evil demons who will be constantly on the alert to attack your every move, your words of encouragement, your acts of defiance to the evil that will become so apparent in the coming days.

You will continue to travel until it is no longer safe to do so. My daughter, your heart is filled with trust in Me and My ability to lead you. Much patience has developed in this waiting, and you realize that all of Us in Heaven and on earth must wait in humble obedience and readiness for the moment the Father chooses to act.

Please, begin to teach all who will listen again and again, through meetings, gatherings of those who pray, those who will also be instrumental in the conversion of the many thousands who come here.

Tell all My young ones that they will not need to wait much longer to reach out to their peers and share all they have learned about Me and My beloved Mother.

You are strong in My Father's Will and in obedience to Our commands. Your preparation has been the one necessary for your soul, to bring your heart and mind to an ultimate readiness to serve Our people.

Please, daughter, be grateful for each event that has

developed in your life that has been a means of teaching you more about yourself and exposing every weakness that needs defending.

In a battle preparation, one needs to inspect the line of defense (the walls) in order to shore up any weak areas. These areas are present in all My people. You know that the quickest way to learn is to experience.

When one falls back from the front lines, it is to shore up, to recover and recoup losses, to rearm, to rest and ready yourself to return to the renewed battle. This will always be necessary, as long as sin and the evil one is allowed to prey on Our people. It is why We have spoken so often and waited so long for each of you to be made ready, strong and prepared for the ultimate battle.

The evil one is cunning and subtle. You cannot know his plans, but you can be ready to combat his evil ways. You know and deeply trust and believe that My strength and the help of My Mother will be enough to sustain each of you who holds out until My coming back into the world.

It is not necessary that My people know more than this at this time. A soldier never knows how a battle will play out, but brings preparedness and obedience to the battle and a willingness to fight alongside the Commander. The outcome of the battle is assured, but it will take many turns before ultimate victory.

Do you think, daughter, that I would ever lead you into danger and then abandon you?

As you can see, it will always be necessary to count on My strength, on the help of the Angels and Saints surrounding you, to carry you through any occasion. The events will seem overwhelming many times, and only trust in Our words will take you beyond apparent defeat."

Retreat continuously to higher ground, allow yourself to be lifted up to a place of new strength and grace in order to lift up others who will need direction.

Do what you can to support My faithful priests and prepare yourself for the time when many will see the error of their ways and be in dire need.

If you ever feel the need of more help and strength, or that you are in danger of being overwhelmed by people and events, you have only to stop and retreat into My Presence (always with you), to be renewed. Whatever you need will always be available to you.

I remind you that an instrument is a lowly, plain tool picked up by the Potter in order to work with the clay while it is soft and pliable. Many such tools are needed to help form and mold the many clay pots in the Master's shop!

Great heat is applied to the lowly containers. They are fired for just the right amount of time to obtain the proper glaze each one needs. These vessels are ornaments at the table of the Master which serve to nourish those who are invited to the Banquet.

My Father and I are preparing the greatest Banquet in the history of Our people! Many vessels are needed to hold the nourishment for Our people starving for the Bread of Life, the Water of Grace, the Meat of Truth.

Many will be used to fashion other vessels in order to set the table for the Banquet. You are made of the finest steel and are sharpened to the proper edge. At times, it is necessary to return you to the fire and burn away impurities which collect. Each time you come out of the fire shining and clean, sharper than before as a result of special honing experiences.

Feel the conviction that courses through your veins, the certitude of all Our promises. It is time to gather around you all the help offered to you. Our words are the honing wheel upon which you will be mostly perfectly sharpened.

Prayer and the protection of My Mother's Mantle are your buckler and shield. I, Myself, am your Commander Who will ride by your side. There will be many more opportunities in the coming months to prepare Our people for each successive battle. You will have less time during which to recover between trips to bolster the hope and trust within Our faithful ones.

You will soon enter into obvious battles and experience new attacks. Remember the subtlety of Satan's approach. Be on guard and ready to go in many directions at a moment's notice. Know that each one of these events has been planned by My Father, that I go before you to prepare the way, that My Mother and the Angels and Saints go with you.

If you feel doubt or fear overcoming you, fly to the arms of My Mother. See her Mantle enfolding you. Feel the embrace of Our Spirit and His strength and gifts coursing through your veins. Know that you are never alone and will never be overcome or abandoned, even though you find yourself alone for the moment.

Let your heart be filled with anticipation at the fulfillment of each great gift that will be a sign and gift given for all. Do not ever doubt that all the promises you await will come to fruition. Believe and be filled with courage and conviction about all that is about to unfold.

Thank you, daughter, for your faithful obedience and patience throughout this long waiting period. It will not be the end of waiting at other times, but more will have occurred by then and the Plan of My Father will unfold, as always, according to the needs of the greatest numbers.

Please continue to offer and consecrate all My people in Our world to Me. You will never understand how much is accomplished by this one act until you enter Eternity and look back over the end of this Age and the beginning of the new Era of Peace and Grace.

My Mother is smiling tenderly at you and nodding her head in great joy and approval for all the gifts being showered upon you now.

Be filled with gratitude, My dear one. Thank My Father with every breath, with every ounce of strength and awareness as the final preparedness before the battle.

We will never leave you. (I felt great emotion in Him with these words.) We will never let you down. We will shower graces on those who come to listen so that hearts will be opened to Our Words and will be healed.

The Holy Spirit showers you with His gifts and bids you be of good cheer, as you wait in joy and hope for My Triumphant return to the world, the Triumph of the Two Hearts and the fulfillment of all of Scripture until that time. Come and Adore!